EXPERT SYSTEM APPLICATIONS

Edited by
SUNIL VADERA,
UNIVERSITY OF SALFORD

SIGMA PRESS
Wilmslow, United Kingdom

First published in 1989 by
Sigma Press 1 South Oak Lane, Wilmslow, SK9 6AR, England.

British Library Cataloguing in Publication Data
A CIP catalogue record for this book is available from the British Library.

ISBN: 1-85058-127-4

Printed by Interprint Limited Malta

Cover design by
Professional Graphics, Warrington, UK

Distributed by
John Wiley & Sons Ltd., Baffins Lane, Chichester, West Sussex, England.

Acknowledgement of copyright names
Within this book, various trade names and names protected by copyright are mentioned for descriptive purposes. These include: DEC and VAX, Digital Research Corporation; GEM, Digital Research; IBM, International Business Machines; Inference ART, Inference Corporation; Lotus 1-2-3, Lotus Development Corporation; MS-DOS, Microsoft Corporation; Smalltalk, Xerox Corporation; Symbolics, Symbolics Inc; TI Explorer, Texas Instruments; UNIX, AT&T, Bell Laboratories; Due acknowledgement is hereby made of all other proprietary names .

Preface

The development of expert systems remains experimental. Unlike traditional software development, we cannot write good specifications and then carry out development steps which can be shown to satisfy the specification. Even in conventional application areas, there are many decisions that have to be taken which are based on experience. For example, the decision as to whether to use a fourth generation package instead of a programming language like COBOL is based on experience rather than some theoretical criteria.

This book contains the experience of designers of expert systems in using various tools, techniques, and languages in developing applications. The book is aimed at readers who want to develop expert systems but have little experience about the applicability of the methods and tools available. It should also be useful for those seeking an application-oriented introduction to expert systems.

We assume that the reader is familiar with computing, and elementary mathematics. Thus, terms like data structures and probabilities are used without explanation.

The book is divided into six parts. The first part outlines the techniques and languages that are often used to develop expert systems. It concentrates on common techniques and languages rather than attempting to be comprehensive.

The chapters in part II of the book describe a selection of tools for developing expert systems. The tools described represent a wide class of similar tools that are available.

The remaining four parts of the book describe the experience of designers in developing expert systems in the areas of:

- Ecology;

- Marketing, and Data Processing;

- Industry;

- Medical Education.

Some of the applications are "live" systems, some are prototypes, and a few are vehicles for research. The applications also vary in their size, complexity, and development cost.

The chapters in parts III to VI can be read independently. However, the reader will gain much more by comparing and contrasting the various applications. Indeed, my main hope in editing this book has been that it will provide a description of a breadth of experience without sacrificing depth.

The Appendix contain a list of expert system tools, their main features, their costs, references to reviews and their distributors.

I wish to express my gratitude to all the authors. It is their willingness to share their experience that has resulted in this book. I would also like to thank Ajit Kumar Halder, Gordon Laws, Eric Irozuru and Marco Jafarian for their comments on some of the chapters. The book was typeset using the wonderful LaTeX system. Bob Phoenix wrote the software which helped to produce the index.

Sunil Vadera

List of Contributors

Dr. Vivienne B. Ambrosiadou,
Department of Electronics and Electrical Engineering,
University of Salford, Salford M5 4WT, U.K.

David R. Bedford,
Knowledge Engineering Group,
Coopers and Lybrand Associates,
Plumtree Court, London EC4A 4HT, U.K.

John Bradshaw,
Department of Computer Science,
Rhodes University, Grahamstown, 6140, South Africa.

Micheal N. Bruton,
JLB Smith Institute of Ichthyology, Grahamstown, 6140, South Africa.

Professor Alan Bundy,
Department of Artificial Intelligence,
University of Edinburgh, 80 South Bridge, Edinburgh EH1 1HN, U.K.

Peter Chalk,
Department of Computing and Mathematics,
South Bank Polytechnic, 103 Borough Road, London SE1 OAA, U.K.

N. Chan,
Artificial Intelligence Applications Institute (AIAI),
University of Edinburgh, 80 South Bridge, Edinburgh EH1 1HN, U.K.

Dr.Paul Wai Hing Chung,
Artificial Intelligence Applications Institute (AIAI),
University of Edinburgh, 80 South Bridge, Edinburgh EH1 1HN, U.K.

Dale Danilewitz,
Department of Computer Science,
Rhodes University, Grahamstown, 6140, South Africa.

Irene J. de Moor,
JLB Smith Institute of Ichthyology, Grahamstown, 6140, South Africa.

Ian Filby,
Artificial Intelligence Applications Institute (AIAI),
University of Edinburgh, 80 South Bridge, Edinburgh EH1 1HN, U.K.

Dr. Nigel J. Holden,
Department of Management,
UMIST, Manchester U.K.

Dr. Robert Inder,
Artificial Intelligence Applications Institute (AIAI),
University of Edinburgh, 80 South Bridge, Edinburgh EH1 1HN, U.K.

Mark Lewis,
Expert Systems International Ltd,
Unit 14, 7 West Way, Oxford, OX2 OJB, U.K.

Tim Lewis,
AI Ltd,
Greycaine Road, Watford, Herts. WD2 4JP, U.K.

Dr. Bob Muetzelfeldt,
Department of Forestry and Natural Resources,
Kings Building, University of Edinburgh, Edinburgh EH1 1HN, U.K.

Jay O'Keefe,
Institute of Fresh Water Studies,
Rhodes University, Grahamstown, 6140, South Africa.

Dr. Jack Ponton,
Department of Chemical Engineering,
University of Edinburgh, 80 South Bridge, Edinburgh EH1 1HN, U.K.

Helen Purchase,
Department of Computer Science,
Rhodes University, Grahamstown, 6140, South Africa.

Denis Riordan,
Department of Computer Science,
Rhodes University, Grahamstown, 6140, South Africa.

Dave Robertson,
Department of Artificial Intelligence,
University of Edinburgh, 80 South Bridge, Edinburgh EH1 1HN, U.K.

Mike Uschold,
Department of Artificial Intelligence,
University of Edinburgh, 80 South Bridge, Edinburgh EH1 1HN,U.K.

Sunil Vadera,
Department of Mathematics and Computer Science,
University of Salford, Salford M5 4WT, U.K.

Anthony Waters,
Department of Chemical Engineering,
University of Edinburgh, 80 South Bridge, Edinburgh EH1 1HN, U.K.

Paul Whip,
AI Ltd,
Greycaine Road, Watford, Herts. WD2 4JP, U.K.

Contents

VI Medical Education 215

Part I

Introduction and Background

Expert systems, like other application areas of computing, have an associated collection of techniques and languages. The first part of the book introduces these techniques and languages. Readers familiar with expert system techniques and methods should skip to the next part of the book.

The first chapter introduces expert systems, and the techniques that are often used to implement expert systems. It introduces the common techniques which are used to represent, structure, and reason with different types of knowledge. It also describes a technique of learning from examples.

One of the most flexible ways of developing expert systems is to use a high level programming language. The second chapter introduces the core of two programming languages, Prolog and Lisp, which are particularly suitable for implementing expert systems.

Chapter 1

An Introduction to Expert Systems

Sunil Vadera

1.1 What is an Expert System?

We define an *expert system* to be a computer based system that can perform some task which requires expertise. Of course, the judgement on whether some task requires expertise is a subjective one. However, such tasks often have one or more of the following characteristics:

- The task may be difficult to specify.

- The task may have incomplete, or uncertain data.

- There may not always be an optimum solution.

- The task cannot be solved in a step-by-step manner.

- Solutions are often obtained by using accumulated experience.

Notice that we do not claim that expert systems model a human expert's mental models. The reader should refer to [53,51] for an approach based on this view.

Expert systems can bring the following benefits:

- They can preserve valuable knowledge which would otherwise be lost when an expert is no longer available.

- They can allow an expert to concentrate on more difficult aspects of the task.

- They can enforce consistency.

- They can perform dangerous tasks which would otherwise be carried out by humans.

As with other application areas of computing, there are a collection of techniques that are often used to implement expert systems (Figure 1.1). In theory, it is possible to ignore these methods and use conventional techniques and languages to develop expert systems. However, in practice, this is like developing business applications in machine code; one simply spends a lot of time reinventing the methods. There is also a danger that we may attempt to use expert system methods when conventional methods would be more suitable. One has to be particularly careful when developing a system that lies at the intersection of various application areas (Figure 1.1).

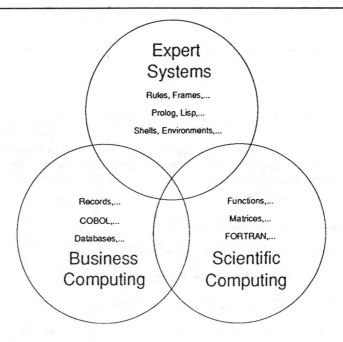

Figure 1.1: Expert systems, Scientific, and Business computing methods

Expert systems can be applied to a wide range of applications. A suitable classification of these applications can often help to identify the methods that are best suited for implementing a particular application. A common classification produces the following four groups.

1. **Diagnostic Systems**

   Problems in diagnosing disease, interpreting geological surveys, and making assessments require a large amount of data to be classified into one or more categories. Such applications are referred to as *diagnostic or classification systems*. Pioneering examples of diagnostic systems include:

   - *MYCIN* which makes suggestions of treatment for bacterial infections in the blood [126];
   - *CADUCEUS* which aids the diagnoses of human disease [92];
   - *PROSPECTOR* which assists in analysing geological data for exploration [50,49].

2. **Design Systems**

   Applications which build models or structures by combining other structures in order to satisfy some goal are often called *design systems*. Pioneering examples of design systems include:

   - *DENDRAL* which determines the structure of a chemical given its formulae and its mass spectrogram [28];
   - *Xcon* which configures DEC VAX systems from orders [89].

3. **Monitoring and Control Systems**

   These applications monitor, and control time dependent events. In addition to tackling the kind of problems encountered by diagnostic, and design systems, these systems have to handle the complexities introduced by time constraints. The use of expert systems in this area is much more recent than in the other categories; it is therefore not surprising that there are no systems that could be regarded as pioneering.

4. **Instruction Systems**

   These applications aim to provide flexible, and sensitive computer based instruction systems. Typically, such systems include the ability to model various styles of learning, monitor a students progress, and explain solutions. Pioneering examples of systems that attempt to attain some these characteristics include:

   - *SCHOLAR* [31] which is a system for teaching South American geography;
   - *BUGGY* [25] which provides teachers with practice in diagnosing students' errors in basic mathematical skills;
   - *NEOMYCIN* [38] which adapts MYCIN's knowledge base so that it can be used to teach medical diagnosis.

1.1.1   Structure of an Expert System

The most common structure of an expert system is shown in Figure 1.2. The *inference engine* (or *control*) uses the *knowledge base* and the *current state* to solve the problem. The *current state* is a dynamic store of information which is known, supplied by a user, or deduced by the inference engine when solving a problem. These divisions allow us to develop a reasonably static inference engine whilst the knowledge base tends to evolve during a *knowledge acquisition phase*.

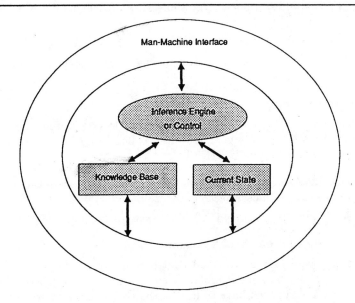

Figure 1.2: A common structure of an expert system

Programs which provide a control for a particular kind of *knowledge representation scheme* but leave the knowledge base empty are called *expert system shells*.

In some applications, we require the combined power of different knowledge representation schemes. A number of tools provide such hybrid *environments* or *toolkits*. These are often called *multiparadigm systems*.

The quality of the man-machine interface will dictate the extent to which a user will trust the system. The system must be capable of explaining its reasoning and justifying its conclusions. Most expert system shells provide a facility for a user to request 'why' a question is being asked, and 'how' a goal is achieved.

Will an expert system be appropriate for your problem? If so, which kind of tool is likely to be suitable for developing your application? Is a shell adequate or is a more sophisticated toolkit necessary? The remaining parts of this book will help you make a more informed decision.

1.2 Knowledge Representation

A system often requires a lot of knowledge before it reaches an expert's level of performance. Hence, the question of how the knowledge is represented is critical to the design of the system.

In this section we describe various schemes for representing knowledge in a computer. Our description is biased towards the methods used in the applications described in this book. A more complete account of knowledge representation schemes can be found in other books (eg. Charniak and McDermott [35]).

Ideally, we would like a knowledge representation scheme to be:

- Well-defined. Its syntax and semantics should be defined.

- Expressive. It should be easy to express and structure knowledge.

- Efficient. There must be efficient computer implementations of the scheme.

Unfortunately, there is no single knowledge representation scheme that is the best in all circumstances. For example, a scheme that is very expressive often requires more powerful computer resources, and more powerful resources can cost more money! Indeed, as already suggested, we sometimes have to use several schemes to develop an application. The most common schemes used to represent knowledge are rules, semantic networks, frames, and logic. We describe each of these in the following sections. We also describe some common approaches of reasoning with uncertain knowledge.

1.2.1 Rules

Rules [104] allow us to represent relationships in the form:

IF antecedent THEN consequent

to express that the consequent is true if the antecedent is true. We say that a rule is *applicable* if its antecedent is known to be true in the current state. An applicable rule whose consequent is used is said to have *fired*. For example, the following list of simple rules can be used to decide whether an applicant for a particular job should be rejected, or invited for an interview:

1. IF applicant is well-qualified AND applicant is neat
    THEN invite applicant for an interview

2. IF NOT(applicant is well-qualified) OR applicant is untidy
    THEN reject applicant

3. IF applicant has a degree
    THEN applicant is well-qualified

4. IF applicant NOT(has a degree)
    THEN NOT(applicant is well-qualified)

> 5.   IF applicant's handwriting is neat
>   THEN applicant is neat
>
> 6.   IF applicant's handwriting is untidy
>   THEN applicant is untidy

Rules are more *declarative* than the use of conventional languages. They state the knowledge without describing how the knowledge should be used. This declarativeness makes it relatively easy to refine and add further knowledge. For example, to add the knowledge that 'A' levels are an acceptable qualification, we change rules 3 and 4 to:

> 3.   IF applicant has a degree OR applicant has 'A' levels
>   THEN applicant is well-qualified
>
> 4.   IF applicant NOT(has a degree) AND NOT(applicant has 'A' levels)
>   THEN NOT(applicant is well-qualified)

In practice, some of the rules may contain calls to imperative routines (like input/output). Such rules reduce the declarativeness of the knowledge.

A uniform collection of rules is probably adequate for small applications. For a larger application, a uniform set of rules is difficult to maintain and can often result in an inefficient system. We can improve the maintainability of such rules by partioning them into subsets of rules. We can improve the efficiency by providing rules to inform the control about which subset of rules might be applicable in a given situation. These rules about rules are called *meta-rules* ([113]).

So how should the control use the rules? The control can forward chain, or backward chain the rules to satisfy some goal. We describe each of these approaches below.

Forward Chaining

Forward chaining works from known facts towards desired goals. In its simplest form, it finds an applicable rule and adds the knowledge in its consequent to the current state. It repeats this process until there is no new knowledge or a goal is reached. To find applicable rules, the control has to *match* facts from the current state to the antecedents of the rules. As an example, consider the above rules together with the information that an applicant's handwriting is untidy. A forward chaining control will search the rules to find that the sixth rule is applicable. It therefore updates the current state to include the fact that the applicant is untidy. The control then rescans the rules to find that the second rule is applicable. It therefore updates the current state to include the fact that the applicant should be rejected. At this stage the control stops since it has reached a goal.

For a small set of rules, the applicable rules can be obtained by scanning all the rules from the first to the last. However, for a large set of rules, whose antecedents often share conditions, this simple approach can be inefficient. In such situations, one should adopt the *Rete match* algorithm (see Forgy [54]).

When there is more than one applicable rule, we must decide which rule to apply. This is known as *conflict resolution*. Possible conflict resolution strategies include:

- *Refractoriness*: avoid applying a rule more than once for the same situation.

- *Recency*: give priority to those rules which use recent knowledge.

- *Specificity*: give priority to rules with more specific antecedents (i.e. antecedents with more conditions).

The choice of an appropriate conflict resolution strategy will depend upon the characteristics of an application. A strategy that reduces the number of rules applied may spend a lot of time selecting the rules. Most tools therefore provide a selection of strategies. For example, the shell used to implement Xcon, known as OPS5 (see [26] for examples), provides two conflict resolution strategies known as LEX and MEA. The LEX strategy applies the above strategies in sequence. The MEA strategy is similar except that it gives more priority to those rules whose antecedent's first condition uses the most recent knowledge.

Backward Chaining

Backward chaining works from goals to subgoals, and then eventually to known facts. Thus given a goal, it finds a rule whose consequent matches the goal. The antecedent of this rule then results in subgoals. This process is then repeated on the subgoals until they are satisfied by the facts in the current state. If at any stage, a particular rule fails to lead to a goal, then backward chaining will back up and attempt to use an alternative rule. The process of finding a rule whose antecedent justifies a goal is known as *abduction*. As an example, consider again the above rules together with the knowledge that an applicant has untidy handwriting. The goals are either to reject the applicant or to invite the applicant for an interview. Suppose we order the goals so that the control first attempts to reject applicants (this might be appropriate if rejection is more likely). The backward chaining control finds that it could use the second rule to reject the applicant provided that either the applicant is not well-qualified, or the applicant is untidy. Suppose it now attempts to establish that the applicant is not well-qualified. It finds that the fourth could establish this provided that the applicant does not have a degree. It now reaches a dead end because it cannot establish that the applicant does not have a degree, and there are no alternative rules which can show that the applicant is not well-qualified. At this point, the control backs up and attempts to show that the applicant is untidy. The sixth rule will establish this provided that the handwriting is untidy. The control knows that the handwriting is untidy, and hence that the applicant should be rejected. Figure 1.3 represents the solution (the path given by the thicker lines in the figure) as an *AND/OR* graph. The nodes of an AND/OR graph are used to denote goals and subgoals,

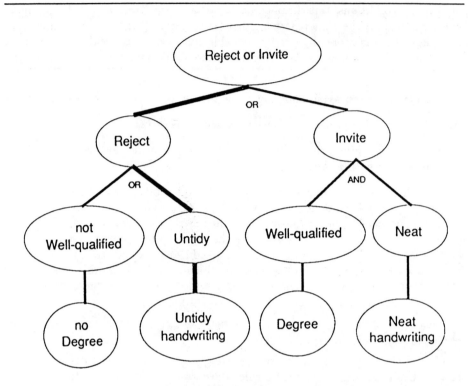

Figure 1.3: Example of an AND/OR graph

while the arcs relate subgoals to their original goal. The arcs of a node can be related to specify whether all the associated subgoals have to be satisfied (labelled AND), or whether satisfying just one of the subgoals is enough (labelled OR).

1.2.2 Semantic Networks

Semantic networks [108] allow us to represent relationships in the form of a graph. Objects are represented by the nodes of a graph whilst relationships between objects are represented by arcs. For example, the relationships:

"Fido is a tiger."

"Tigers eat men."

"Joe is man."

"All men are human."

"All tigers are animals."

would be represented by the graph shown in Figure 1.4; where the instance_of link is used to relate objects to their type, and the is_a link is used to relate different types of objects.

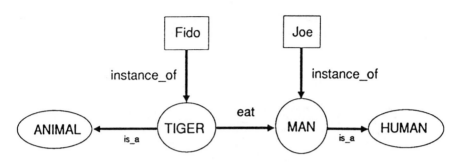

Figure 1.4: Example of a semantic network

The major advantage of using semantic networks is that they give a good structural overview of the relationships involved. They have, however, been criticised over the lack of meaning expressed by the arcs and nodes [147].

1.2.3 Frames

Frames (also known as *schemas*) are record-like structures which can be used to represent and structure previous experience about objects, and concepts [93]. For example, a frame representing a particular car might take the form:

MY-VOLKSWAGEN is an instance_of Object with:

Registration no.	W3D 987T
Colour	blue
No. Wheels	
Mileage	60000

A frame has *slots* which can be *filled* or *unfilled*. Thus, the No.Wheels slot is unfilled.

This frame represents one car. There are certain features which are true of most Volkswagens, and of most cars. For example, all Volkswagens are made in Germany and have four wheels. We can represent this knowledge by creating frames to represent typical cars and Volkswagens:

CAR is_a Object with:

Colour	
No. Wheels	4
Mileage	

VOLKSWAGEN is a CAR with:

Country	Germany

The relationship that a Volkswagen is a car is expressed in the second frame by using the is a relationship. The frame for a particular Volkswagen might now take the form:

MY-VOLKSWAGEN is an instance of VOLKSWAGEN with:

Registration no.	W3D 987T
Colour	blue
No. Wheels	
Mileage	60000

Where the No. Wheels slot can inherit its value from the VOLKSWAGEN frame. The VOLKSWAGEN frame, in turn, inherits its No. Wheels slot from the CAR frame. This kind of inheritance, where we represent concepts by relating them to more general concepts, is a powerful technique which allows us to represent knowledge very succinctly.

In addition to values, we can attach the following kind of information to slots.

- *Units* to give the units of the slot. For example, we could attach the qualifying units (miles or km) to the Mileage slot.

- *Range checks* which specify that a slot must only be filled with values in a given range. For example, the value of the No. Wheels slot must be in the range [0,4].

- *Rules* to carry out some action under some conditions. Thus we might attach a rule to the Colour slot which says IF the colour is unknown THEN ask the user.

- *Demons* which are activated when the value of a slot changes. For example, if the Mileage slot changes, a demon might be activated to raise an alarm if the mileage reduces.

1.2.4   Logic

Logic is the most well defined way of expressing, and reasoning about knowledge. In this section, we give an informal introduction to *predicate logic*. Gallier [58] gives a formal account of logic, whilst Turner [137] gives a good introduction to other types of logic used in artificial intelligence (AI).

We can use logic to express knowledge in the form of propositions. A *proposition* can either be *true* or *false*. Propositions can be combined by using connectives. Given two propositions P and Q, we can form their:

- *conjunction*: $P \wedge Q$ to express that both P and Q are true. If either P or Q is false, their conjunction is also false;

- *disjunction*: $P \vee Q$ to express that either P or Q is true. If both P and Q are false then their disjunction is false;

- *implication*: $P \Rightarrow Q$ to express a relationship that Q is true when P is true. If P is true and Q is false then the implication is false;

- *equivalence*: $P \Leftrightarrow Q$ to express that P is equivalent to Q.

- *negation*: $\neg P$ to express that P is false. If P is true, then its negation is false.

Example

"The sun is round" $\wedge$ "The sun is red-hot"

"The sun is red-hot" $\Rightarrow$ "There is no life on the sun"

The above rules can be used recursively to form more complex statements. A statement which conforms to the syntax rules of a logic is called a *well-formed formula* (wff). Apart from providing syntax rules, a logic provides rules which allow us to make legal deductions. These rules are called the *inference rules* of the logic. Examples of inference rules are:

$\wedge$-elimination: from $S1 \wedge S2$ we can legally infer $S2$

$\Rightarrow$-elimination: from $S1$; $S1 \Rightarrow S2$ we can legally infer $S2$

Thus, the $\wedge$-elimination rule can be used on the first statement to infer:

"The sun is red-hot".

Now applying the $\Rightarrow$-elimination rule on this statement and the second statement above allows us to infer:

"There is no life on the sun".

Clearly, the inference rules of a logic must be carefully chosen. If we start with statements that are true, then any inferences we make with the inference rules must also be true. This property is known as the *soundness* of a logic. We would also like to be capable of inferring anything that is true from a collection of true statements. This property is known as *completeness*.

This language of propositions together with its rules of inference is called *propositional calculus*. This language has the property that it is *decidable*. That is, there is an algorithm which given any wff statement will decide whether the statement is true or false.

Propositional calculus, is however, not very expressive. It is difficult to express statements like:

"All planets are round";
"There is a planet that is flat".

The best we can do is to list all the planets:

"mars is round" $\wedge$ "venus is round" $\wedge$ ...

"mars is round" $\vee$ "venus is flat" $\vee$ "planet-x is flat" $\vee$ ...

We can, however, express these statements in *predicate calculus*. In addition to the connectives, predicate calculus allows us to use the following:

- *Variables* to denote indefinite objects. Thus formulae like $flat(x)$ and $round(y)$ are wff where x and y are *free* variables.

- *Predicates* to express relationships. Thus to express that something is flat, we would introduce a predicate $flat(x)$, where the x is a *free variable* which can be filled in by suitable objects. For example, $flat(board)$ is true but $flat(moon)$ is false.

- *Functions* to express mappings. Thus, $radius(moon)$ could denote a mapping from the object *moon* to its radius.

- *Quantifiers*
  A formulae $P(x)$ can be *universally quantified* by writing $\forall x \cdot P(x)$. This expresses the statment that all values of x possess the property P. A formula $P(x)$ can be *existentially quantified* by writing $\exists x \cdot P(x)$ to express the statement that there is at least one value of x which possesses the property P. The quantifier $\forall$ is read as "for all", the $\exists$ is read as "there exists", and the dot is read as "such that". We can now express the above statements by:

$$\forall x \cdot planet(x) \Rightarrow round(x)$$

$$\exists x \cdot planet(x) \wedge flat(x)$$

The price we pay for this expressiveness is that predicate calculus is not decidable. It is only semi-decidable. That is, there is only an algorithm for statements that are true.

In the above example, we used the predicate $planet(x)$ to express that x must be a planet. In computer science, we would say that x must be a *type* of planet. We can use a *sorted logic* to express the above statements more compactly:

$$\forall x \in Planets \cdot round(x)$$

$$\exists x \subset Planets \cdot flat(x)$$

1.2.5 Inexact Reasoning

There are many approaches for representing uncertain knowledge; none of which are universally applicable. In this section we describe how some basic probability theory leads to one approach that is sometimes used. We also summarise other approaches that have been advocated.

Consider the following (hypothetical) situation:

> A housewife finds a stain on her husband's shirt. Her husband denies that it is a lipstick stain. She knows that applying a little methylated spirit to a stain, and softening it with washing-up liquid almost always removes lipstick stains. She also knows that this method hardly ever works on other stains. She applies this method to the shirt and finds that it removes the stain. As a result she concludes that it was almost certainly a lipstick stain.

How do we represent this type of knowledge and reasoning? We can represent the uncertain aspects of the knowledge by assigning subjective probabilities to statements. We will use the notation $P(X|Y)$ to mean the subjective probability of X occurring given that Y has occurred. Thus, in our examples we may assign the probabilities:

$$P(works|lipstick) = 0.9$$

$$P(works) = 0.2$$

Where we use *works* to mean that the method works, and *lipstick* to mean that it is a lipstick stain.

We can now pose the housewife's goal as first finding:

$$P(lipstick|works)$$

But how can we find this from the probabilities that we know? We can use the following rule known as *Bayes' rule* (see [103] for a tutorial account):

$$P(X|Y) = \frac{P(X) * P(Y|X)}{P(Y)}$$

That is,

$$P(lipstick|works) = \frac{P(lipstick) * P(works|lipstick)}{P(works)}$$

The only value which is not available in this formula is $P(lipstick)$. However, the housewife can estimate the proportion of previous stains that were lipstick. Suppose she believes it to be about 0.25, then we obtain:

$$P(lipstick|works) = \frac{0.25 * 0.9}{0.3} = 0.75$$

This shows how we can use one piece of evidence. Suppose that the housewife also knew that the husband was late from work when he wore the shirt. Using Bayes' rule again:

$$P(lipstick|works\,and\,late) = \frac{P(lipstick) * P(works\,and\,late|lipstick)}{P(works\,and\,late)}$$

Now since the method working, and the husband being late are independent pieces of evidence (even when there is a lipstick stain), we can use:

$$P(works\,and\,late) = P(works) * P(late)$$

and

$$P(works\,and\,late|lipstick) = P(works|lipstick) * P(late|lipstick)$$

to simplify the above formula to:

$$P(lipstick|works\,and\,late) = P(lipstick) * \frac{P(works|lipstick)}{P(works)} * \frac{P(late|lipstick)}{P(late)}$$

Thus, we can see that to incorporate this additional evidence, we simply multiply the current probability of the stain being lipstick (i.e. the probability after the first piece of evidence) by an additional factor. Thus if $P(late|lipstick) = 0.6$ and $P(late) = 0.5$ we obtain:

$$P(lipstick|works\,and\,late) = 0.75 * \frac{0.6}{0.5} = 0.9$$

However, it is worth emphasising that this method assumes that the different pieces of evidence are *independent* of each other. If we do not assume independence we find that the number of probabilities that are required becomes prohibitive. For example, for just 5 pieces of evidence and one possible hypothesis (eg. *lipstick*) we could require as many as 6251 probabilities!

Approaches which use Bayes' rule as a basis of combining evidence are called *Bayesian*. Duda et al. [115] describe the use of a Bayesian approach in PROSPEC-TOR. A drawback of such approaches is that there is no indication of whether the probability is a wild guess, or a judgement based on experience. For example, in the above situation, the housewife suggested that the probability of the husband being late from work was 0.5. Did she mean that she did not know, or that the husband is late 50% of the time?

Several alternative approaches have been advocated to overcome such deficiencies. The applicability of these approaches remains the subject of research. However, we summarise four approaches below.

Dempster-Shafer Theory

The Dempster-Shafer approach can be used to express belief in a subset of hypotheses. For example, given the possible hypotheses:

{strawberry stain, lipstick stain, blue ink stain}

the evidence that a stain looks red could be represented by associating a belief of 0.8 (say) with the subset:

{strawberry stain, lipstick stain}

The approach allows the narrowing and revision of such beliefs in the light of more evidence. It also maintains a measure of plausibility for the subset of hypotheses. This measure, together with the belief in a set of hypotheses, gives an interval which expresses the confidence in the set of hypotheses.

Gorden and Shortliffe [59] describe how the Dempster-Shafer approach can be used in MYCIN. They also point out that the approach is inefficient when applied to situations which require reasoning about high-level concepts in knowledge bases which have a hierarchical structure.

A detailed account of this approach is given in [123], whilst a more recent account can be found in [122].

Fuzzy logic

Zadeh [149] develops an approach which allows us to represent and reason with vague and fuzzy knowledge. To accommodate informal arguments, fuzzy set theory provides a framework in which membership of a category is graded rather than simply definite. Thus, for example, the husband being late could be a function of time into the range [0,1]. Fuzzy logic takes this a step further by arguing that there is no clear boundary between a statement being true and a statement being false. It allows fuzzy truth values by employing *linguistic truth-values* like 'very true', 'not very true', and 'more or less true'. Each of these values is a fuzzy subset of the range [0,1]. Thus, in the above example, the housewife could conclude that 'the stain is lipstick' is more or less true.

In analogy with predicate logic, Fuzzy logic provides fuzzy operators like ∧ and ∨ to enable us to express and reason about fuzzy knowledge. The interested reader can refer to Zadeh [148] for a more detailed account. Kohout and Bandler [80] describe some uses of fuzzy logic in expert systems.

Interval based approaches

These approaches use an interval to represent the likelyhood of some statement. Thus the housewife would say that the probability of the husband being late is in the range [0, 1] to express that she does not know; or in the range [0.5, 0.5] to say that he is late 50 percent of the time. This approach is used in the P.R.O. shell in part two of this book. Quinlan also makes use of intervals in INFERNO [110].

Logic based approaches

Advocates of logic based approaches argue that assigning probabilities is not a natural way of reasoning for human experts. They advocate approaches which provide operators together with legal ways of reasoning about statements containing the operators. For example, we could provide an operator 'likely' so that the statements:

      lipstick 'likely' when late

and

      method works 'likely' when lipstick

could be combined to

      method works 'likely' when late

An example of such an approach can be found in [63].

A mathematical comparison of these methods is beyond the scope of this book. Prade [105] gives a good review of the methods of handling uncertainty. Lee [85] provides a more recent comparison of the Dempster-Shafer and the Bayesian approach.

1.3   Learning from examples

To develop an expert system, we have to acquire the knowledge which will make it expert. We can often acquire this knowledge from human experts. However, human experts are invariably scarce, and costly. Thus the time spent in obtaining knowledge from human experts can greatly increase the cost of developing a system. An alternative to using experts' valuable time is to use a history of previous decisions to develop a system. One approach that is often used is to learn a decision tree from a table of examples (see [91] and [20] for other approaches). This approach is based on Quinlan's algorithm known as ID3 [112].

ID3 takes a table of examples as input and produces a decision tree which is consistent with the examples. We describe ID3 with the aid of the following example.

Example

A recruitment agency which specialises in recruiting trainee programmers wants to develop a decision tree to filter out unsuitable applicants. The agency use three criteria to make this decision: *programming ability (Prog)*, *communication ability (Com)*, and *presentation (Pres)*. Suppose the agency provide the examples in Table 1.1.

No.	Prog	Com	Pres	Decision
1.	good	ok	neat	yes
2.	average	ok	fair	yes
3.	poor	liar	scruffy	no
4.	average	liar	fair	no
5.	good	boring	scruffy	yes
6.	good	ok	scruffy	yes
7.	average	boring	scruffy	no
8.	good	liar	scruffy	no
9.	poor	boring	fair	no
10.	poor	boring	scruffy	no

Table 1.1: Table of examples

A decision tree which is consistent with these examples can be obtained by applying the following procedure:

1. Choose an attribute as the root. Only those attributes that are not ancestors are eligible. Initially, all the attributes except the 'Decision' attribute are eligible.

2. Create an arc for each possible value of the root. Label the arcs with their value.

3. Partition the table into subtables; one for each arc. A subtable for a particular arc must have exactly those examples of the table whose root has the value labelling the arc.

4. Repeat the process on those subtables whose 'Decision' attribute has different values.

Figures 1.5 and 1.6 show two different decision trees that result when different attributes are chosen as the root (the example numbers in brackets correspond to the subtables obtained in the third step of the procedure).

Notice that although both these trees are consistent with the examples, they are not equivalent. Thus, for example, a candidate who is neat but a liar and a poor programmer is accepted by the first tree. However, the candidate would (rightly?) be rejected by the second tree. This problem occurs in the first tree because we chose an attribute which does not give much information about the final classification.

How can we choose an attribute which will result in a good tree? We should choose an attribute which gives us the most information. That is, we should choose that attribute which results in the least uncertainty about the final classification. Information theory provides a suitable measure.

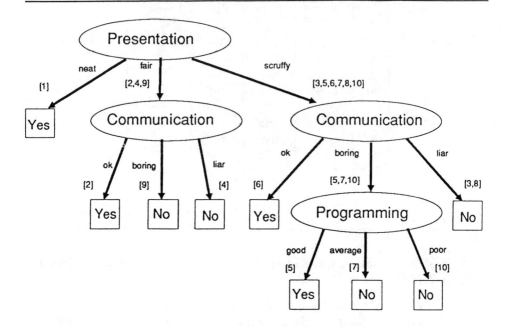

Figure 1.5: Decision tree when *Pres* is chosen as root

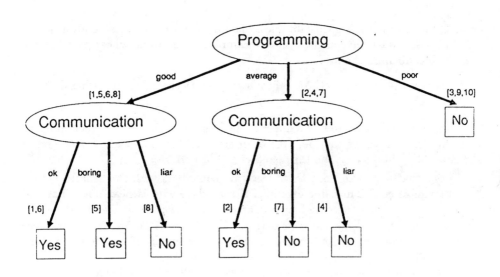

Figure 1.6: Decision tree when *Prog* is chosen as root

In information theory, the information obtained by knowing that an event has occurred is given by:

$$- \log_2 P$$

where P is the probability of the event occurring. This measure of information is motivated by the fact that knowing something that has a low likelyhood gives us more information. For example, learning that you have won the pools would give you more information than learning that the sun will rise tomorrow.

The average information obtained when a number of events occur is given by the *entropy* (H):

$$H = - \sum_i P_i \log_2 P_i$$

We are interested in the entropy of classification given the choice of a particular attribute. For example, how much information would we gain by knowing whether the decision is a 'yes' or a 'no' if we already know how good the candidate is at programming. This conditional entropy is given by:

$$H(C|A) = \sum_{j=1}^{n} P(a_j)H(C|a_j)$$

where

$$H(C|a_j) = - \sum_{i=1}^{m} P(c_i|aj) \log_2 P(c_i|aj)$$

Where the a_j are the n values of the attribute **A**, and the c_i are the m values of the decision **C**. For example, we can calculate $H(Decision|Prog)$ by first using the latter formula to obtain $H(Decision|a_j)$ for each value of *programming ability* (last column of the table):

a_j	$P(yes|a_j)$	$P(no|a_j)$	$P(a_j)$	$H(Decision|a_j)$
good	3/4	1/4	4/10	0.811
average	1/3	2/3	3/10	0.919
poor	0/3	3/3	3/10	0.000

and then use the former formula to obtain:

$$H(Decision|Prog) = \sum_j P(a_j)H(Decision|a_j) = 0.600$$

In a similar way, we can obtain:

$$H(Decision|Comm) = 0.325$$

1.	good	neat	yes
2.	average	fair	yes
6.	good	scruffy	yes

Table 1.2: Partition when communication ability is ok

5.	good	scruffy	yes
7.	average	scruffy	no
9.	poor	fair	no
10.	poor	scruffy	no

Table 1.3: Partition when applicant is boring

3.	poor	scruffy	no
4.	average	fair	no
8.	good	scruffy	no

Table 1.4: Partion when applicant is a liar

and

$$H(Decision|Pres) = 0.827.$$

Thus knowing the *communication ability* would give us the least uncertainty about the final classification. We now partition the examples into the above three tables (Tables 1.2, 1.3, 1.4); one for each value of *communication ability*. The decision given for an example in Table 1.2 is 'yes', whilst the decision for an example in Table 1.4 is 'no'. We repeat the process on Table 1.3 to find that

$$H(Decision|Prog) = 0$$

and

$$H(Decision|Pres) = 0.690$$

Hence we choose *programming ability* as the next criteria and find that no further partitioning is necessary. The resulting decision, which also rejects the neat liar, is given in Figure 1.7.

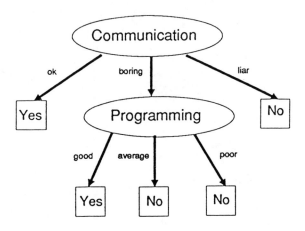

Figure 1.7: Decision tree obtained by ID3

Chapter 2

An Introduction to Prolog and Lisp

Sunil Vadera

The most flexible way of developing expert systems is to use a programming language. Two of the most common languages used are Prolog, and Lisp. In this chapter we introduce Prolog, and summarise Lisp. More complete accounts of these languages can be found in other books (e.g. [133] and [144]).

2.1 A Taste of Prolog

Prolog is yet to be standardised. As a result, there are numerous versions of Prolog. Two common styles are the Edinburgh syntax, and the Micro-Prolog syntax. We concentrate on the Edinburgh syntax, which is the basis of current standardisation efforts by the British Standards Institution [4]. However, we describe how the other versions differ from the Edinburgh style. We also mention the techniques used to develop shells in Prolog.

2.1.1 Representing Relationships

We begin with a small example. Suppose we have the information:

"methylated spirits removes lipstick stains"

"methylated spirits removes ink stains"

"white vinegar removes alcohol stains"

We can represent this in Prolog as *facts*:

```
removes(methylated_spirits,lipstick_stains).
removes(methylated_spirits,ink_stains).
removes(white_vinegar, alcohol_stains).
```

We can access this information by *queries*. Thus, we can ask whether a particular fact exists:

```
? removes(methylated_spirits,ink_stains).
```

results in:

```
yes
```

and the query:

```
? removes(methylated_spirits,alcohol_stains).
```

results in:

```
no
```

We can also use variables in queries. For example the query:

"find a way of removing lipstick stains"

can be posed as:

```
? removes(X,lipstick_stains).
```

Prolog can *satisfy* this query by setting the variable X to methylated_spirits. The variable X together with its associated value is called a *substitution*. We say that X has been *instantiated* with methylated_spirits. The process of finding a suitable substitution is called *unification* (see [139] for more details). Prolog answers this query by displaying the substitution, and then asking if an alternative answer is required:

```
X = methylated_spirits
more (y/n) ?y
No further solutions
```

In general, variable names must begin with a capital letter, whilst names of atoms (like alcohol_stains) must begin with a lower case letter. An anonymous variable, written _ (underscore), can be used to denote variables whose values are not significant.

Now suppose that we require our program to be capable of determining the kind of stain. For example, one way of recognising an ink stain might be:

"It is an ink stain if it is red, and the item is normally worn by a person who owns a red pen."

We can add this as a *rule*:

```
stain(Item,ink_stains) :-
        colour_stain(Item,red),
        worn(Person,Item),
        owns(Person,red_pen).
```

The left hand side of a rule is called the *head* and the right hand side of a rule is called its *body*. The ':-' can be read as 'if', whilst the commas in the body denote conjunction (and). Rules and facts are called *clauses*. Assuming the following facts:

```
colour_stain(shirt2,blue).
colour_stain(shirt1,red).

worn(first_twin,shirt1).
worn(second_twin,shirt1).

owns(first_twin,blue_pen).
owns(second_twin,red_pen).
```

A query:

```
? stain(shirt1,X).
```

results in:

```
X = ink_stains
```

How does Prolog produce this answer? It begins by unifying the query with the head of the stain rule. This results in Item being instantiated to shirt1. It now proceeds to satisfy the goals in the body of the stain rule:

```
colour_stain(shirt1,red),
worn(Person,shirt1),
owns(Person,red_pen).
```

The first of these conjuncts is satisfied by the second colour_stain fact. The second conjunct can be satisfied by both the first, and the second worn facts. To proceed with, Prolog chooses the first worn fact and instantiates Person to first_twin. It now attempts to satisfy the third conjunct. However, it fails to find a fact to confirm that the first twin owns a red pen. At this stage, Prolog *backtracks* to the second conjunct and attempts to *resatisfy* it. It now chooses the second worn fact and instantiates Person to second_twin. It again attempts to satisfy the third conjunct. This time it succeeds because there is a fact which confirms that the second twin owns a red pen.

As this example illustrates, the inclusion of backtracking enables us to express relationships much more naturally than in conventional programming languages. However, Prolog attempts to backtrack even when it is not necessary. To avoid this inefficiency, Prolog provides an operator called the *cut* (written !). The cut specifies that Prolog must not backtrack beyond the point that it is placed.

For example, suppose we now want to write a procedure to recommend a method of removing a stain on a given item:

> "A stain on an Item can be removed by a Method if the stain is X, and a Method removes X stains."

We can add this as a Prolog rule:

> removes_stain(Item,Method) :- stain(Item,X), removes(Method,X).

Prolog would attempt to satisfy a query

> ? removes_stain(Item,Method).

by first finding the kind of stain and then finding a method of removing the stain. If it fails to find a method of removing a particular stain, it will backtrack and attempt to reclassify the kind of stain. Assuming that our classification of the kind of stain is reliable, Prolog will not find an alternative classification. We can avoid this unnecessary backtracking by placing the cut appropriately:

> removes_stain(Item,Method) :- stain(Item,X), !, removes(Method,X).

Thus, when Prolog fails to find a method of removing a particular kind of stain, the cut will stop it from backtracking to reclassify the stain. The cut will also stop Prolog from considering any alternative removes_stain clauses (if there are any).

2.1.2   Lists in Prolog

In the above example, we represented ownership of an item by a fact which related the owner and the item. A more succinct representation would be to list all the items owned by a person. Thus instead of:

> owns(husband,blue_shirt).
> owns(husband,red_shirt).
> owns(husband,yellow_socks).

we can write:

> ownslist(husband,[blue_shirt,red_shirt,yellow_socks]).

where the list is the second component of this fact. In general, lists are a sequence of terms separated by commas and enclosed in brackets. Each term can also be a list.

Of course, this different representation requires different procedures to access individual items. How can we write a procedure equivalent to the original owns relationship? We can formulate it as:

"Person owns an Item if it is in the list of items owned by the Person."

which translates to the Prolog rule:

owns(Person,Item) :- ownslist(Person,List), member(Item,List).

where member(X,L) succeeds if X is in the list L.

To allow us to develop predicates like member we need a way of accessing and creating lists. The notation [H | T] defines a list whose first element is H and whose remaining elements are given by the list T. We say that H is the *head*, and T is the *tail* of this list.

We can use this notation together with unification (written =) to both access elements of a list, as well as to construct lists. For example:

? X = [blue_shirt |[white_shirt, yellow_socks]].

gives

X = [blue_shirt, white_shirt, yellow_socks]

and the query

? [X|Y] = [red_shirt,white_shirt,yellow_socks].

gives

X = red_shirt
Y= [white_shirt,yellow_socks]

We are now in a position to develop the member predicate. An item is a member of a list if:

- it is the same as the head of the list;

- or it is a member of the tail of the list.

This translate to the Prolog clauses:

member(X,List) :- [H|_] = List, H = X.
member(X,List) :- [_|T] = List, member(X,T).

We can improve this code by using the fact that Prolog attempts to unify the head of a clause with the goal that it is trying to satisfy. In this case, we can factor the unifications into the head of the clauses:

```
member(X,[X|_]).
member(X,[_|T]) :- member(X,T).
```

Prolog normally provides a rich set of built-in predicates for handling lists (including member). These predicates, together with unification, backtracking, and predicates for processing other predicates makes Prolog a very expressive language.

2.1.3   Turbo-Prolog and Micro-Prolog

Implementations of Edinburgh Prolog vary in the range of facilities for I/O and for defining modules. They can even differ in the meaning of particular predicates. Figure 2.1 shows how far one implementation of the Edinburgh style of Prolog (Expert System Int. Ltd's Prolog2) is from another (Salford University's Prologix). It displays the results of over 800 tests based on Prologix (see [12] for further details). Each test can succeed as expected (sae), fail as expected (fae), fail unexpectedly (fu), or succeed unexpectedly (su). The differences between different styles of Prolog are even greater. In this section we outline how Turbo-Prolog, and Micro-Prolog differ from the Edinburgh style. More complete accounts of these languages can be found elsewhere (e.g. [74,64]).

Turbo-Prolog

The major difference between Turbo-Prolog and the Edinburgh style of Prolog is that Turbo Prolog requires the type of objects to be declared. The various types are declared in a section with the heading domains, and the types of objects in relations are declared in a section with the heading predicates. The clauses follow a section with the heading clauses. Thus the program of Section 2.1.1 takes the form:

```
Domains

person_type , stain_type , colour_type ,
method_type , item_type = symbol

Predicates

removes(method_type,stain_type)
colour_stain(item_type,stain_type)
worn(person_type,item_type)
owns(person_type,item_type)
stain(item_type,stain_type)
removes_stain(item_type,method_type)
```

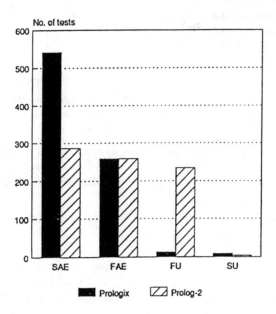

Figure 2.1: A comparison of Prologix and Prolog2

Clauses

/******************* Facts *********************/

removes(methylated_spirits,lipstick_stains).
removes(methylated_spirits,ink_stains).
removes(white_vinegar,alcohol_stains).

colour_stain(shirt2,blue).
colour_stain(shirt1,red).

worn(first_twin,shirt).
worn(second_twin,shirt1).

owns(first_twin,blue_pen).
owns(second_twin,red_pen).

/******************* Rules *********************/

removes_stain(Item,Method) :-
    stain(Item,X),
    removes(Method,X).

```
stain(Item,ink_stains) :-
        colour_stain(Item,red),
        worn(Person,Item),
        owns(Person,red_pen).
```

Thus all the domains are symbols (rather than numbers). The owns relationship's first component has a domain person-type, and a second component whose domain is item_type. Turbo-Prolog provides other standard types like char, integer, real, and string. It also allows the use of union, and list types.

The major advantages gained by the use of types are that type errors can be detected, and the code produced is often faster and more compact. The major disadvantage is that programs that require the use of mixed types are more awkward to code in Turbo-Prolog.

Even when this difference in types is ignored, there are a number of other differences between Turbo-Prolog and the Edinburgh style. Figure 2.2 shows how far Turbo-Prolog is from an implementation of the Edinburgh style of Prolog when type and naming differences are ignored (see [75] for further details). The test suite used to obtain Figure 2.2 was adapted from the one used to obtain Figure 2.1. The tests are a measure of closeness and do not reveal which style is better.

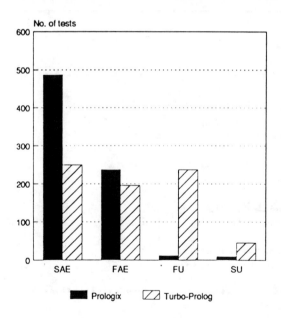

Figure 2.2: A comparison of Prologix and Turbo-Prolog

Micro-Prolog

The major difference between Micro-Prolog and the Edinburgh style of Prolog is its syntax. Micro-Prolog requires that parenthesis are used to group things. Thus the query:

> ? removes_stain(X,Y).

is typed as:

> ? (removes X Y)

and the rule:

> owns(Person,Item) :- ownslist(Person,List), member(Item,List).

is typed as:

> ((owns X Y) (ownslist X Z) (member Y Z))

where the first element is assumed to be the head of the rule. In addition to the use of parenthesis, the names of several built-in predicates are different. However, most of the predicates in Micro-Prolog are similar to those in the Edinburgh style.

2.1.4   Shells in Prolog

Prolog is not capable of explaining how it obtains a particular solution. Thus when we ask:

> ? removes_stain(shirt1,Y).

and obtain:

> Y = methylated_spirits

we are not given an explanation like:

> This was shown by the rule:
>
> removes_stain(shirt1,methylated_spirits) :-
>   stain(shirt1,ink_stains),
>   removes(methylated_spirits,ink_stains).
>
> stain(shirt1,ink_stains) was shown by the rule:
>
> stain(shirt1,ink_stains) :-
>   colour_stain(shirt1,red),
>   worn(second_twin,shirt1),
>   owns(second_twin,red_pen).
>
> The following are facts:
>
>   removes(methylated_spirits,ink_stains)
>   colour_stain(shirt1,red),
>   worn(second_twin,shirt1),
>   owns(second_twin,red_pen).

A number of shells which extend Prolog so that such facilities are available have been developed. Hammond and Sergot [64] describe the APES (**A**ugmented **P**rolog for **E**xpert **S**ystems) shell which incorporates explanations, as well as a facility for obtaining information from a user.

A technique, known as *meta-interpretation*, can also be used to extend Prolog to include such explanation facilities. Meta-interpretation works by interpreting Prolog programs in Prolog and is described by Sterling and Shapiro [133].

2.2   Lisp in brief

Lisp (**List P**rocessing) is the oldest language used in artificial intelligence. Despite its maturity, Lisp has not yet been standardised. Our brief introduction is based on Common Lisp ([131]).

A Lisp program's objects are known as *symbolic expressions*. In its simplest form, a symbolic expression is an atom (e.g. blue-shirt, owns, 1, +, etc.). A symbolic expression may also be a list. A list is defined as a sequence of symbolic expressions enclosed in parenthesis. The empty list is denoted by nil or by (). Thus, our Prolog list:

> [blue_shirt, red_shirt, yellow_socks]

is represented as the following list in Lisp:

> '(blue-shirt red-shirt yellow-socks)

The quote (') informs Lisp to treat the list as data rather than as a function application. Due to the importance of lists, Lisp provides many predefined list handling functions. The head of a list can be obtained by applying the function car, while the tail of list can be obtained by applying cdr. The function null returns true (T) if its argument is an empty list and returns nil otherwise.

Examples

> (car '(blue-shirt red-shirt yellow-socks))

gives

> blue-shirt

> (cdr '(blue-shirt red-shirt yellow-socks))

returns

> (red-shirt yellow-socks)

> (null '())

returns T

We can define our own Lisp functions by using a form called defun; an acronym for **define function**. For example a function to double a number can be defined by:

```
(defun double (x) (times x 2) )
```

and used:

```
(double 6)
```

returns 12.

Atoms like **defun** are called *special forms* to distinguish them from predefined functions like car and cdr. A special form, called cond, allows us to code conditional functions. In general, cond takes a form:

```
(cond
        (condition-1 action-1a action1b ...)
        (condition-2 action-2a action2b ...)
        ... )
```

Cond evaluates the conditions in sequence until it finds a condition that evaluates to a nonnil value. The associated action forms are then evaluated, and the result of the last action is returned as the result of applying cond. If all the conditions evaluate to nil, then cond returns nil.

As an example, the following function defines the list membership function:

```
(defun member (x lst)
        (cond ((null lst) nil)
              ((eq x (car lst)) T)
              (T (member x (cdr lst))) ) )
```

Thus, in this example, cond has three lists as arguments. The first list specifies that x cannot be in an empty list. The second list specifies that x is a member of lst if x is equal to the head of lst. The third list makes a recursive call to find out if x is in the tail of lst.

There are many situations when the generality of the cond form is not needed. Most versions of Lisp provide forms like if, case, and when which lead to better code.

The popularity of Lisp in artificial intelligence stems from the fact that it was the first system to provide many powerful predefined functions (including member) for symbolic manipulation. Unlike Prolog, Lisp does not provide backtracking, or unification. This means that some problems are more natural to express in Prolog than in Lisp. However, Lisp allows an imperative style of programming. Thus for example, Lisp provides assignments statements which allow a variable to be overwritten. In most implementations of Prolog, programmers are often forced to add extra arguments to their predicates or to record values in a database!

Part II
Expert System Shells and Environments

There are many expert system development tools. These tools provide a framework in which various knowledge representation techniques are already available. These vary from simple PC-based tools called shells to the more sophisticated and more expensive workstation based environments called toolkits.

The simple PC-based shells often provide one particular knowledge representation technique, while the workstation based environments or toolkits provide a broad range of knowledge representation, and development aids.

This part of the book gives an indication of the kind of facilities, and power offered by the shells and the toolkits.

Chapter 3 describes a PC-based shell called Advisor-2. It gives a good indication of the kind of facilities that are offered by expert system shells, as well as how Advisor-2's facilities can be used to represent and structure knowledge.

Chapter 4 provides an extensive review of one of the most powerful toolkits currently available, known as Inference ART. It gives a detailed account of the broad range of facilities offered by Inference ART and comments on their suitability. It also describes the experience of using and installing several versions of ART.

Most of the available expert system tools are general purpose. A trend that is increasing is to provide more specialised development tools for particular areas of application. Chapter 5 describes an expert system shell that was developed primarily for applications in ecology. The main feature of the shell is the pragmatic manner in which it handles uncertainty.

An expert system will not be used unless its recommendations are trusted by a user. Chapter 6 describes how the integration of simulations can improve the reliability, and capabilities of expert systems. It also describes a simulation tool called STEM which can be integrated into an expert system.

Chapter 3

An Introduction to Advisor-2

Mark Lewis

3.1 What is Advisor-2 ?

Advisor-2 is an enhanced version ESP Advisor, one of the first expert system shells in the world. Advisor-2 is an ideal tool for the first-time developer of expert systems who demands ease of use, as well as for the experienced developer who insists on sufficient power to build advanced systems and to interface to a wide variety of other packages. To date, ESP Advisor and Advisor-2 have been used to develop a wide range of expert systems including:

- Diagnosing causes and recommending treatment of bacteriological problems in gas plants.

- Illustrating a design process for a telecommunication network.

- Advising on the storage of dangerous chemicals on ships

- Advising on IEE wiring regulations.

- A model of a pension fund.

- Formalising well-defined management decision aid techniques.

- Selecting an appropriate computer.

Advisor-2 provides four main tools for the development of an expert system:

1. A formal language which may be used to code the raw knowledge of the application in a concise but readable and easy-to-understand form. This is the Knowledge Representation Language (KRL).

2. A KRL compiler which converts the high-level knowledge base into a compact and efficient form.

3. A Knowledge Base Analyser which produces a parameter dependency report and detects circular dependencies and nested repeats.

4. A Consultation Shell which uses a compiled knowledge base and provides a friendly, interactive system with which to access and use the stored knowledge.

The following four sections describe each of these tools whilst Section 3.6 lists some further features of Advisor-2.

3.2   The Advisor-2 Knowledge Base

An Advisor-2 knowledge base consists of rules, and advice or information which may be displayed during a consultation session. An Advisor-2 expert system proceeds by working through its knowledge base, selecting relevant advice and presenting this information to the user. In order to determine which information is relevant at any particular time, the system will use the rules to deduce answers or ask questions of the user in a friendly and helpful manner.

A knowledge base for Advisor-2 may be divided into one or more sections; each section being concerned with a particular self-contained aspect of the application. The ability to decompose a large or complex knowledge base into a set of well-defined sections greatly simplifies its design, development and subsequent maintenance. Using the sectioning facility, it is possible to make the knowledge base reflect the inherent structure of the knowledge of the application domain. For example, knowledge about faults in cars might be divided as in Figure 3.1.

Each section of the knowledge base might contain:

- A number of paragraphs of text.

- References to other sections.

- A declaration of the parameters of the problem.

- A repeat statement.

The following sections describe each of these in further detail.

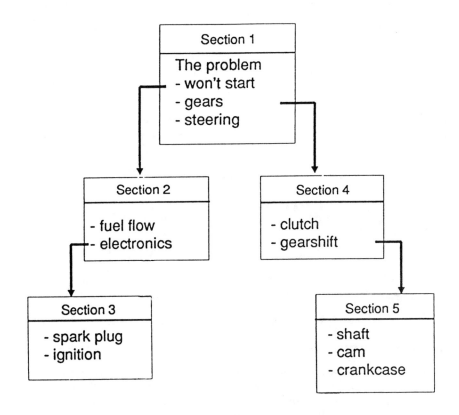

Figure 3.1: An example of sectioning

3.2.1 Paragraphs

A paragraph is a convenient way of representing advice or information that must be displayed.

For example, the following production rule:

```
IF      fuel flows into the carburettor
AND   the spark plug is not wet
THEN Check carburettor for air leakage .. etc
```

can be represented by including the condition in brackets and following it with the advice:

```
{ fuel_flows and not spark_plug_wet }
```

```
'Check carburettor for air leakage at cylinder base,'&
'crankshaft oil seals, crankcase joint and carburettor joint.'.
```

3.2.2   Section References

The KRL allows the designer to specify that control should move from one section to another by following the keyword reference by the name of the section. Each section reference may be unconditional or conditional. For example, we can represent the rule:

```
IF     fuel flows into the carburettor
AND    the spark plug is wet
THEN reference the section called spark_test
```

by the statement:

```
{ fuel_flows and spark_plug_wet } reference spark_test.
```

which specifies that if the parameters within the brackets are satisfied the system will enter another section within the knowledge base called spark_test which deals with a separate aspect of the application.

3.2.3   Parameters

A parameter is a variable or circumstance which has a bearing on the problem domain. A parameter is declared by naming it, providing a description of the parameter, and specifying its type. A simple type of a parameter is a fact which can have a boolean value (true or false). The value of a parameter can be obtained from a user if it is marked as askable. Thus, for the above example, we can declare the parameters as follows:

```
( fuel_flows and spark_plug_wet ) reference spark_test.

fuel_flows: 'fuel flows into the carburettor'
fact
askable
        'Is there fuel flowing into the carburettor?'.

spark_plug_wet: 'the condition of the spark plug'
fact
askable
        'Is the spark plug wet?'.
```

where fuel_flows, and spark_plug_wet are parameters which are facts. These facts are marked as askable, and the text of the question is provided.

In general a parameter can also be a number; a phrase providing a short piece of text; a category providing a small number of fixed options; or help text which can be used for providing further explanations. We can also attach rules to parameters, and define the acceptable values of a parameter. Thus, for example, some of the reasons for a car not starting might be coded as follows:

```
'The' ..@problem .. 'is responsible for the engine not starting.'.

problem: 'the possible faults'
category
options
        fuel_tank, spark_plug
rules
        fuel_tank if air_vent_clogged,
        spark_plug if wet or gap <> 0.8.

air_vent_clogged: 'the condition of the air vent'
fact
askable
        'Is the air vent clogged?'.

wet: 'the condition of the spark plug'
fact
askable
        'Is the spark plug wet?'.

gap: 'the spark plug gap'
number
askable
        'What is the size of the spark plug gap?'.
```

Note that the order in which parameter definitions are presented in the knowledge base is not significant. The system decides when and what questions to ask.

3.2.4 Iteration

A particularly powerful feature of the Advisor-2 KRL is the ability to repeat sections using the repeated until control specifier. All the parameters in a repeated section can be used multiple times, and for each iteration the value of a parameter is saved. It is then possible to carry out list functions on the saved values, such as find the minimum, maximum or average.

Iteration allows the building and comparing of a number of scenarios — a number of alternative business plans for example.

3.3 The KRL Compiler

The purpose of the compiler is to convert the high-level English-like form of the knowledge base into a compact form which can be efficiently accessed by the

Consultation Shell when running the finished expert system. Another function of the compiler is to check the content of the knowledge base for syntactic correctness and for self-consistency. In checking the syntactic correctness of the knowledge base, the compiler will identify any mistakes with a helpful message which should allow the error to be easily located and corrected.

3.4   The Knowledge Base Analyser

The Knowledge Base Analyser is a very useful debugging tool. It cross references a knowledge base and generates a report of which parameters depend on which parameters. The analyser also detects circular parameter dependencies, circular section references and nested repeats.

3.5   Consultation Shell

The Advisor-2 Consultation Shell provides friendly and interactive access to the knowledge base, allowing the expertise and information to be inspected and used in a conversational style and has a set of powerful commands conveniently attached to the function keys which allow the internal operation of the system to be examined and questioned. There is also an on-line help facility providing help with the use of the commands. The commands include:

- F1 Help: context sensitive help system;

- F2 Explain: explain the question;

- F2 Explain/More: information on related topics;

- F3 Status: display status of consultation;

- F4 Show: display a parameter;

- F4 How: display how a parameter value was obtained;

- F5 Why Question: why is a question being asked;

- F5 Why Advice: why was advice given;

- F6 Recap: recap on last or all advice;

- F7 Forget: a flexible 'What-if' facility;

- F8 Print: print advice to a file or printer;

- F9 DOS: calls to DOS;

- F10 Save: save, restart or quit a consultation.

3.6   Further features of Advisor-2

3.6.1   The External Interface

Many expert system builders wish to make better, and more intelligent use of their existing software. The external interface is used as an escape mechanism to implement various features without adding extra constructs to the KRL.

Interfaces to Advisor-2 come as standard and are included in the price. The interfaces include: Prolog-2, C, Fortran, Pascal, Assembler, Lotus 123, dBase III, and Gem Graphics.

With the Prolog interface certain functions are accessible via the interface regardless of whether the system is supplied with Prolog-2. These facilities include the ability to save a consultation and start with the saved session, and interface to DOS.

3.6.2   The Packager

Once a knowledge base has been completed the packager can be used to package the application as a stand-alone system. During the packaging procedure it is possible to specify the level at which the system should be run, i.e. should the user be allowed access to the How and Why functions. Password protection can also be included which is particularly useful if the system is only to be used by authorised persons.

3.6.3   The Window Configurer

The user interface of an expert system is extremely important. The end-user must be happy with it if it is going to be used effectively. In addition to features like How and Why, Advisor-2 allows windows to be configured. For example, it allows the foreground and background colours of all the windows to be configured to the users preference.

Chapter 4

The State of the ART

Robert Inder

4.1 Introduction

This is a review of **Inference ART**, the **A**utomated **R**easoning **T**ool, a programming system for the development of expert systems. It began as a two-part article which described and discussed the features of Version 2.0 of ART, in the light of several months experience of using the tool for a number of small projects at the AI Applications Institute in Edinburgh,[1] mostly through the KRSTL facility.[2] This appeared in Issues 1 and 2 of *AIring*.[3]

Subsequently, after about six months experience of using ART 3.0 on a SUN workstation, a third part was written for Issue 4 of *AIring*, describing the extra features found in the new release of the tool. Finally, after installing Version

---

[1] The **A**rtificial **I**ntelligence **A**pplications **I**nstitute (AIAI) is a self-funding technology transfer group within the University of Edinburgh. It is distinct from, but has close ties with, the Department of Artificial Intelligence, which is the only department dedicated to the subject that has been established in any European University. The Institute can provide courses and consultancy in many aspects of Artificial Intelligence, but is also keen participate in collaborative project work.

[2] The **K**nowledge **R**epresentation **S**ystems **T**rials **L**aboratory (KRSTL) is a government-supported facility operated by the AIAI. It aims to support the use of the specialised Knowledge Representation toolkits, such as ART, by providing advice and assistance, together with access to the tools themselves for trial projects.

[3] *AIring* is a magazine produced by the AIAI three times per year and copies can be obtained by contacting the Institute's External Relations Manager.

3.1 and experimenting briefly with it, the three parts were combined to produce this chapter. The most obvious anachronisms were removed during the merging process, and the resulting seams were smoothed to a some extent, so that hopefully the final result is not seriously impaired by its development.

The next section gives a very brief overview of the entire system, mentioning all the main kinds of facilities it offers. The following sections then expand on each of these in turn, aiming to provide a picture of their operation that is complete enough to be accessible to those with only limited knowledge of AI tools and techniques. For the sake of brevity of explanation, some liberties have been taken with the syntax! These descriptions of the specific facilities provided by the tool are followed by a discussion of some more general aspects of its use and a summary of the impression it gives In addition to bare descriptions of the facilities that the system provides, there are also a number of observations on their usability or shortcomings. While these are based on a number of months of both using the tool and helping others to do so, they are, or course, personal opinions.

4.2   An Overview of ART

Inference ART is an example of what is sometimes called an AI Toolkit or a Knowledge Representation System: a powerful program development system specialised to facilitate the writing of knowledge-based (or expert) systems. It is a very large program developed originally on the Symbolics Lisp Machine, and now also available under (Lucid) Common Lisp on SUN 3 (and shortly DEC Micro-Vax) workstations. It offers its users both a language that supports the use and combination of a number of different programming styles, or *paradigms*, together with a sophisticated programming and debugging environment that is based around a high-resolution graphics display. However, ART users are easily able and occasionally forced to program the underlying Lisp system directly.

At the heart of ART's programming language is a rule-based system. That is, ART contains a mechanism which allows the user to specify certain features of the (kind of) situation that he wants the system to work with, together with a number of *rules* which describe the behaviour that is appropriate to a particular type of situation. The system will then determine the results of behaving in accordance with these rules in the situation specified, and carrying out these actions constitutes the execution of the program. Of course, in ART programs, as in life, there are often a number of rules that are applicable to any given situation, and the choice of which to follow at any moment can dramatically affect the behaviour produced by the system. As a result, ART's rule engine provides features that allow the programmer some control over these decisions. Most importantly, it provides the ability to give each rule a priority, or *salience*, and to specify that it is to be used in a goal-directed manner.

In addition to allowing the programmer control over the sequencing of rules, ART has a number of features designed to facilitate the description of situations. Foremost amongst these is the ability to accept descriptions of objects and concepts and the relations between them in terms of what ART calls *schemata*. Moreover, once the programmer has specified the properties of relations, such as their inverses or their transitivity, the system will automatically determine the consequences of these properties whenever the relation is used. In particular, ART knows that certain relations between objects — such as one being an instance of the other — involve the sharing, or *inheritance*, of properties between the entities involved. By using these features to describe the concepts and relations to be considered, it is possible to get ART to do a considerable amount of reasoning (and consistency checking) automatically.

In addition to handling the inheritance of attributes and values, ART also supports object-oriented and access oriented programming styles. It allows the programmer to associate the applicability of any arbitrary procedures, or *actions*, with specific classes of objects. These procedures can then be invoked by operating on the object (by sending it a message). Alternatively, actions can be associated with some attribute of objects of a given class, resulting in an *active value* In this case the procedure is invoked by accessing the value of the relevant attribute in the appropriate way (e.g. reading or changing it).

So far, program execution has been described as the carrying out of actions that rules have specified are appropriate to the situation under consideration. However, one of the most powerful features of ART is its ability to support the simultaneous manipulation of a number of different descriptions of situations, known as *contexts*. Not surprisingly, the situations considered within most programs are generally not independent, but are alternatives, specialisations or continuations of one another. As a result, ART provides the programmer with a sophisticated mechanism, based on what are called *viewpoints*, for specifying and organising the inter-relationships between the states being considered. On the basis of this specification, ART is able to ensure the efficient manipulation of the information within inter-related contexts while maintaining the appropriate degree of independence or consistency between them. This feature is particularly useful for evaluating the consequences of decisions, checking the consistency of hypotheses or handling of uncertain information.

Finally, the system provides the ability to smoothly integrate the use of mouse, keyboard and high-resolution graphics within its rule-based programming paradigm, thus allowing the construction of sophisticated user interfaces.

4.3   Basic Rule-based Programming in ART

Since the operation of the system has been described in terms of the application of rules to situation, it seems most natural to start by considering how ART represents situations. Any represented state of the world is characterised by the set of *facts* which hold in it, with each fact indicating a commitment to the truth of a particular *proposition* in all the states (i.e. contexts) to which it applies. In ART, a proposition is typically an arbitrary sequence of words, numbers or indeed other propositions: thus the following are all propositions (although, of course, there is no sense in which ART can be said to understand them):

```
(THIS IS A PROPOSITION)
(SO IS THIS)
((THIS IS A PROPOSITION) IS A PROPOSITION)
(THE VALUE OF PI IS 3.14159)
(EVALUATING (+ 2 2.142) GIVES 4.142)
```

In addition to a proposition, a fact has a unique system-generated identifier and an indication of the range of contexts (possible states of affairs) to which it applies. A state, therefore, is specified by indicating the collection of propositions that are true in it. Thus if one were inclined to construct a system for reasoning about how to shuffle blocks about a table, one might choose to specify the initial state, STATE-1, by the following collection of facts:

```
fact-1: (ON BLOCK-B TABLE) in [STATE-1]
fact-2: (ON BLOCK-A BLOCK-B) in [STATE-1]
fact-3: (ON BLOCK-C TABLE) in [STATE-1]
fact-4: (OBJECTIVE ((ON BLOCK-C TABLE)
                    (ON BLOCK-B BLOCK-C)
                    (ON BLOCK-A BLOCK-B))) in [STATE-1]
```

For the most part, the interpretation of this notation should be intuitively obvious. The possible exception is fact-4, which indicates that the objective in STATE-1 is characterised by the sequence of three further propositions.

Having outlined the way ART represents the state of the world, it is now possible to consider how rules can be written to interact with it. ART's rules have two parts: a set of actions, and a pattern characterising when those actions are appropriate in terms of the facts that are present within the various contexts that the system may be considering. Because of the way that these parts are written, separated by an arrow, they are usually known respectively as the right and left hand sides of a rule.

Most often, the action part (or right hand side) of a rule is intended either to change the system's description of a situation it is considering, by adding or removing facts from the relevant context, or to cause the consideration of a completely new state of affairs, by creating a new context. When either of these happen, it will usually affect the set of other rules which are able to fire, thus giving rise to the basic execution cycle of the system, in which a rule fires, changes the state of the system and thus enables another rule to fire. However, in addition to simply modifying a context, a rule's actions can also present information to the user, accept information from him or indeed call arbitrary Lisp functions. This last option allows the programmer to carry out any computation or action that is possible on the machine, either directly, in the case of Lisp Machines, or through the operating system (and possibly calls to processes written in other languages) on a general purpose workstation.

At its simplest, the pattern part, or left hand side, of a rule comprises a list of propositions, and ART will consider that it is appropriate to execute the rule's actions any time the description of a state comes to contain all those propositions. For instance, given the following pattern component of a rule, ART would decide that its associated actions should be carried out in STATE-1 above:

```
(DEFRULE EXAMPLE-RULE
    (ON BLOCK-B TABLE)
    (ON BLOCK-A BLOCK-B)
=>   ... some action or other
```

Notice that, as with all production systems, the order of the proposition patterns within the rule does not have to match that of the facts. Notice also that the pattern matches even though there are features of the state which the rule does not mention.

In addition to allowing rule patterns composed of a number of simple propositions, ART allows very much more complex pattern matching. The feature which makes the greatest contribution to the flexibility of pattern matching is the ability to make use of *variables*. These are denoted by names that begin with "?", and the following is an example of a rule using them:

```
(DEFRULE EXAMPLE-RULE-2
    (ON ?X TABLE)
    (ON ?Y ?X)
    (ON ?Z ?Y)
=>   (ASSERT (ONE BIG PILE)))
```

The pattern component of this rule states that it should fire when there is a state in which there is something (?X) on the table, something else (?Y) on top of it and something else again (?Z) on top of that. The action component, incidentally, states that the system should add to the description of the state a fact asserting the proposition (ONE BIG PILE).

There are two key points about the use of variables in ART's pattern matching which are strongly reminiscent of their use in Prolog. First, variables are entirely local to the rule (clause) in which they are used: they cannot be accessed in any way from outside the rule, and there is never any interaction with any variable of the same name in any other rule. Second, at the point it is first used in matching against a fact, a variable can be matched against any single item in its proposition. However, in doing so it will acquire a *binding* to that item which cannot subsequently be changed or removed (at least within the LHS of a rule). If the bound variable appears elsewhere in the pattern part of the rule, it will only match against precisely the same item to which it has been bound. Thus a rule is only considered appropriate to fire if the facts in a context will allow a complete match of every pattern in its left hand side using only a single fixed binding per variable. These bindings are then available in the RHS of the rule in order to shape the actions that it specifies to reflect the precise details of the context to which it is being applied.

In fact, life is slightly more complicated than this, since it is often possible to find more than one set of bindings of the variables present within the LHS of a rule: that is, a rule's pattern component can be satisfied in more than one way. When this happens, ART will simultaneously determine every possible set of variable bindings, and consider firing the rule once for each. Notice that when ART is deciding what to do next, it considers not just rules, but rules in combination with acceptable variable bindings. Precisely how ART chooses a particular rule-and-binding combination will be the topic of the next section, but crucially there is only ever one that is selected at any point. Once a set of variable bindings has been chosen then, unless the programmer deliberately specifies otherwise, all possible implications of this choice will be explored. Should it transpire that this does not allow the program to achieve its objectives, ART will select another of the possible bindings of the variables and pursue its consequences in turn. However, this behaviour can be disrupted if some action taken while evaluating the implications of one possibility modifies the state and disrupts any remaining matches.

This style of behaviour is similar to that of Prolog. Where there is more than one possible instantiation of a variable, Prolog will make a note of the existence of alternatives (a backtrack point) and select one for immediate attention. Should the choice made prove unsatisfactory, Prolog will undo everything it did in discovering this, return to the backtrack point and attempt to search for any other possible bindings. Prolog also provides a mechanism, called the cut, by which the actions taken in exploring one possibility can prevent the consideration of others. However, there are a number of differences between the two approaches. Prolog is more explicit, which means that it is easier to see the order in which things will be searched, at the expense of having to specify it. It also does less work before opting for one possibility, since it only notes that others (may) exist, without evaluating what they may be, although any performance implications of this are largely obscured by the details of the implementations. Finally, the Prolog approach may require less storage, since it is able to discard any information stored in exploring one possibility before considering the next. ART's approach on the other hand, allows it a greater measure of flexibility. Since it does keep information about its earlier explorations, it is possible to compare them, or even go back to them, and as a result of this it is very easy to get a limited breadth-first exploration of the possibilities. However, full breadth-first search (exploring all viable alternatives equally until a solution is found) still requires to be programmed in both systems.

As well as variables, ART has a number of other features that contribute to the flexibility of its pattern matching. To begin with, it allows (groups of) proposition patterns to be negated; thus making the rule only eligible to fire in a context if there are no (groups of) facts with propositions that match the negated pattern(s). It also has facilities for binding variables to multiple items within a fact's proposition, although having been so bound it will subsequently only match against precisely the same sequence of items occurring elsewhere. In addition, it allows the user to impose restrictions on what can be bound to any individual variable. At its simplest, this can be done by listing a range of possible bindings that are to be permitted or excluded. Alternatively, it is possible to specify the invocation of any procedure written in Lisp in order to determine the acceptability of any given binding (or indeed combination of bindings). Finally, ART supports a range of constructs which cause any rule containing them to automatically generate a number of other rules. In some cases the generated rules are each slight modifications or specialisations of the function described by the original rule. In others, the created rules form a coordinated set that carry out conceptually familiar tests that are tricky to implement in production systems.

4.4   Flow of Control

One of the key benefits claimed for rule-based systems is that the user is not obliged to explicitly specify, or even consider, the flow of control as the program (rule base) is executed. Ideally it is possible to simply regard each rule as being invoked whenever it is appropriate (i.e. when its LHS pattern matches the current state). Unfortunately, in a system of any size it is often the case that there are several rule patterns which suggest that their actions are appropriate in the same situation. In addition, as pointed out in the previous section, one rule may be able to fire with more than one variable binding, and indeed all discussion of rules being able to fire actually refers to rule-and-binding combinations. Since the actions of any of these rules may change the situation to the extent that the other rules are no longer appropriate, the choice of which rule to follow first can have a dramatic effect on the behaviour of the system.

To understand this situation, it is useful to think in terms of what ART terms the *agenda* (the *conflict set* in the terminology of OPS-5, one of ART's conceptual ancestors) — the queue of rules waiting to be fired. Whenever a state is created that allows the pattern component of a rule to be completely matched, that rule is placed on the agenda, where it remains until either it is fired, or the state changes in such a way as its pattern is no longer matched. Once a rule is fired, the corresponding rule-and-binding combination is removed from the agenda and will never be fired again on precisely the same facts. When ART discovers that a rule pattern can be completely matched, it will, in the absence of any reason to behave otherwise, place an entry for that rule at the head of the agenda — at the front of the queue of rules waiting to fire. This has the effect that ART will normally fire (execute the actions of) the rule that has matched most recently — i.e. against the fact most recently added to the context. This strategy, which is used in OPS-5, has the effect of basing the selection of the next action on the result of the most recent action. This tends to focus processing on a depth-first exploration of the possibilities open to the program: that is, the consequences of one option are exhaustively pursued before another is tackled.

Flow control, and the strategy used for choosing which rule to fire in any given circumstances, obviously have an enormous effect on the results of program execution. Within ART's rule-based system there are a number of techniques for directing this choice that the programmer can adopt. For instance, it is possible to generate facts to indicate the current stage of processing and use additional LHS patterns to ensure that rules fire only in particular stages. However, in addition to supporting these techniques, ART offers the user two further mechanisms for influencing its rule selection behaviour, namely salience and backward chaining rules.

In ART, every rule can be associated with a numerical *salience* which is taken to be a measure of its priority. When rules are added to the agenda, they are not necessarily added to the very front, but only to the front of those that share the same salience. This means that the rules that can fire are considered primarily in order of their salience, and only within that is recency of addition to the agenda considered. As a result, no rule is ever fired while another of higher salience is applicable. This is useful for a number of reasons, not least for specifying flow of control. It is a simple matter to separate control rules — those responsible for moving from phase to phase or for controlling cyclic behaviour — from the rules that actually carry out the process being controlled, simply by giving them a lower salience.

The other major mechanism for controlling inference affects the circumstances under which rules are moved to the agenda. Normally, production systems operate in a *forward chaining* manner, with rules being fired as soon as their preconditions, as specified on the LHS of the rule, are satisfied. This means that program execution can be seen as finding out what follows from what is known. The alternative is known as *backward chaining*, and execution using such a strategy is more a matter of finding out whether some known result can be achieved. In other words, rules are only considered when some fact that they may be able to supply is known to be wanted. Within its essentially forward chaining paradigm, ART achieves this by adding the desire to know a conclusion to the preconditions of rule. It does this by using *goal patterns*. To a very good approximation these can be thought of as normal facts which happen to have a proposition that states that some other proposition is a goal — i.e. of the form:

(GOAL (SOME PROPOSITION OR OTHER))

A rule is made backward chaining simply by including within its left hand side a goal pattern, similar to the above example, specifying the kind of proposition that the rule is able to provide. If this is done, then ART will ensure that whenever the left hand side of any rule would be satisfied by the presence of such a proposition, a suitable *goal fact* is automatically created. This goal fact could then, in the presence of facts to satisfy all the other patterns in its preconditions, advance a backward chaining rule to the agenda, where it can take its place among the other rules that are waiting to be fired in the normal way. Once it has fired, it can assert an appropriate normal fact by way of a reply. If this corresponds to the goal — in this case by having the proposition (SOME PROPOSITION OR OTHER) — it will immediately satisfy the pattern that caused the goal to be generated, and thus allow that rule to proceed on its way to the agenda.

Judging from the emphasis that backward chaining receives, both in the tutorials and the vendor course, people seem to find it difficult.[4] Possibly as a result of this, ART also provides a special syntax for backward chaining rules. However, this form only provides access to a limited subset of the possibilities open when using goal patterns directly in forward chaining rules. Moreover, it is expanded into the equivalent forward chaining form as soon as it is loaded, and this is the form in which it appears through any of the debugging tools that the ART environment provides. This means that familiarity with the underlying mechanism of goal patterns in forward chaining rules remains more or less essential, and as a result the provision of the special format for backward chaining rules seems to be of minimal utility.

Given the visibility of the underlying forward chaining mechanism, one may be tempted to interpret this suggestion that ART's backward chaining rule syntax is unnecessary as impugning its ability to backward chain. ART is able to invoke a rule whenever the result it offers is relevant, provided that its other preconditions hold. Moreover, if one of these preconditions itself turns out to be a potential result of some other backward chaining rule, then the system will create another goal fact which in its turn may either allow rules to reach the agenda or create still further goals.... Admittedly each rule is restricted to being used in either a forward or a backward chaining manner. However, it is still fair to say that ART **can** backward chain, and the mechanism of intermixing goal patterns with other pre-suppositions seems a very natural way of integrating such behaviour within an essentially forward chaining paradigm.

4.5   Objects and Relations

In addition to providing very flexible pattern matching, ART offers the programmer some powerful facilities for representing situations through the definition of what ART terms *schemata*. An ART schema is an information structure describing a given object or concept in terms of a collection of slots with values. To a good but not perfect approximation, the value for each slot of each object appears as an ordinary fact, just as described above, with the added restriction that the fact's proposition contains precisely three terms, the middle of which is the name of the schema. For instance, ART might display the facts in a particular schema as follows:

```
(INSTANCE-OF CLYDE ELEPHANT)
(COLOUR-OF CLYDE GREY)
(FAVOURITE-FOOD CLYDE BUNS)
(WEIGHT-OF CLYDE (1023 LBS))
```
[5]

At the trivial level, ART's support for schemata includes some syntactic sugar which allows a schema to be written in a more compact form that avoids the

---

[4] I must admit that I found it comparatively straightforward, although perhaps this is a result of extensive exposure to Prolog.

[5] Note here that this particular schema fact does indeed contain precisely three terms, the third of which (the value) happens to be a sequence of other items.

repetition of its name (see below). However, the key thing is that the slots that make up each schema are themselves each described by another schema, which the ART system examines when it needs to determine how to manipulate any instances of that slot. As a result, by putting suitable values in the slots of the schema that describes a slot (!), the programmer can have ART manipulate it appropriately for the property he wants it to represent. For instance, it is possible to specify whether or not a particular slot can have multiple values (compare a garment's *colour* and its *price*). It is also possible to tell ART that a particular slot represents a *relation* between schemata. In this case, it will know that whatever fills the slot is itself another schema, which ART will automatically create if it does not exist already. Indeed ART is also able to handle the fact that a relation has an *inverse*, or that it is *transitive* or *reflexive*, and even that under certain specified conditions it implies some other arbitrary relation. In each case it will automatically generate additional facts to represent the implications of these properties. Finally, if the slot represents a relation, it is also possible to specify that it is an *inheritance* relation. In this case, if ART is told that schema A is related to schema B by an inheritance relation, it will automatically ensure that A acquires all the slots (and their values) possessed by B.[6]

It is possible to illustrate many of these facilities by looking at the way they operate within ART, which uses them to define the well-known *is-a* and *instance-of* relations. Consider the following description of Clyde, written using ART's schema notation:

```
(DEFSCHEMA ELEPHANT
    (IS-A MAMMAL)
    (COLOUR GREY)
    (FAVOURITE-FOOD LEAVES))

(DEFSCHEMA CLYDE
    (WEIGHT-OF (1023 LBS))
    (INSTANCE-OF ELEPHANT)
    (FAVOURITE-FOOD BUNS))
```

When these definitions are interpreted by the system, they produce a total of 10 facts supporting the following propositions:

```
(COLOUR ELEPHANT GREY)
(IS-A ELEPHANT MAMMAL)
(FAVOURITE-FOOD ELEPHANT LEAVES)
(WEIGHT-OF CLYDE (1023 LBS))
(INSTANCE-OF CLYDE ELEPHANT)
(FAVOURITE-FOOD CLYDE BUNS)
(COLOUR CLYDE GREY)
(INSTANCE-OF CLYDE MAMMAL)
(HAS-KINDS MAMMAL ELEPHANT)
(HAS-INSTANCES MAMMAL CLYDE)
```

---

[6] In fact, only the slots that are known to be inheritable are inherited, and the inheritance behaviour of a slot is one of the properties specified in the schema describing it.

The first six simply come from normalising the syntax of ART's schema shorthand. The fact that Clyde is grey has been inherited from the definition of an elephant, while the fact that Clyde is an instance of a mammal has been inferred from the fact that Clyde is an elephant and specified properties of the relation INSTANCE-OF. Finally, the last two facts were inferred by ART from the definition of the inverses of the IS-A and INSTANCE-OF relations. Notice, incidentally, that Clyde's favourite food illustrates that inheritance is by default. That is, the specification of an attribute value that is specific to Clyde overrides the value that would otherwise have been assumed.

Once a schema has been defined, ART will continually check to ensure that its slots are being manipulated in line with their declared properties. In particular, whenever inferences of the kind illustrated concerning inverse relations, inheritance and so forth become possible, they will be made automatically and immediately — that is, independently of the rule-firing cycle. Similarly, ART will continually check for attempts to assign multiple values to slots that have been defined as being necessarily single-valued, and will prevent this happening. Because it operates without involving the rule engine, the schema mechanism can make considerable inferencing power available directly from Lisp, and ART provides special functions for accessing, setting and clearing slot values. In addition, there is a modify function which applies to single-valued slots and which first retracts any (fact specifying an) existing value, and then asserts a new one. This can also be invoked from a rule through a special action, and this allows the slot to be changed without first pattern matching against its current value, a facility which can help control execution under certain circumstances.

There are, of course, limitations on what can be done with schemata. One of the least expected, and therefore most irritating, is the fact that ART imposes special restrictions on matches against slot names. It is only possible to use literals or (new in ART3) variables that are already bound, and in the latter case the normally-optional schema "wrapper" is obligatory. However, this new feature does not interact at all well with backward chaining. Although the syntax might invite one to assume otherwise, it is not possible to use bound variables in goal patterns (trying to do so produces compiler errors, and indeed the BNF forbids it), which is a shame since it prevents writing backward chaining rules for finding values for classes of attributes. More insidiously, bound variables used as slot names do not **trigger** goals either, and no warning or error messages are produced. It is quite possible that these abilities have been deliberately omitted because of their potentially serious efficiency implications, but their omission surely warrants being explicitly highlighted. In any case, their absence is to be regretted, since they constitute real lapses in the otherwise very pleasing productivity (in the sense of uniformity) of the language.

Having pointed out this limitation on using variables as the slot or relation name in a schema, it is important to stress that it is not a limitation of ART itself. ART always displays facts relating to schema slots in precisely the same way as other facts with three-element propositions. However, it actually draws a sharp distinction between the two types of fact. Simple facts, those unrelated to schema slots, are perfectly well behaved with appropriately bound variables in any position, including the first, and as a result it is possible to use them to generalise over all aspects of a proposition, including the relationship involved. Moreover, a number of the other facilities that are available for schemata are also implemented for ordinary *propositional* facts. Thus without making any use of the schema mechanism it is possible to declare relations to ART and associate properties with them. One such property is arity — the number of items it interrelates — and on the basis of this information ART will check any propositions using that relation and warn if the arity is violated. In addition, ART can interpret specifications of the standard mathematical properties of relations — transitivity, symmetry or an inverse relation. Finally, as with schema slots, any relation can have the property of implying arbitrary other facts.

However, despite the fact that these facilities for propositional facts so closely mirror those provided for schemata, they are implemented by a completely independent mechanism. Facts capturing the consequences of schema slot properties are simply generated by ART as soon as they can be deduced. In contrast, the properties of non-schema relations are handled by automatically generating rules to assert the appropriate implications, which must then take their turn on the agenda along with those written by the user.

Why ART provides two mechanisms which seem to overlap so substantially in the facilities they provide is not obvious. Moreover, it can lead to difficulties, particularly if one does not realise the sharp distinction between facts representing schema slots and those representing other propositions. It is quite possible to create two apparently identical facts, one of which will appear as a part of a schema but will not match against a particular rule, while the other simultaneously matches the rule but is not recognised as belonging to the schema. Admittedly getting into such a state requires trying to be "clever", but not to the point of perversity, and the fact that it is possible is a definite misfeature of the system.

4.6   Object Oriented Programming

The most conspicuous facility added to release 3 of ART is explicit support for Object Oriented Programming. This is an approach based on a metaphor of a collection of autonomous objects interacting with each other by sending messages, which may be requests for information or instructions to do something. At its simplest, an object oriented system allows the programmer to write procedures for handling certain types of messages, and associate them with classes of objects. The applicability of these procedures will then be treated as a property of such objects that is inherited throughout the class hierarchy in the same way as any other attribute. Procedure applicability can also be over-ridden by the specific provision of a new procedure for the same message, again just like any other inherited attribute, but note that procedures associated with different messages are treated as independent attributes. Whenever an object is sent a message, its response is determined by whatever procedure has been assigned to or inherited by that object for dealing with such messages. The procedure relevant to the type of message is called (and passed any arguments given in the message) and any value it returns is passed back to the originator of the message. From this it should be clear that message passing is a conceptual re-packaging of function calling, with the function to be executed being determined by the message and object types.

The schema mechanism in ART has always been capable of handling the specification of a class hierarchy of objects and handling the inheritance of their static attributes (i.e. slots and values as fillers). To this, ART 3 adds the ability to specify the inheritance of the procedures (written, needless to say, as Lisp functions and called *actions*) together with some extensions to the programmer's interface to explore what actions are inherited by any object.

To the mechanism described, the object oriented system offered by ART adds a number of additional features which have clear conceptual ties to those provided by the *Flavors* object-oriented package in Symbolics Lisp. Quite apart from what message they are specified to handle, actions can be of one of four quite distinct types. A *primary* action is essentially as described above: a single procedure (function) which specifies what should be done when a particular (class of) object is sent a particular type of message. In addition, though, an object can be associated with *before* and *after* actions for the same message, which are called in addition to the primary action (determining the relative timing is left as an exercise for the reader). These do not interfere in any way with the behaviour of the primary action, but can, of course, have side-effects. Note that if a primary action is assigned to an object, it supercedes any other primary action for handling the same message that would otherwise be inherited. In contrast, new actions of the other three are interpreted as applying in addition to any that are inherited.

Finally, in addition to primary, before and after actions, there are *whoppers*.[7] If an object is sent a message for which it has a whopper, the most specific such action (i.e. the one declared lowest in the inheritance hierarchy) is invoked. The whopper may explicitly trigger the normal processing of the message (i.e. the invocation of the primary, any before or after actions, or any less specific whoppers), possibly passing it a modified form of the message, but if it does not, these actions are not invoked. When the whopper finishes, it returns a result to the sender of the original message which may simply be the result generated by the primary action, but may instead be something completely different. In short, a whopper can change the messages that other actions receive, or keep them from them altogether, and either change or invent their replies.

To all of this, the ART messages system adds yet another feature, in the form of *multi-methods* (not, curiously, multi-*actions* ...). Whereas a normal action specifies the handling of a type of message sent to a class of object, a multi-method specifies

---

[7] The only explanation for this distracting nomenclature yet encountered is the (highly unofficial) suggestion that it relates to a hamburger. This would be in line with the general food orientation of the Flavors system (vanilla, mixins etc.), but I prefer to think of a connection with telling whoppers...

what happens when a type of message is sent to a number of objects. This seems to me to be straining the analogy of message sending beyond the point of usefulness, and it is perhaps more sensible to simply talk in terms of applying a function to them. In any event, invoking a multi-methodical action causes ART to choose and apply the definition that is best able to handle the relevant types of entity. For a simple action the appropriate definition is simply the one associated with the lowest point in the class hierarchy, (and thus most specific to the object receiving the message). In the case of multi-methods, which involve a number of objects positioned within different inheritance hierarchies, ART selects an action on the basis of closeness to the objects that are specified first.

Whereas the actions discussed so far are associated with objects, and are triggered by sending messages to them (i.e. by explicit invocation), ART also supports another category, which are termed *active values*. Active values are associated with specific attributes (or slots) of an object, and are triggered by accessing those values. ART recognises four different kinds of access to slot values: getting them, setting them, changing them and removing them. For each of these operations, it is possible to carry out an action either before or after the actual access to the slot, and thus ART has eight kinds of actions that can be attached to any slot. Thus a *get-before* action would be invoked immediately before a something was allowed access to the value in its associated schema slot, while a *modify-after* action would be invoked immediately after the value in its slot had been changed. Note that the "before" and "after" in these names are quite distinct from the types of actions already discussed, and indeed a sufficiently determined programmer could actually combine the two mechanisms. It is quite possible to declare an action to be a "modify-after before" which is an action that is run before a modify-after primary. Perhaps fortunately, it does not seem to be possible to define active multi-values.

When an action is executed, any inferences it makes will by default affect the context/viewpoint that triggered its invocation, though it appears possible for the programmer to direct them elsewhere if necessary.

The combination of ART's rules and schema mechanism, together with the ability to invoke arbitrary Lisp functions, already allowed most of the capabilities provided by the object oriented facilities to be expressed reasonably concisely. As a result, their appearance in the tool did not seem to add significantly to it. However, growing familiarity, rather than breeding contempt, is suggesting that they may well have a valuable contribution to make. It seems likely that the new control structures they offer can be used to greatly simplify the handling of many of the situations in which pure production rules are clumsy. Unfortunately, though, there are a number of details that make them harder to use than they could be, particularly relating to their integration with other facilities of the tool. For instance, there does not seem to be any way for an active value to make any use of the logical dependency mechanism, since there is no obvious way for it to get at the identity of the fact (as opposed to its constituents) that triggered it. Other difficulties relate to the sub-optimal range of conditions under which actions can be invoked and the overhead of inheriting them.

The main (rule-firing) inference engine does not invoke any *get-* actions when it matches a schema slot on a left-hand-side pattern. This means that these actions cannot be seen as *guarding* **all** accesses to the slot. However, it is fairly easy to guess why this should be so, since the timing and frequency of such accesses would be horrendously difficult to predict or control, so it is probably best to accept this as a significant but necessary violation of the spirit of the actions. Less excusable, and more annoying, is the fact that a modify operation on a slot, a process that retracts the fact for one value and asserts one for another, does not invoke any retract- or put- actions. This means one has either to be careful not to modify slots or to specify additional actions to make sure that this eventuality is covered.

Finally, there is a peculiar aspect of the implementation of active values which makes them decidedly less convenient to use. Before an active value can be assigned to a slot in a schema, the programmer must first declare that it is-a active-value, which is done by asserting a normal fact to this effect. If some other schema is inheriting from the schema where the active value is attached, ART does not handle the required inheritance of its applicability simply by attaching the action again lower down. Instead it automatically creates a new active value, which it duly declares is-a descendant of the original active value, and attaches that to the inheriting object's slot. This is repeated each time an active value is inherited: a new active value is created, and facts are inserted to show its inheritance from some existing one. This means that the system is quietly building up a second complete inheritance hierarchy which is isomorphic to the one through which the active value is being inherited, but which contains nodes which have no properties and are quite meaningless to the programmer. Moreover, because this is being done using the normal schema mechanism, the consequences of is-a being transitive and having an inverse are all being automatically asserted as well. This means that the shadow hierarchy for the inheritance of a single active value can easily contain several hundred facts, and quite possibly a significant percentage of the total number in the system. At least in the absence of guidance from any documentation, these facts appear completely useless and since presumably they each impose as much load on the system as any other fact, their presence seems glaring and inexplicable.

4.7   Contexts and Viewpoints

As was suggested in the introduction, one of the most powerful features of ART is its ability to handle more than one situation at a time. This is particularly useful whenever a program is confronted with a decision that cannot be taken with certainty given the information currently available. ART makes it very easy to create a separate description of the state of the world — a *context* — for each possible choice. These can be used to independently generate the consequences of each potential course of action, which can then be compared in any way that seems appropriate. Equally, the ability to create contexts can facilitate temporal reasoning, with separate contexts being used to represent not alternative but **subsequent** states of the world. In addition, ART allows for the complex combination of contexts relating to different kinds of information using its *viewpoint* mechanism. This section outlines the features provided by this mechanism, first in terms of ART's facilities for manipulating contexts, and then their combination to form viewpoints.

4.7.1   Contexts

As these example uses of contexts — for alternatives and continuations — may suggest, when a single program has to deal with more than one state of the world, they will usually be **related** states. As such, their descriptions will usually have a great deal of information in common. For instance, even though alternative choices may differ in the consequences of the actions to which they correspond, they will still share the description of the situation in which the decision is being made. Similarly, although the description of the world is different at each moment in time, most of it remains the same. ART makes use of this interrelation to allow various contexts to be specified concisely and reasoned about efficiently. It allows the user to construct a hierarchy of world states and provides for the controlled sharing of information between them, primarily by a form of *inheritance*. By default, each context will contain all the facts that are present in its *parent* (i.e. the state above it in the hierarchy).

One of the essential concepts underlying ART is that when the system finds a context describing a state in which all the LHS patterns of a rule can be satisfied, that rule is said to be able to fire "in" that context. This means that any actions taken by that rule will have their effect on that particular context. In particular, any fact that the rule asserts will be given an extent (see below) that indicates that it is true only in that context and any other contexts that may (come to) inherit from it. The basic mechanism by which an ART program can consider more than one situation involves a rule firing in an existing context and instructing the system to create a new context which will be a child of the one in which the rule is firing. If nothing more were done, this new context would inherit all the facts from the existing parent context (where the rule just fired), and would contain no others — that is, it would describe an identical situation to the context in which it was created. However, when a rule creates a context, it is usual for it also to specify at least one fact which is present in that context alone (it can also specify that facts that are present in the parent context are missing from the new one, which ART calls *shadowing*). Should this fact, together with any that the new context is inheriting from its parent, be able to satisfy the LHS pattern for any rule, that rule will fire in the new context and give rise to further differences between it and its parent. On the other hand, should any rule subsequently add information to a parent context, this will immediately become available in all the other contexts inheriting from it.

To control what information can be accessed in each context, ART tags every fact it creates with an *extent*, which indicates both the context in which the fact is created and a record of any descendent contexts in which it has been shadowed. Because the effects of rule actions are inherited between contexts, a single firing of a rule can have the same effect as firing that rule in every context in which its preconditions are satisfied. Every new fact that is deduced by firing a rule is given an extent which indicates that it holds in all and only the contexts in which every pattern on the rule's LHS can be satisfied. This approach allows ART to extract the maximum information from every rule firing, and thus to handle multiple contexts as efficiently as possible.

Although the essential purpose of the viewpoint mechanism is to allow the system to reason about any number of distinct states, the way ART allows information to be inherited means that it usually doesn't reason about them one at a time. While each rule firing is associated with a particular context, all its conclusions will be propagated into any other context that may be appropriate, in any of which the new facts may complete satisfaction of the LHS of a rule and thus advance it to the agenda. As a result the programmer does not have to think about controlling which context is to be considered at any moment, since by default they all are! In practice, because ART defaults to reasoning with the most recently added facts it will tend to explore one context at a time, in a depth-first exploration of the hierarchy of possible contexts. However, this can readily be controlled by using salience or by explicit reasoning with control facts.

Since there is no need to control the focus of attention, much of a program's reasoning can be specified without needing to take account of the fact that it may be dealing with an arbitrary number of situations. Indeed for the most part the programmer need not even know which ones will or might exist! Of course the rules that actually set up or manipulate the world structure must use special language features for doing so. ART provides procedures both for constructing new viewpoints and specifying their position within the existing hierarchy, and also for deliberately making comparisons between multiple existing contexts. However, ART's use of contexts ensures that the actual manipulation of the state represented in each context is carried out by normal rules making no mention of context.

In addition to creating new contexts, it is also possible to destroy them when they are found not to be useful — for instance, when one is recognised to be internally inconsistent or no longer capable of contributing to a successful solution of the problem in hand. One of the actions a rule can take is to *poison* the context in which it fired. When this happens, that context is deleted from the system, along with every context that inherits from it. This prevents the system from wasting effort on further evaluating the details of a state which has already been recognised to be irrelevant.

As well as creating and manipulating contexts precisely as and when a program explicitly tells it to, ART is also able to take a more active role in context manipulation. When a world is created, it is possible to explicitly identify a number of facts which constitute its *assumptive base*. These facts are taken to characterise the context, and ART will interpret any denial (retraction) of these assumptions as indicating the inconsistency of the state it represents and will thus poison it. Moreover, ART will keep track of the assumptive bases of contexts and ensure that they are manipulated consistently with them. It will ensure that any context with a specified assumptive base will be optimally positioned within the context hierarchy. This means it will not always create a context precisely where the program called for it. Instead it may either create it below some existing descendant that shares part of its assumptive base, or even create nothing at all if a context depending on identical assumptions already exists or has already been poisoned. This allows it to maximise the extent to which computation can be avoided by sharing (inheriting) results between viewpoints.

4.7.2   Merging Contexts

Discussion so far has been in terms of a tree of inheriting contexts, with each being specified in terms of its differences from a parent state. However, ART's context mechanism is also able to allow two distinct existing contexts to be *merged* to create a new context which inherits facts from both of them. When the different contexts are being used to represent subsequent moments in time, the result of this is generally meaningless,[8] but when they are being used to evaluate alternative assumed circumstances or courses of action, the new context represents the effect of assuming or taking both. If the contexts being merged have been given assumptive bases, then ART will recognise that the assumptive base of the merge is the union of the assumptive bases of the parents.

It is possible to tell ART that merging is not appropriate to a particular context hierarchy, in which case it will remain strictly a context tree. However, if this is not done then whenever a program explicitly creates two contexts, ART will by default also recognise the possible existence of a third, which is the result of merging them. This recognition remains implicit unless ART discovers a rule that is able to fire in the merged state but not in either of the parents, at which point the existence of the merged state will be made explicit. In fact ART will carry out any number of pairwise merges that may be needed to make a rule fire — that is, if the LHS of a rule has three patterns that are present in three separate contexts, ART will automatically combine one of these with the result of merging the other two, and thus create a context in which the rule can fire.

When the programmer specifies contexts in terms of assumptions, ART ensures that all possible combinations of them are considered. Quite often the consequences of the assumptions characterising the state are not independent, and hence their combination will represent a state which is inconsistent. If nothing were done about this, the system could squander its time worthlessly evaluating the consequences of inconsistent states of affairs. To prevent this, the programmer should construct rules to recognise unacceptable states as quickly as possible and poison them. ART itself provides some assistance in this, in that by default it will automatically poison any context which is inheriting multiple values for a schema

---

[8] It is usually pointless to merge a context with one of its ancestors, since doing so has no effect because all the facts from the older context are already being inherited by its descendant.

slot which is declared as only able to hold one.[9] Whenever a merged context is poisoned, ART recognises this to mean that its parent contexts are inconsistent, and remembers never to bother considering any other merge between them or any of their descendents.

The vendor training course for ART places considerable emphasis on the existence of the automatic merging mechanism and the possibility of its use for generating conclusions from the combination of their characteristic features. A separate context is created for each possible value for each parameter that specifies a conclusion, together with a number of rules for recognising and poisoning inconsistent states. Finally, a rule is written which will recognise an acceptable solution, and the merging triggered by ART's attempt to fire this rule will generate every possible combination of those components. In this way the space of possible parameter combinations can be searched for acceptable solutions on the basis of only a description of the problem domain itself, and without explicitly specifying anything to do with how the search should be carried out.

Despite the obvious attractions of this approach, its applicability would appear not to be as widespread as this emphasis would suggest. Problems in AI typically involve confronting a very large number of possible conclusions, and knowledge-based programming can be reasonably characterised as trying to use domain-specific information to control the way they are considered. However, using the merging mechanism to generate possible solutions for consideration involves entrusting the responsibility for searching the problem space (of possible combinations of assumptions) to ART. However fast this inference engine may be, and however efficiently it may be able to handle the relationships between states of affairs, it is not obviously worthy of this responsibility. Of course, the order in which such possible states can be generated is not random, and can no doubt be influenced by certain subtle features of the code. In particular the the ordering of the patterns on the LHS of the conclusion-recognising rule will interact with the sequence in which the various contexts are created to determine the opportunities for poisoning inappropriate contexts. However, to the extent that controlling execution is important in **any** programming system, the wisdom of endorsing a policy of programming-by-nuance is not obvious.

Moreover, programs that reason by indiscriminate merging and poisoning can be very difficult to debug, not least because the basis for the ordering of the creation of contexts is not obvious, and the system does not display anything pertaining to those that are poisoned. This means that when a program stops without finding a conclusion, it can be very difficult to tell whether this is because some crucial state was created and erroneously poisoned (and if so, by what), or was simply never created. Indeed this is a general problem with the debugging programs that make use of the context facility, since the corpses of those poisoned are collected with the garbage, and there is nothing left to post-mortem! Recognising that this may well arise as a direct result of the operation of the Truth Maintenance System underlying the context mechanism, but that doesn't make it

---

[9] It is also possible to instruct it to spawn two new contexts, each assuming one of the two possible states of the slot.

any nicer.

4.7.3   Viewpoints

The discussion of contexts has outlined how ART can support a hierarchy of inter-related state descriptions, each inheriting from its parent(s), and thus in turn from all its ancestors. In fact, ART is able to simultaneously support **multiple**[10] distinct but interacting context hierarchies. These are intended to be used for different **kinds** of information. Thus if one were simulating the behaviour of a group of taxis transporting passengers to their destinations, one might consider comparing two strategies for allocating taxis to bookings. While it would be possible to include an indication of the strategy being used along with the taxi positions that result from following it, there is a real sense in which the choice of strategy is outside the state to which it is applied. Similarly, a program for making any complex decision might create a network of contexts to allow it to evaluate the consequences the possibilities open to it. However, it could well be sensible to evaluate these consequences in the light of a number of possible assumptions. At the very least it might want to make best case and worst-case analyses, and considering (all possible interactions of) a number of explicit external factors might well be desirable. While it would be possible to include these factors with those that directly determine the decision to be made, the viewpoint mechanism is well suited to factor apart the different sorts of information. It can cleanly handle the combinations of related factors — decision parameters or assumed circumstances — and to allow the controlled interaction of the resulting situations and possible decisions. In each case the use of multiple context trees can be used to separate information at different levels of abstraction.

   In line with the idea of using it for information at different levels of abstraction, ART's context hierarchy is conceptually layered. Contexts at lower levels can only be accessed with respect to a context at each higher level, and the position chosen within the context tree at each level governs all interactions with any context trees lower down. In a sense it serves to determine a "point of view" from which to interact with state(s) represented in the lower levels. The appearance of lower level contexts — the facts they contain, and even their very existence — is inherited between higher level contexts much like normal facts.

   ART's ability to handle multiple levels of contexts is another of its features that is loudly proclaimed. The ability to separate different kinds of knowledge can clearly improve the clarity of the code, which is, after all, one of the most important aspects of any program. Moreover, with increasing familiarity with the tool I am becoming more able to see ways in which the complex inter-relation between the context levels could bring savings in computational or conceptual effort. However, this has taken time, and I am still not convinced that the benefits the mechanism offers to the approaches I can now imagine justify the enthusiasm that the ART's proponents wish to instill within me. This leaves me with the feeling that even

---

[10] ART's viewpoint mechanism can only support 9 levels of contexts. However, this must not be mistaken for a limit on the number of actual contexts there can be.

though I am pretty clear about what the tool can **do**, I still have only a murky perception of what it is **for**. The new documentation is better, but I still feel that a bit more work on the tutorial/explanation side would not go amiss.

4.8   Consistency Within Contexts

ART provides essentially two mechanisms for maintaining the consistency of the description of a single state. One is the automatic monitoring for any attempt to put a second value into a schema slot that has not been explicitly stated to be able to have multiple values. In addition, it is possible for the programmer to define additional, application specific, "contradictions", although the mechanism for doing so is essentially only a use of the normal mechanisms for attaching salience to rules whose action is to poison the inconsistent viewpoint. In both these cases the effect of the detection of the contradiction is to *poison* the state in which the contradiction has occurred. When a program is considering multiple states of affairs, this has the obvious benefit of preventing it from spending time elaborating the intricacies of a state that has been found to be inconsistent. In addition, ART will also remember the viewpoint's position within the hierarchy of possible states, and will ensure that it will not waste any further time creating or considering any other viewpoint which is dependent on it. Unfortunately, when a program is only dealing with a single state of affairs the contradiction detection mechanism is somewhat less useful, since it brings processing to a grinding and somewhat uninformative halt that merely indicates that something somewhere got it wrong.

The other facility concerned with the maintenance of the consistency within a single state of affairs is the ability to make the facts asserted by particular rule firings logically dependent on some (or all) of the conditions on its LHS. This ensures that whenever any depended-upon fact that allowed a rule to fire is removed from a viewpoint, so too are all the facts asserted by that rule. For instance, in the case of the rule

```
(DEFRULE EXAMPLE-RULE-3
    (LOGICAL
         (ON ?X TABLE)
         (ON ?Y ?X)
         (ON ?Z ?Y))
=>   (ASSERT (ONE BIG PILE)))
```

the fact recording the proposition (ONE BIG PILE) is made to depend on the facts representing the three ON relations. As a result, if any of these are retracted (for instance, if any of the blocks were moved), then the fact indicating (ONE BIG PILE) would also be automatically removed from the state. Logical dependencies are also fully integrated with the viewpoint mechanism, with the extent of the dependent fact being created to precisely match the intersection of the extents of its supports. Moreover, it is automatically adjusted to take account of any subsequent modification to those extents, thereby ensuring the correct behaviour of the dependent fact in every viewpoint in the system.

The logical dependency mechanism is used by the ART system itself to support its schema processing. All inherited properties of a schema are declared to be dependent on the inheritance relation, so that if Clyde were to cease to be an elephant, he would also cease to be grey. It is also possible to make asserted facts dependent on a **negative** condition that enables a rule to fire, in which case they are automatically retracted as soon as any fact that falsifies the negation is asserted. Thus it is possible to make the continued presence of a fact depend on the presence of some other fact or the absence of any fact able to match particular patterns. However, once the fact is removed, it is never automatically re-asserted, even if the fact that led to its retraction is itself removed or re-asserted. Fortunately this is not the limitation that it might appear, since under precisely the conditions in which one might expect this automatic re-assertion to take place, the rule that was responsible for the fact's creation in the first place will be able to fire again.

Unfortunately, there are some frustrating limitations on the logical dependency mechanism. For no apparent reason the logical preconditions of a rule must be the first of the patterns on its LHS. This can make expressiveness awkward, particularly when schemata are involved, and can have implications for efficiency (although how is beyond the scope of this review). In addition, every fact created by the rule is dependent on all the logical supports mentioned on its LHS. However, there are circumstances when it would be desirable to be able to make only some of the assertions of a rule dependent on the logical supports. In contrast, there is no obvious way of obtaining the information needed to use the logical dependency effectively from an active value action. Finally, logical dependencies are not accessible to programs in any way, and indeed are not even shown by any of ART's code or state browsing facilities. This means that there is no way of telling whether a fact is dependent on another, except by retracting one and seeing if the other goes away!

4.9   User Interface Facilities

One of the most significant aspects by which any programming tool is judged is the range of features it provides for constructing sophisticated user interfaces, which should ideally be able to use graphics, menus and mouse. Being a child of the Symbolics, ART is able to provide good access to a sophisticated graphics environment based on the powerful facilities offered by such hosts. Moreover, all aspects of the user interface are represented in the same form as the data the system normally handles (i.e. facts), and are thus all accessible by all the operations available within ART's normal paradigm of fact manipulation by rules. This makes it comparatively straightforward to build up sophisticated interfaces using only the normal control constructs of ART.

Within ART programs, screen icons are generated by creating normal schemata within a hierarchy of pre-defined standard types of *atomic* icons, such as ellipses, splines and polygons, thus making use of ART's ability to handle the inheritance of properties between such objects. A programmer wishing to display a particular icon can simply declare it to be an instance-of one of the known types (for instance, an ellipse, with a particular pair of values in its radii slot), and fill in appropriate slots to specify other features such as line thickness, screen position, scaling etc. It is possible to create new atomic icons, provided one is prepared to write a few (tens of) lines of straightforward Lisp detailing what lines should be drawn where. The code required is usually only a sequence of parameterised procedure calls and can be created by modifying the example given in the ART manual. Once they have been created, such user-created atomic icons can easily be linked into the system's hierarchy of icon types simply by asserting the appropriate schema relations. Alternatively, the programmer can create *composite* icons, which are composed of a number of other icons (atomic or composite) appropriately arranged. For instance, a percentage sign could be specified as two circles appropriately positioned relative to a line. ART is able to handle these as entities, creating moving and scaling them appropriately.

In addition to specifying icons by asserting values for schema slots, the programmer may also make use of ARTIST. This is a powerful icon creation and modification tool that allows the mouse to be used for defining and positioning icons, with the relevant schemata being automatically created by the system. It allows the programmer to convert any arrangement of icons to a raster image, which removes the need to store all the sub-structure that led to its creation. It also has facilities for modifying images which seem to be fairly typical of the kind one expects from MacPaint or its clones.

One of the properties of an icon that a programmer may specify by filling slots in its schema is whether it should be mouse-sensitive. When a user clicks on a mouse-sensitive icon, ART automatically generates (and asserts) a particular form of fact, with the relation name *utterance*. These utterance facts contain assorted information about the position and timing of a mouse click, together with a proposition specified in the *input* slot of the icon's schema. The same approach is applied to handling user selections from menus (but see below), which makes the whole menu handling process very simple. All the programmer needs to do is specify the list of elements that are to be included in the menu, and request it to be displayed in a particular window, and ART will then ensure that when any item is selected, an utterance is generated which contains (among other things) the name of the item moused. Finally, the utterance fact mechanism can also be used for handling other kinds of asynchronous events, such as input from other processes (in a real-time system) or spontaneous typing by the user.

Given that such facts will be asserted, it is of course very easy to write rules that will be triggered by them, simply by pattern matching against the expected form of the utterance fact in the left hand side of a normal rule. The actual utterance facts that are asserted by the system contain a great deal of information about the precise nature of the event that triggered them (e.g. event type, timing, mouse position, what was typed or selected). This means that although the basic mechanism is the same for all these types of asynchronous input, the precise format of the utterance facts varies. Nevertheless, ART's pattern matching is sufficiently flexible to allow them all to be easily recognised and the various classes either distinguished or conflated as required. Moreover, because response to utterance facts is mediated by the rule firing mechanism, the full flexibility of ART's normal control facilities (e.g. *goals, salience, control facts* etc.) can be used to integrate the response to unexpected events with any other processing that may already be underway. This makes the basic mechanics of providing interfaces that allow the user great flexibility very easy, although the issues relating to deciding what should actually be done obviously remain.

Obviously, handling input by asserting facts which trigger rules only gives acceptable response times if the inference engine is running. To get around this problem, ART provides a second, almost unrelated, way of handling menus, which is made available only when the inference engine is **not** running. Once again the user supplies the system with a list of items which are to appear in the menu, but in this case the system expects them to be the names of other menus or of commands. If the selected item names another menu, then that menu is *pushed* into the window in place of the one already being displayed, thus building up a stack of menus associated with the window, and ART offers standard mechanisms for the user to move about such a stack. On the other hand, if the selected item has been declared as naming a command, the function associated with that command is executed. In either case there is support for providing longer documentation or additional help menus. Taken together, these facilities make it very easy to construct an interface based around using an inter-connected system of menus for guiding access to commands.

Even though each of the two mechanisms for handling menus is very powerful, it seems a shame that there have to be two! While it is perfectly clear why the utterance fact method cannot be used when the inference engine is not running, it is not at all obvious why the command-based approach has to be disabled when it is. While it is in fact possible to specify both commands and utterance-related rules for a single menu, the programmer would probably feel the system to be more integrated if it offered a menu system that could operate in the same way whatever the state of the inference engine.

Finally, release 3.1 of ART can be used from a normal VDU (or emulation thereof). It is obviously not possible to use graphics or a mouse when operating in this way, and this inevitably reduces the range of interface-building facilities that can used. However, being able to easily access ART programs (with suitably restricted interfaces) from a (remote) terminal or another program is a qualitative increase in the functionality of the tool, and is very much to be welcomed.

4.10   Programming Environment

As might be expected in the light of the existence of these features, the ART system itself offers an impressive programming environment, the "ART STUDIO", which is heavily based on windows, mouse and menus. As an alternative, from release 3.1 there is an alternative "scrolling studio" which is usable from a terminal (as opposed to a graphical workstation). This is definitely the poor relation of the full graphics studio. It does not support any of the graphical debugging displays (see below), and the restricted screen size limits the amount of information that can be presented at any time. These shortcomings undoubtably restrict programmer productivity (not to mention enjoyment!), arguably to the point where one might deem it an inadequate tool for system development. However, this does not detract from its usefulness for testing terminal interfaces or for making minor modifications to a (non-graphical) system.

Menu interfaces are obviously very well suited to getting beginners started with a system, and certainly that offered by ART is reasonably straightforward to get to grips with. There were, of course, a number of menu items that were not where they were expected, although this is probably the same feeling one encounters when cooking in someone else's kitchen, and it did not present any real obstacle to using the system. However, it is generally accepted that more advanced users tend to find a rigid menu structure somewhat restrictive, and the provision of an alternative or supporting command interface is often thought desirable. In fact, ART does provide single-character short-cuts for a scattering of commands, and it also allows any command to be typed, though unfortunately it will often only interpret typed commands appropriately if they are currently on the menu being displayed.[11] This makes it generally impossible to give a command without first working through the menu network to an appropriate point, and having given it, one has to repeat the chore to get back to the point where issuing the command seemed like a good idea. Interestingly, by typing the appropriate pair of Lisp functions it is possible (within the graphics studio) to create additional windows onto the command menu tree. This seems to greatly alleviate this problem, and must surely be a candidate for addition to the basic graphics studio.

Regardless of any misgivings about the mechanism for invoking them, ART supports a comprehensive kit of program inspection tools. At any time it is possible to interrupt the program, either from the keyboard or by setting a break-point on a rule which will cause the system to suspend execution just prior to firing. Having done so, it is possible to use a number of powerful tools to inspect or change the state of the system before allowing it to continue. In particular, it is possible to see what rules exist and the current state of the agenda and to call up the text of any rule and the (possibly partial) matches that have been found against its LHS patterns. It is also possible to request a graphical representation of any arbitrary set of inter-relations between the schemata the system knows about and mouse on it to focus on any that deserve further attention. Similarly, the system can provide a diagram of the current state of any context hierarchies it is handling, and allow

---

[11] Although a facility that allows you to type in full any entry on a mouse-sensitive menu that is currently on screen may sound entirely pointless, it is in fact useful when the menu does not all fit within the screen window. This often happens with menus of schema or rule names, and it is often faster to type the name of a known entry than to grub down the menu to find it.

the user to interrogate the states described within each. In particular, ART can supply the programmer with a *justification* for any fact. This takes the form of a diagram that shows the rule that led to it being asserted and the facts that allowed that rule to fire, together with the justification for each of those facts. However, while this facility is very useful, the information it provides is somewhat terse, and it is only available and useful to someone who is competent at manipulating ART's sophisticated menu-based programming environment. This makes it an excellent debugging tool for the program developer, but quite unsuitable for use by a user, which is curious given the widespread belief that expert systems should (or even must) be able to explain themselves. The anomaly is emphasised by the fact that ART can provide a program with only very restricted access to the kind of information it would require to support any kind of user-oriented explanation facility.

My most serious worry about the user interface concerns the fact that although it is excellent for small demonstration systems, a number of its facilities do not scale up to larger programs as well as might be hoped. For instance, the system tends to invite the programmer to select facts, schemata, and rules from a menu in the same window as commands are normally presented. This makes perfect sense when the number of rules is at least vaguely comparable to the number of commands (i.e. about ten), but in a large system this is not the case, and the window size requirements of the two applications do not go together well and one is often offered a tiny window to select from a very large menu. Fortunately, experience is beginning to suggest that the problem may often be avoidable. The menu system is sufficiently rich that when the obvious approach for getting information involves an excessively cumbersome menu, there is often a way of using the less common options to obtain it more neatly. This suggests that although the vendor training course covers the actual contents of the various menus, it should perhaps devote some further effort to illustrating the importance of the less obviously useful options.

A more serious failure to scale up to large programs relates to the various graphical displays offered by the system: its justification networks, schema relation diagrams and context trees. These are superb aids to understanding and examining what is happening in small programs. However, as matters get more complex (and therefore the diagrams get more important and potentially useful) the time taken to draw them becomes first annoying, and then unacceptable. Moreover, when they finally do appear so little of the total network will fit on the screen that there is very little benefit from the fact that it is a graph, particularly if the system is set to display any of the content of each state on the graph.

It would be churlish to suggest that the environment is bad or that there is always an alternative which would be obviously better. However, I am still left with a faintly disappointed feeling that a number of its features do not seem to be as useful or pleasant for big systems as they appear to be when dealing with small problems.

4.11   General Matters

4.11.1   Documentation and Training

To accompany ART, Inference produce a primer, three programming tutorials written by Bruce Clayton, and a reference manual. In addition, the purchase price of the system includes two weeks of training for two people, which at the time of writing is provided in the U.K. by Ferranti at Cwmbran.

The tutorials are eminently readable and give an excellent, if at times rather laboured, introduction to the concepts of the system and its syntax. The only exception to this is the treatment of backward chaining in Tutorial One, a defect which is remedied by the devotion of most of Tutorial Three to the same topic.

The vendor's course that I attended was a little patchy. It offered about an equal mix of lectures (which closely followed course material provided by Inference) and practical time based around writing a set of independent, more or less illustrative programs. Unfortunately, having read the tutorials before the course I found much of the lecture material too laboured. The course seemed to make minimal assumptions about (and therefore to take minimal advantage of) attendees' background in AI techniques or systems, and seemed to be aimed at presenting ART programming almost from scratch. The main course hand-out is a collection of the (copious) slides used during the lecture presentations, although perhaps because of my personal foibles I have never found such take-aways of much use. A set of "model answers" to the practical exercises are also provided.

The last aspect of coming to grips with ART is the reference manual, which is now supplied in two large loose-leaf binders. The first volume covers the core of the system: rules, schemata, logical dependencies, contexts, viewpoints and support for object and access oriented programming. The second volume is machine specific (i.e. there are different versions for the SUN and Symbolics), and it covers the programming environment, user interface facilities and using ART from Lisp.

Whereas I liked the tutorials very much indeed, I initially found the reference manual very difficult to get on with. With experience, it seems to have become more manageable, although I gather that this attitude is also common among those obliged to use an artificial limb, and even after almost two years it is still an effort to find information. Part of the problem seems to stem from the fact that the manual aims to be a combination of a reference document and an explanatory text, which means that reference material is distributed among discursive explanation. The situation is exacerbated by the index. At times I feel that actually finding a reference to the topic of interest counts as one of lifes pleasant little surprises, while discovering that the indicated text contains the relevant information at the appropriate level of detail is a cause for active celebration. Despite the considerable improvements that have accompanied Release 3, the manual still seems one of the weakest aspects of the system.

4.11.2   Performance

The most immediately daunting aspect of the performance of ART is the time taken to load programs, which can easily take well over a quarter of an hour for a demonstration system. Inference seem (now!) to have recognised this as a serious shortcoming, and ART 3 has introduced some facilities for saving the state of the system. However, it is still not possible to save everything: ART 3.0 can save only rules, and 3.1 cannot save Lisp code. As a result, in order to run a saved state, it is in general necessary to load some parts of the system from other files, some before the state is restored, and some after. This of course means that either the relevant pieces of the system must be duplicated, or the original sources must be structured to fit in with the restoring process, rather than for clarity or maintainability. Arranging files in this way seems a frustrating and error-prone task, and the sooner it can be handed over to the computer the better!

Once it is running, ART can give excellent response times (e.g. to mouse activity) provided paging can be avoided, and delays remain acceptable even when the system is dealing with fairly large applications. In addition, ART provides a number of features which are aimed at allowing programmers to improve the efficiency of their creations. One of these allows patterns on the LHS of a rule to be prevented from triggering any backward chaining rules that may be applicable. Another provides the ability to warn the compiler that facts with a particular relation or slot name will be potentially supplied by a backward chaining rule. The compiler has always been able to recognise this for itself at the point when it processes a relevant backward chaining rule, but any rules with patterns matching the relevant relations that were compiled before this point was reached have to be re-compiled. By warning the compiler in advance, this re-compilation can now be avoided. Finally, a third new feature allows the programmer to optimise the construction of the join net required by the Rete algorithm that underlies rule matching and firing. This is a facility which, depending on the precise nature of the program, could well have a considerable influence on performance.

4.11.3   Upgrading

When looking to choose a programming tool, it is obviously pleasing to see new versions appearing, bringing additional facilities and features. However, once one reaches the stage of using a tool on a day to day business, the negative side of new releases becomes apparent. The most direct drawback is simply the effort of installing the new version: by the time we had encountered and overcome one or two minor setbacks, and modified Inference's recommended installation procedure to make it acceptable to our system manager, installing ART 3.1 on our network of SUN's (some 6 months after 3.0) took a little over two days. More importantly, anybody who is intending to develop or use substantial pieces of software is inevitably going to be concerned with ensuring that it will remain usable on any new releases of the programming tool. We have found that the transition between ART 2 and ART 3 has required some (very straightforward) modifications to some low-level (icon-definition) code. In addition, a number of functions related to the command-style menu system have without comment ceased to be documented. However, the bulk of the changes appear to be strictly upgrades (i.e. ART 3 is a super-set of ART 2).

4.11.4 Bugs

Given the facts of software life, it would be surprising if a system the size of ART were entirely bug free, and indeed work at the Institute has thrown up a handful of specific and repeatable faults, some in ART 2, and some in ART 3. One or two of these have been sufficiently intrusive to need to be worked around, and to require significant effort to do so. Those in ART 3 on the SUN have primarily been related to interfacing functions, and can no doubt be regarded as an indication of the scale of the task of confronting an entirely new machine and operating system.

In addition to these problems, we have always found that inexperienced users (at least on the Symbolics) tend to suffer from system failures which give them uninterpretable error messages and cannot be reproduced. This phenomenon can no doubt be ascribed, at least in part, to the complexity of the tool. However, it seems certain that some of the difficulty arises from the fragility of ART's error handling.

Finally, we found that under certain circumstances ART 2 used to invoke the Symbolics debugger for no obvious reason, and since all variables and procedure names within ART are scrambled, there was not much that could be done to diagnose or remedy the situation. The only plausible explanation seemed to involve some kind of interaction with the activities of the (Release 6) garbage collector. The use we have so far made of ART 3 has not shown any similar problems.

Of course, it would be quite inappropriate to give the impression that the system is perpetually falling over — for the most part it runs perfectly, and the problems mentioned would only be of relevance to safety-critical real-time applications.

4.11.5 ART on the SUN

It is perhaps worth pointing out that this is the Lisp-based version of ART, running under Lucid Common Lisp (version 2.0.3). Inference have in the past announced an intention to translate ART from Lisp (in which it was written on the Symbolics) into 'C', a move intended to enhance both its portability to and its efficiency on conventional (i.e. non Lisp-machine) computing engines. Indeed, a version of ART in 'C' has been seen (in the USA) for the micro-VAX. However, achieving this was apparently considerably more difficult that expected, and the resulting system appears to have had severe reliability problems. Unfortunately, despite Inference diverting still further resources from other porting or product enhancement projects, these difficulties have not been resolved. In addition, while this development has been underway there have been considerable improvements in the Lisp systems available on general purpose processors, and a continuing improvement in the performance available from acceptably priced workstations. Both factors have lessened the requirement for the 'C' based system, and it appears that, despite the significant effort already committed, the entire exercise may well have been abandoned.

When ART is invoked on the console of a SUN, it begins by creating a shell window running Lisp, and if the scrolling studio is selected, this is where it runs. If, on the other hand, the graphics studio is selected, ART invokes a second, window-handling, process. This creates a single background window which by default occupies most of the SUN's physical screen, and all normal ART input and output takes place through sub-windows within this. However, if there are any messages produced directly from Lisp, such as file loading reports, garbage collection statistics or (more importantly) debugger prompts, these appear within the Lisp window.

Within the main window, ART on the SUN is very like the implementation on the Symbolics. Inference have re-created the window system very closely, even down to the style of characters, the way of reshaping sub-windows and the continuously changing mouse documentation line near the foot of the screen, though they have left behind the ability to scroll by dragging the mouse and (thankfully) the sticky-sided windows! This obviously demonstrates considerable commitment to provide consistency within the tool across machines. However, it seems reasonable to assume that people who use SUN's would have preferred ART to have adopted the SUN's style of window behaviour, which they already know well. This would obviously compromise the uniform appearance of the tool, and would probably upset those who use the tool on more than one type of machine. But for every such user, how many are there who will be using only one? Inference have followed what appeared to them (and indeed others) to be the most obvious approach: whether an alternative might have been better seems worthy of debate.

One of the nicest features of ART on the Symbolics is the close coupling with the editor, ZMACS, which allows one to have the system find particular portions of code, and once they have been edited, incrementally recompile only what has changed. On the Sun, Inference have attempted to provide similar facilities by making use of GNU Emacs,[12] which they supply with the system. This editor is (obviously) a separate process from ART itself, and the communication between the two is achieved by writing scratch files, with one of the two processes always suspending while the other is running. The communication files between the processes pass enough information to allow GNU Emacs to find the required rule or schema definition automatically. They also allow incremental compilations, although compiler messages are split (albeit fairly sensibly) between an ART window and an editor buffer. The change-over is reasonably fast, but the editor window closes when it is not active, and it is frustrating not to be able to leave the editor screen in view while browsing about within ART. This is probably a manifestation of the fact that the UNIX environment is much less geared towards supporting

---

[12]GNU Emacs is a piece of software licenced free of charge by the Free Software Foundation for use or redistribution by anyone, on the condition that no attempt is made to charge for the use of the software.

closely integrated processes than the Symbolics, but it seems reasonable to hope for close interaction in future releases.

Finally, system errors are handled by exiting to UNIX, behaviour that makes one appreciate being in the Symbolics debugger surrounded by gensymmed code.

4.12   General Impressions

4.12.1   Language versus Toolkit

There appears to be a spectrum of ways one can regard sophisticated programming systems like ART. At one extreme it is possible to treat them as collections of tools or library routines which can be used to add functionality to a (Lisp) program written to do what is required. To support this style of use, ART provides a number of functions for carrying out the basic operations of storing and retrieving information under the control of the viewpoint and schema processing mechanisms. It can invoke arbitrary Lisp from the RHS of any rule,[13] thus allowing the rule engine to be used simply to control the execution of a Lisp program.

On the other hand, it is possible to consider these systems as languages in their own right, in which one writes a program to solve a problem. Of the major systems in its league, ART has probably the best claim to being regarded as an independent programming language and as being usable without a knowledge of Lisp. This is certainly the attitude which pervades the ART training course and its supporting materials, where the interfaces for using ART from Lisp programs are scarcely more than mentioned. Indeed, it seems a perfectly reasonable approach to the implementation of small demonstration systems. However, it is not clear that building systems in this way will necessarily result in the best structured or most efficient solutions, and this may become a serious restriction when writing larger programs: it may be possible to play the piano with two fingers, but that is not the way to produce the most interesting music. Moreover, it is necessary to write at least some Lisp when integrating with existing software or data. For instance, the provision of file handling within ART itself leaves something to be desired (i.e. it is simply not mentioned) and so the programmer is forced to use the facilities provided by Lisp. While this may be a perfectly natural way to proceed for a tool written for Lisp Machine users, it does constitute a significant additional obstacle to be overcome by potential users who are unfamiliar with the language. Nevertheless, experience suggests that in a environment where suitable support is available (i.e. there is at least some Lisp expertise available to be applied to particular tasks) it is possible to come to grips with and fruitfully use ART without having to be particularly proficient in Lisp.

---

[13] It is also possible to call arbitrary Lisp code from the pattern side of any rule. However, the number of implicit factors that would affect the timing of its executions argues for strict limitations on any actions taken by this code.

4.12.2   Uniformity

One of the most obvious features of ART's schema mechanism is the way it is used
by the system itself, to support its graphics facilities and active values and indeed
the schema system itself. Except for the case of the active values, there are a
number of clear advantages to doing this, since it makes all the information available for inspection and alteration by programs written in ART's normal rule-based
formalism. However, there are also disadvantages, in that this same information
tends to get under foot! As soon as a program defines any schema (which includes
any graphics icon) all the schema information is immediately (and laboriously)
loaded, and as a result hundreds of facts and dozens of schemata appear on all
the system browsing menus. On balance, the flexibility that the explicit representation brings is probably well worthwhile, although one is left wondering whether
it might be possible to have unmodified system schemata somehow segregated or
invisible.

However, in contrast to the internal uniformity of the schema mechanism, ART
draws a sharp distinction between it and other facts. For the most part the former
are simply presented as facts which happen to have three element propositions,
the first of which is taken to be the name of the slot and the second to identify
the schema to which it belongs. Slots appear the same as other facts in rules, and
are freely intermixed with them when the fact database is examined. This uniformity is deceptive. Although both types of facts allow properties of relations to
be specified and subsequently enforced, they use unrelated mechanisms for doing
so. Similarly they differ in the way they match against patterns with variables in
the first position, when the normally optional schema wrapper becomes obligatory
and backward chaining rules are not triggered. Indeed, it is even possible to have
two apparently identical facts coexisting simultaneously and exhibiting different
matching behaviour! Admittedly this is unlikely to be a problem under normal
circumstances, but the apparently unmotivated inclusion of two distinct mechanisms for doing what appears to be the same job still constitutes a misfeature of
the language.

Similar but more frustrating confusion is caused by the distinction between
ART sequences and Lisp lists. Both appear to be intended for essentially the
same task: namely allowing an ordered collection of independent entities to be
treated as a single object. Moreover, they even share the same notation: both are
represented to (and by) the system by enclosing their members in round brackets.
Nevertheless ART insists that the programmer maintain a rigid distinction between instances of the two types. Admittedly the system documentation contains
perfectly clear statements that the two are different and non-interchangeable, and
identifies and describes the routines for translating between the two forms. However, the documentation for early Fortran systems was equally explicit about the
need to precede every string to be printed with a precise count of the number of
characters it contained. In neither case does highlighting the requirement make the
additional programmer effort involved any less irksome or error prone. That the
system cannot carry out any necessary translations automatically is frustrating.

That the programmer is obliged to distinguish between two data structures which appear identical is ridiculous. There seems to be no justification for obscuring a distinction to which the programmer must be sensitive by delimiting sequences in the same way as lists, particularly given the obvious range of conspicuously distinct forms of brackets.

4.12.3 Additional Features

When comparing ART to more modest tools available on PCs, many people are surprised to find that it provides no facilities for handling certainty factors or probabilities. Instead ART offers the viewpoint mechanism, which allows the programmer to entertain alternatives in isolation. This makes it very straightforward to associate them with some kind of explicit numerical certainty factor which can be manipulated in whatever manner seems most appropriate to the particular domain. Nevertheless the lack of provision for any facilities to handle uncertainty remains a surprising omission. Similarly, most expert system shells offer the user (as opposed to the programmer) some kind of explanation tool, to give some kind of indication of what the system is doing or has done. ART, however, offers no such facility, and it is very difficult to even wrest from it the information needed to program one.

Another area where ART's facilities fall somewhat short of what might perhaps be expected of such a sophisticated tool concerns the scheduling of rule firings. The only control offered to the user is the ability to specify a single fixed salience for all instances of any rule. If this is not sufficient, then the user is of course at liberty to implement a *declarative agenda* — that is, to write program code to assemble the set of possibly appropriate actions and brood upon which ought to be taken next. However, modest experimenting with this approach showed that it can have a disconcerting effect upon execution speed, which suggests that at best it is a technique that requires more subtlety than is at first apparent. It is also comparatively easy to think of mechanisms that appear to be easily (and efficiently) incorporated within the system, and which would allow the programmer useful additional control without having to resort to full meta-level reasoning. The most obvious is to allow a rule to calculate its salience based on the precise facts it has matched against. This would allow different invocations of the same rule to have different saliences. Another attractive idea is the *specificity* mechanism present in OPS5, which is one of ART's ancestors. The number of patterns on the left hand side of a rule is taken as an indication of how tightly the rule defines the class of situations it applies to, and OPS discriminates in favour of those that can handle the current situation as an example of a "special case", rather than those handling it as an example of a more general concept.

ART provides excellent support for debugging rule-based code: the ability to set break-points and thence single step, and facilities to determine which rule was responsible for the appearance of every fact, and which facts are currently contributing to the possible activity of which rules. However, rule firing is not the only mechanism by which things happen in ART programs — facts can also come and go as a result of the schema processor and the firing of actions. However, it is much harder to track this kind of "behind the scenes" activity, and the user is forced to rely on (and thus find out about) the powerful but complex facilities offered by the Lisp environment. As a result, there would seem to be some scope for further debugging tools for these facilities.

Finally, when a viewpoint is poisoned, it disappears without trace, which not only makes debugging more difficult, but also hampers any kind of meta-level reasoning. When the approach being considered has been found to be unsatisfactory, it is not possible to reason about the nature of the problem encountered, because the possible world in which it was recognised has gone. It would be very nice to be able to "stun", rather than kill, a world, so that it could not contribute to any further merges (and would prevent its ancestors from doing so), but was still available for a post-mortem.

4.13   Conclusions

I find ART a powerful and unrestricting programming tool that is pleasing to use, and these impressions that are generally shared by those who have used it within the Institute. Achieving this requires a considerable investment, both in computing equipment and in user training. While I found its basic concepts and operations very natural and easy to grasp, others seem to find it more effort to come to grips with. However, it has proved perfectly possible to use ART for building demonstrator systems with only a basic grasp of Lisp, and this seems likely to be repeatable, at least given limited access to Lisp expertise for particular problems.

Chapter 5

The P.R.O. Expert System Shell

John Bradshaw

5.1 Introduction

P.R.O. is an expert system shell designed primarily, though not exclusively, for use in ecological domains. To date, it has been used in the development of the following applications (described in Chapter 8):

- RCS - The river conservation system.

- FISHFARMER - An aquaculture expert system.

- PISCES - An expert system to assess the impact of the introduction of alien fish.

Initially, we considered using a commercial expert system shell. However, we found that these lacked the flexibility which was required for ecological applications. The need for a general expert system shell for use in ecological applications was clearly identified, resulting in the development of the P.R.O. expert system shell [18]. In this chapter we describe the motivation for developing P.R.O., and describe its main features.

A major reason for developing P.R.O. was that the shells available could not handle the different kinds of uncertain knowledge that is present in ecological problems. Thus a major emphasis of the work was devoted to the the development of an efficient and effective algorithm to handle uncertainty. The method adopted allows conditions to be interrelated, which is important when considering ecological applications, and also attempts to overcome some of the computationally expensive problems which are associated with other methods commonly used.

In ecology, many of the measures which other statistical models require, are simply not available. More subjective knowledge is often used by the ecologist in his deliberations. Starfield et al [129] summarise the problem:

> "On the one hand, the numerical models required information about the process and rates of change that the biologists could not provide; on the other hand, the biologists were in fact reacting to field observations which were very different from the substance of the models being built".

The fundamental design approach has been to create the most flexible system possible without degrading its performance. This has been achieved by including in the knowledge base additional control information, which is used by the inference engine to guide it through the knowledge base.

In order to achieve the desired degree of flexibility, as many of the variables as possible have been placed in the knowledge base. This provides the expert with a framework which can be readily tailored to suit his individual requirements. The mechanism of the shell has been kept as simple and as transparent as possible, which in turn reduces the conceptual problems which experts may have in using the system.

Considering the nature of ecological work it was decided to target the system at a PC based environment. An efficient, compact system was thus required. This was achieved by implementing P.R.O. in Turbo Prolog. Hence P.R.O. runs on an IBM PC (or compatible) and requires 640k of RAM.

The architecture of the P.R.O. expert system shell closely follows the normal expert system architecture. The shell consists of an inference engine, a method of defining a knowledge base, and a user interface. Essentially, it is a backward chaining, rule based system capable of handling uncertainty.

This chapter is divided into four main sections. Section 5.2 describes the inference engine, Section 5.3 describes the method of defining the knowledge base, and Section 5.4 describes the user interface. Section 5.5 touches on the problems of handling uncertainty and outlines the method implemented in the P.R.O. system.

5.2   Inference Engine

In keeping with our design philosophy, the inference engine is fairly simple. The order in which the 'top level' rules (goals) are examined is determined by the order in which they appear in the knowledge base. Consequently, the order in which potential solutions are considered is under the direct control of the knowledge engineer. At any point in time, the next rule investigated is the one which appears next in the knowledge base. No evaluation is done to find the 'best' remaining rule. The expense of running a more sophisticated system was found to outweigh the benefits which might accrue.

The system only asks a question or fires a rule once. The only proviso is that the certainty value associated with the answer should be above a minimum (3, on a scale of 1 to 10) to justify remembering the answer. Very uncertain answers hold little benefit.

The P.R.O. system inference engine can act in two different modes; either as a diagnostic type system or as a system to compute a composite index value of all the contributing numeric data. We describe each of these modes below.

5.2.1 Diagnostic Type Expert Systems

Diagnostic systems are the most common form of expert system. Essentially the expert represents a number of alternative solutions in the knowledge base. The inference engine wheels through these in turn by asking the user questions and trying to find an acceptable solution. This usually takes the form of a simple assertion of a fact, for example "your tax rebate is £xxx", or "you are an incurable hypercondriac!".

In a diagnostic expert system, therefore, the results are generated directly from the knowledge base. Systems which compute an index, based on the numeric attributes, operate slightly differently.

5.2.2 Expert Systems producing an Index Figure

The P.R.O. system provides an alternative mechanism to the 'standard' diagnostic system, namely the index system. This system calculates an index figure based on the combined effect of the numeric attributes in a particular domain. A contributing factor, known as the rating, is calculated for each contributing attribute. These ratings are then used to compute a final score in the range zero to one hundred. This type of system is thought to be particularly useful in ecological applications and may not hold very much wider appeal. The RCS system is a good example of the use of this inference system.

Index systems only have one uppermost goal which identifies subgoals, that is subsections of the main problem. In addition to producing an overall index, the system also computes an index figure for each of these subsections. The attributes to be included in a subsection index are recognised by name. A double naming convention is used to group like attributes. In the RCS system this has been a useful feature as it gives the users answers which are much more detailed than 'conventional' systems might manage. For example the RCS system problem is split into three subproblems: the river's physical attributes, the catchment and the biota. Thus the double name 'biota, introduced-fish' is used in the calculation of the biota's subsection index.

The rating is calculated according to the mechanism described in the next section. Each attribute is assigned a rating according to the class in which the attribute's value falls, the maximum weight of the attribute and the weighting algorithm used (described in Section 5.3.3). It should be noted that the absence of a deleterious attribute (that is, an attribute with a negative weighting) will produce the greatest possible positive contribution to the final index value.

The final index value is calculated as the sum of the ratings divided by the sum of the maximum possible ratings. For a system to achieve an index value of 100 (the maximum possible), requires the total absence of deleterious attributes and the presence of a maximum quantity of the positive attributes.

When using an index system, the knowledge base assumes a rather different function to that when using the diagnostic system. In a diagnostic system, the knowledge base produces the solution directly. The index system uses the knowledge base only to identify those attributes whose values make up part of the final index and also perhaps to determine the effect of these attributes.

5.3   The Knowledge Base

As already mentioned, the knowledge base follows the production system format. A number of expert systems have used this format and have shown that it works well. Systems such as MYCIN [27] and Prospector [48] are successful production systems housed on large powerful machines. Micro Expert [42] and Exsys [70] are examples of the production system based shells available for microcomputers.

In practice, it has been found that the knowledge base needs to consist of more than 'pure' rules and questions. The need for general introductory information and extra information about rules has also been identified. Additional data on numeric attributes is also necessary to check bounds and to assign weights. The various structures, and their format is described in the following sections.

We illustrate the various formats by representing the rules of a simple tax rebate system. The amount of rebate calculated is based on four basic criteria, namely age, marital status, number of children and number of dependents. Although the P.R.O. system has been developed for use in ecological applications, this 'toy' system illustrates the main features of the knowledge base.

5.3.1   Introductory Knowledge Structure

As described in Section 5.2, P.R.O. can work in either a diagnostic mode, or in an an index mode. The mode required, together with introductory information to be displayed at the start of a consultation, is represented by a Prolog fact of the form:

>   introinfo(*the type of expert system* - diagnose *or* index,
>   *title of the expert system,*
>   *introductory remarks to the expert system*).

Thus, for our tax rebate system, this might take the form:

>   introinfo(diagnose,
>   "A Tax system to calculate rebates",

```
[["This is a system designed to calculate tax rebates. Rebates are",
  "calculated according to four categories - Age, Number of dependents,",
  "Marital status of the person and the Number of",
  "children the person has. Answers to the questions should",
  "reflect the status at the end of the tax year."],
 ["This is not an accurate system and the result produced should not be",
  "taken seriously. This system was written only to demonstrate the ",
  "features of the P.R.O. expert system shell."],
 ["The system was written by John Bradshaw and is based on the TES",
  "system designed by Martin Steinhobel."]]).
```

Notice that all text is represented as lists of strings. As strings in Prolog may not extend from one line to the next, the use of lists enables the knowledge engineer to provide any number of lines of text. Within the shell there is a small word processing function which ensures that all text is neatly formatted to the screen with lists representing paragraphs and lists of lists chapters.

5.3.2 Rules

A pure rule is represented as a Prolog clause of the form:

```
rule(name1, name2,
     the answer which the rule will either test or return -
     n indicates numeric range and c yes/no type answers) :-

     the conditions needed to satisfy the rule.
```

For example, a rule:

IF a person is married THEN allow a rebate of £880

is represented by:

```
rule(primary, rebate, n(880, 880)) :-
     checkres(person, married, 100, c(y)).
```

Where the condition part is represented by using a predicate cd checkres that is provided by P.R.O. In general checkres takes the form:

```
checkres(name1, name2,
         the relative importance of the condition,
         the non-numeric answer).
```

where the *relative importance* of a condition indicates its importance with respect to the other conditions in that rule. The sum of the relative importances in a rule must equal one hundred (100). The relative importance of a condition is the amount of influence the condition has within the rule. In different rules the same condition may have different relative importance values. These values are

determined by the influence the condition exercises in the individual rule, with no
regard to its overall importance in the rest of the system.

Apart from checkres, P.R.O. also provides predicates for checking numeric results, and for collecting numeric values. All three may invoke either questions or
rules. The first time a user is asked a question the result is returned as well as
being saved. Subsequent enquires will, of course, use the saved result.

As we mentioned earlier, simply representing a pure rule is not enough. We
must also provide a description of the rule, explanation text, and some measures
to be used to handle uncertainty. This additional information, is represented as a
Prolog fact of the form:

> ruleinfo(*name1, name2,*
> > *type of answer expected,*
> > *minimum threshold,*
> > *positive threshold,*
> > *negative threshold,*
> > *measure of the goodness of the rule,*
> > *introductory message,*
> > *message given on completion of the rule,*
> > *question text,*
> > *why, how, explain texts).*

For example, for the above rule, we might provide the following information:

> ruleinfo(primary, rebate, n, 0, 100, 0, 8,
> > "Calculating the primary rebate",
> > [],
> > ["How much primary rebate can you claim?"],
> > ["In order to calculate the total rebate the system must calculate",
> > "the primary rebate which the person may claim."],
> > ["Depending on whether or not the person is married ",
> > "they may claim either £620 or £880 primary rebate."],
> > ["A person is married if he or she is married in terms of any law of",
> > "custom and is living permanently with his spouse, or if the person is",
> > "a widow or widower, or if the person qualifies for a child rebate and",
> > "is responsible for the maintenance of the child."]).

Thus to allow various kinds of uncertainty to be represented, P.R.O. requires
the knowledge engineer to specify four numbers for each rule.

The fourth number allows a knowledge engineer to state how good he thinks
his rule is. This value reflects the confidence which the expert has in the results
that will be produced by the rule. Rules with a low confidence rating will produce
low confidence answers. In the above example, the rating is only fairly high (8
out of 10), reflecting the experts uncertainty that the user will always correctly
interpret the law on marital status.

The first three numbers are thresholds levels which are used to determine the
final confidence figure. As the system examines each of the condition parts of the
rule, it is not only working towards a final answer, but is also computing a value

which reflects the evolving confidence the system has in the final answer. The threshold values enable the rule to stop before all conditions have been examined because enough is known about the final answer, with sufficient confidence, not to require any further investigation. The positive threshold indicates the amount of confidence that is enough for the rule to be satisfied. Once this level is exceeded, the rule's answer is returned with a confidence equal to the 'goodness of the rule'. The negative threshold operates in the same way as the positive threshold value but provides an upper limit for the confidence in the conditions which disprove the rule. Once this level is exceeded the rule fails and the system attaches the maximum possible confidence value to the result. If neither the positive nor the negative levels are breached and once all the conditions have been examined, the evaluated confidence figure is compared against this minimum threshold level. If the confidence value is less than the minimum threshold, the answer will be recorded as unsure. If the minimum threshold value has been exceeded, the rule will succeed and the computed confidence value will be associated with the result.

The ruleinfo structure also allows the knowledge engineer the option of attaching a question to a rule. Before the conditions are tested, the system will ask the attached question. This is a short cut method of obtaining the answer from the user instead of by computation. The longer method evaluates the conditions in the body of the rule to compute the answer. The short cut has been included because semi-expert users find it frustrating to answer numerous low level, trivial questions which enable the expert system to deduce what they already know and could have told it in the first instance. The problems these users have are often of a higher conceptual nature. They are, therefore, more interested in benefiting from (and seeing) the global problem solving strategy used by the expert system. Answering many simple questions obscures the general methodology. Only rules which are goals need have any text in the answer field.

If the answer to a question linked to a rule is too uncertain the system will overrule the given answer and attempt to compute a better result by examining the condition parts of the rule. The user may also indicate that a particular question is not applicable for a given situation and the system will ignore that attribute. Associated with questions are three structures which provide the user with explanations.

Besides being syntactically defined by the P.R.O. system, the knowledge base comprises syntactically correct Prolog clauses. Rules are legal Prolog clauses. This gives the knowledge engineer the freedom and flexibility to recreate exactly the same problem solving methodology as used by the expert. If the expert performs simple calculations, these can be defined in the rule. If the calculations are more complex, he can define his own functions to perform them. These functions can then be called from the rule. Although the knowledge engineer can create his own functions, the three defined 'statement types' (checkres, checkvalue, and getvalue) link the knowledge base and the inference engine.

5.3.3   Questions

In general a question is represented by a Prolog fact of the form:

> question(*name1, name2,*
> *the type of answer expected,*
> *question text,*
> *why, how, explain texts*).

The question text contains the question to be put to the user. The why, how and explain texts contain information about the question. Their function is to explain why the question is being asked, how the answer will effect the final result and explain in more detail what the question means. The use of these three fields is discussed as part of the user interface in Section 5.4.

For example, a question for our tax rebate system might be:

> question(person, married, c,
> ["Are you married in terms of the act?"],
> ["The amount of primary rebate and thus the total rebate will differ",
> "if the person is a married person in terms of the act or not."],
> ["If the person is a married person in terms of the act they will be",
> "allowed a rebate of £880 otherwise the receiver will allow them a",
> "rebate of £620."],
> ["The act states that a person is married if he is married in terms",
> "of any law of custom and is living permanently with his spouse, or",
> "if the person is a widow or widower, or if the person qualifies for a",
> "child rebate and is responsible for the maintenance of the child."]).

All questions which yield numeric results require an additional knowledge structure, which contains extra information for use by the inference engine. In general this takes the form:

> weight(*name1, name2,*
> *the range of the answer and the demarcation of different categories,*
> *the weighting factor of the attribute,*
> *the scaling method to be used*).

For example:

> weight(dependents, number, class(0, 1,2,4,7, 10), 0, 0).

The values held in the range parameter are required at two stages in the system. At the questioning stage, use of the maximum and minimum values ensures that the answers received are within range. Index type systems use the four intermediate bound values, the weight and the scaling method to determine the contributing factor of the attribute.

Different attributes become significant at different levels. The P.R.O. system provides three weighting methods to allow this fact to be represented in the knowledge base. In some cases the effect that an attribute has on the system as a whole is proportional to the amount of attribute present (method 1). In other cases, the difference between the presence of none and a small amount of an attribute is much more significant than the difference between a lot and a little bit more of the attribute (method 2). (This method is used in the case of endemic fish in the RCS system [100]. An endemic species is found in only one ecosystem in the world. Therefore the difference between having none and one endemic species present effects the conservation status of the ecosystem greatly. This effect is much greater than the difference between having nine or ten endemic species.) In still other cases the existence of a small quantity of an attribute may be unimportant. The change in the amount of the attribute may, however, become increasingly significant as the amount of the attribute present increases (method 3). For example, If the percentage of water extracted from a river system is low, this attribute cannot be considered a significant feature of the river. As the percentage rises, the significance of this attribute becomes exponentially greater, until such a time as 100% of the water is extracted. This would ensure that this feature becomes the overriding attribute of the whole system. The four 'inner' values of the class parameter are used to determine how the total range should be divided and this associated with the weighting method will combine to produce the weight of the attribute. A more detailed discussion on the attributes mentioned here can be found in the RCS user manual [99].

5.4   The User Interface

The approach taken in providing a user interface is very simple. The user is severely restricted in the type of answer which he might offer since the system allows only two forms of input at any stage, either a single real number or a single character. It was felt that the inclusion of even a simple natural language system would not permit the optimum use of the limited computational power available within our target environment and, moreover, the lack of a more sophisticated interface does not seem to impair the execution of the P.R.O. system.

Questions requiring single character answers can be answered with a y or n ('yes' or 'no'), together with an associated confidence in the answer.

All numeric questions require the user to supply a range (minimum and maximum values) as the answer. The user must be sure that the actual answer lies within the range he has given. If the two values given are the same, the system assumes that the user is totally certain about his answer and will ascribe the maximum confidence to the answer when it calculates its own results. If, however, the bounds differ, the system will assign a confidence value which is a function of the actual range with respect to the maximum possible range and also the number of classes which are covered by the answer range.

If the user is unsure of the answer, a 'don't know' option may be used. In this case the system takes the default upper and lower bounds as the answer.

The knowledge base contains sets of explanation texts associated with the questions. These explanations are used to give the user background information about the questions. The text is supplied by the expert and should tell the user how his answer will effect the final result, why the question has being asked and also explain the meaning of the question and possibly terms within it. The 'why' and 'how' texts are aimed at highlighting the decision making methodology embodied within the knowledge base.

The explanation routines offered in the P.R.O. systems are simple to use, yet their effectiveness is a direct function of the thoroughness of the knowledge engineer. The options are invoked by answering any question with a letter in the set {w, h, e}. These are interpreted as requests to the system to explain 'why', 'how' and 'explain' respectively. These options are available for both questions requiring numeric answers and those requiring single character responses.

The P.R.O. system displays all currently active portions of the knowledge base. Windows, which contract towards the lower right corner, give the user a sense of perspective. Each new rule initiates the creation of a new, smaller, 'inner' window and when rules terminate their window is removed. Outer rules thus remain visible and a feeling of purpose is maintained. The user can see how the system moves through the knowledge base.

All text displayed on the screen is taken directly from the knowledge base. It is therefore the knowledge engineer's responsibility to provide the information at a level suitable for the anticipated users of the system. A simple word processing facility is available in the P.R.O. system to format the text neatly on the screen.

Once the system has collected sufficient information to produce a solution it will display the answer text supplied. The option then exists for the user to send the expert system back to look for alternative solutions or to terminate the consultation. At this stage it is possible to save the given answers on disk for future reference. It is also possible to change certain answers and to observe the effect these changes have on the final solution. It is important to remember that the P.R.O. system will not necessarily produce the 'best' answer first. The system simply reports the first answer it finds. The onus is on the user to instruct the system to look for other solutions. If there are no solutions about which the system is sufficiently confident, it will display those solutions which were produced but which had too low a level of confidence.

The results produced by the index system not only give the index values for the whole system and for the subgoals, but also provide full information on every attribute. The influence of each attribute on the final score can be readily seen. This facility has proven most useful in the RCS system where it has been used to highlight the most important attributes of the river.

5.5   Handling Uncertainty

The P.R.O. system is able to handle both uncertainty which users have about their information and also uncertainty which experts have about their knowledge. The first of these is perhaps more obvious and prevalent than the latter, but there are still many areas, including ecology, in which experts do not have all the answers

[130]. The P.R.O. system also allows the expert to show that different conditions within a rule carry different weights according to their relative importance in that rule. In certain instances if important factors are obviously present experts tend to forgo the extra expense of doing any further investigations and simply make their decisions on what they already clearly know. A system of thresholds has been implemented which allows a rule to terminate before all conditions have been evaluated. An intuitively simple numeric system which both experts and users seem to find acceptable has been developed.

5.5.1 The Bayesian, and the Dempster-Shafer approaches

The two most commonly used numeric systems are Bayes' theorem [48] and the Dempster-Shafer system [60]. Both these systems, however, have been criticized for features which make them unacceptable for use in expert systems [143].

The Bayesian approach makes the initial assumption that in the event of there being multiple conditions, there should be no relationship between these conditions. In even the simplest expert systems, relationships will in all probability exist between conditions; in ecology this is especially true — there is, for example, some relationship between the size of a river's catchment area and the amount of water that flows down the river. This deficiency has been highlighted before [8] and yet expert systems are still designed using Bayes' theorem or a derivative thereof. Because conditions are often inter related and because Bayes' theorem is not easy to conceptualize, there was a clear need to develop an alternative system. This view was strengthened by the additional fact that experts may be hard pressed in some domains (e.g. ecology [130]) to supply all the figures which Bayes' theorem requires.

The Dempster-Shafer approach suffers from the problem of intractability. Gordon and Shortliffe [60] state that the scheme used for combining evidence means that computational time will increase exponentially as the size of the hypothesis set increases. Given our intended target environment, it was self evident that a 'pure' Dempster-Shafer approach was not a contender. Barnet [14] has shown that for a single hypothesis set, computational time is reduced to polynomial proportions. Gordon and Shortliffe have adapted the Dempster-Shafer model in the light of Barnet's findings to propose a system which will execute in polynomial time for hypothesis sets of more than one element [60]. Although the new method has significantly reduced the time required, time is still significant. The Dempster-Shafer method requires that the domain expert be able to articulate precisely the global effects of each contributing attribute on the system. The domain expert cannot provide a hierarchical representation of his problem solving methodology. Perhaps this global view is possible in some domains, but in ecology experts simply cannot do this [100] — usually because the field does not have fixed, well researched solutions. The Dempster-Shafer method also takes no cognizance of the different weights which different pieces of evidence have on the final solution, something all experts seem to do. It was felt that this was an important concept which ought to be represented. The desire to implement a simple, transparent architecture lead

```
rule(tax, rebate, n(H, L)):-
        getvalue(person, status, 65, n(Hs, Ls)),
        getvalue(person, age, 20, n(Ha, La)),
        getvalue(person, children, 10, n(Hc, Lc)),
        getvalue(person, dependents, 5, n(Hd, Ld)),
        H is Hs + Ha + Hc + Hd,
        L is Ls + La + Lc + Ld.
```

Tax Rebate	Ri	Cf	$Ri*Cf/10$	$PosCf$	$NegCf$
Status	65	8	52	52	0
Age	20	10	20	72	0
Children	10	2	2	74	0
Dependents	5	6	3	77	0

$ruleCf = 77/10 * 8/10 = 6.16$

Threshold values: $Post = 84$; $Negt = 0$ and $Mint = 30$

Figure 5.1: Example calculation of a confidence value

to the development of the novel P.R.O. mechanism for handling uncertainty.

5.5.2   The P.R.O. Mechanism

The main objective in the design of the P.R.O. mechanism has been to allow the expert as much flexibility as possible by giving him the power in the knowledge base to control significant aspects of the inference system. The inference system has been designed so that it provides the expert with a basic operational framework and leaves him free to specify the precise nature of each operation in each rule. As a result rules in the P.R.O. system contain more information than the 'normal' production rules of other systems. The expert must attach a relative importance rating to each condition in each rule, he must supply three threshold values for each rule and he must give his own rating of the goodness of the rule.

The relative importance (Ri) value for each condition is a unique value applying to a particular condition in a particular rule. The sum of all the Ri values within a rule must be 100. The confidence rating of a rule $(ruleCf)$ is calculated by multiplying each condition's Ri value with that condition's confidence rating (Cf) and taking the sum of these products. It is then moderated by the 'Goodness of the rule' value (Gr) which the expert gives as a rating of his rule. The confidence value generated by the rule is compared against the threshold values and the final value produced according to the manner described earlier. As an example, Figure 5.1 illustrate how this system works

This simple 'Tax Rebate' rule is used to calculate a persons tax rebate according to four criteria: 'Status'; 'Age'; number of 'Children' and number of 'Dependents'. 'Age' is twice as important as 'Children' because it potentially yields a rebate twice as large. Once 'Status' has been positively answered and been given a Cf rating of 8 by the user, $PosCf$ is set to 52, and $NegCf$ is unchanged at zero. The new $PosCf$ value is calculated by adding a proportion of the Ri value to the old $PosCf$ value. This proportion is indicated by the proportion of the confidence of the user (Cf) compared to the maximum confidence level possible (10). Thus $PosCf = 0 + 65 * 8/10 = 52$. If the condition was not positively satisfied then this product (52) would have been added to the old $NegCf$ score to give a new $NegCf$ value. $PosCf$ is not greater than $Post$, nor is $NegCf$ greater than $Negt$, nor have all the conditions been examined so the next condition is evaluated. This process continues until there are no more conditions. $PosCf$ is then greater than $Mint$ so the $ruleCf$ value is set to the $PosCf$ value moderated by the Gr value, and the rule succeeds. The $ruleCf$ value is calculated by taking a proportion of one tenth of the $PosCf$ value, this proportion is the same as the proportion of the Gr value compared to the maximum Gr level possible (10). Thus $ruleCf = ((77/10) * (8/10)) = 6.16$. If 'Status' had been satisfied with a Cf value of 10 then this rule would have only considered the first two conditions. After the 'Age' condition $PosCf$ would have been 85 and this is greater than 84 ($Post$). $RuleCf$ would then have been 8 — the measure of goodness of the rule (Gr) as defined by the expert.

The expert supplies the threshold figures ($Post$, $Negt$ and $Mint$), the relative importance weighting for each condition (Ri) and the measure of the goodness of the rule (Gr). Some people have expressed scepticism that experts can in fact quantify their knowledge in this way. Experience with the RCS, FISHFARMER and PISCES systems, has shown that not only is this true, but that in fact they find this a natural form of representing this type of expertise.

The P.R.O. system also neatly handles the problem illustrated by Bundy [30]:

> An uncertainty value of 3 (on a scale of 1 to 5) associated with the fact 'John hates Mary' is ambiguous, could mean either, yes he hates her but only moderately, or that it is uncertain whether he hates her or not.

In the P.R.O. system the approach has been to handle different aspects of evidence separately. In other words the state of the attribute is recorded separately from the user's confidence in his answer.

The P.R.O. system embodies a simple, inexpensive, method for handling uncertainty effectively. The two objectives, transparency and simplicity, have been fulfilled without any loss in accuracy which might have been expected.

5.6 Extensions to P.R.O.

There have been two major extensions to the P.R.O. system since its initial development. Purchase [106] has extended the range of permissible answers and generally improved the questioning routines. These extensions include:

- the facility to request textual responses and direct numerical answers instead of being limited to character answers or numerical ranges;

- the ability to read in a file of data at the start of a session, refer to it where necessary using special "look up" commands in the knowledge base, and update it with information gathered during the consultation;

- a more efficient and effective screen layout;

- the use of menu driven questions during the consultation.

Carden [32] has built into the original system an extended explanation system which P.R.O. generates itself. This allows the user to ask the system to explain how it has arrived at its final answer. The system graphically displays the knowledge base as a tree and shows how it was traversed.

5.7   Conclusion

The emphasis in the design and development of the P.R.O. system has been the desire to produce an expert system shell of practical value. The development of the RCS, FISHFARMER and PISCES systems has helped achieve this objective and has shown that it has been met. There was also the desire to produce a flexible and powerful system which could run within the confines of a microcomputer environment. An important factor considered was the need for an expert system shell targeted at ecological applications and which was able to handle uncertainty effectively.

In order to increase the flexibility of the system, variables which are normally not represented in the knowledge base have been placed in the knowledge base. The knowledge engineer thus has greater control over the workings of the system. The relative importance parameter and the threshold levels are the most important figures in this regard and their use is one of the novel features built into the P.R.O. system. The knowledge base is also more flexible than those used by other system because it consists of a set of syntactically correct Prolog facts and clauses. Thus the expert is able to define his own routines and embed these into the more formal structure of the rules. The RCS system uses this facility to good effect.

The other important design consideration, namely the provision of an effective method of handling uncertainty, has been satisfied by the design of a simple mechanism. This mechanism has been shown to work well and to produce intuitively acceptable answers.

The P.R.O. system is simple to understand. Thus the problems which some users have with the answers that expert systems produce are minimized. The mechanisms which produce the final answer are easily understood, enabling the users to see the relationship between the answers and the data.

Acknowledgements

I am grateful to Denis Riordan for help and advice during the development of the P.R.O. system, also to Jay O'Keeffe, Dale Danilewitz and Nick Dean for comments and suggestions. Thanks also to Karen Wrench and Helen Purchase for reading early drafts of this and other papers.

Chapter 6

Model Based Reasoning and Simulation

Paul Whipp, Tim Lewis

6.1 Introduction

Although expert systems have been around for a number of years, their implementation and use in the commercial world has not been without difficulty. There are two major reasons for this:

- the initial impression during the development of rule based systems is invariably good. It is possible to rapidly generate diagnosis systems which perform reasonably well using a small numbers of rules. However, when these systems are extended to cope with real tasks, the problems associated with the performance and maintenance of the rule base soon become a severe limitation;

- a large number of the expert systems in existence are not fully capitalised on because although they may be reliable 90 % of the time, it is not possible to differentiate the erroneous output from the correct output.

The first of these problems has been addressed by the new generation of high level expert system toolkits (ART, KEE, LOOPS, Goldworks, etc.). These toolkits provide a variety of paradigms including rules which can be used to represent and process knowledge in a convenient form which can scale up to handle real world problems.

The second problem can be alleviated by developing expert systems based on some suitable underlying model, an appropriate simulation is one method which may be employed to provide this model. The use of a simulation permits the verification of an expert system's output by comparing, for example, the simulation data for a diagnosed fault with the real observed data. Standard statistical comparison techniques to produce a confidence figure for the fault being a correct interpretation of the real observations are then possible. The use of simulations within expert systems is the subject of this chapter.

In the past, the development of simulations and models has been a costly and a time consuming exercise. Modern prototyping techniques and toolkits have reduced the development times substantially, allowing the development of simulations to be considered as a practical solution to a large number of problems where the complexity of the simulation would previously have prohibited its development.

Expert system applications can be categorised into two types when considering the uses of modelling and simulation. Firstly, applications which reason about a complete model of the system being considered and secondly applications which reason about a partial or unknown model of the system: a circuit board fault diagnosis application is reasoning about a known system, whereas a credit worthiness advice application is reasoning about a system which is unknown.

In the latter example, we do not know enough about the underlying system (the individual, his future, economics, etc.) to model it with sufficient accuracy. It is therefore convenient to rely on expert systems which allow us to describe what we know empirically about the system.

In the former case, we have the capability to model the circuit in sufficient detail to cover all of the likely faults but it would be impossible to use the model directly for diagnosis. Such a diagnosis would require a massive search involving simulating all possible faults and combinations of faults to establish which model output is equivalent to the observed output. We would end up waiting forever for the diagnosis. As a result of this, we rely on expert systems technology which can produce solutions from the smaller search space, specified by rules, to cover the most commonly encountered faults.

This chapter only considers those expert systems which can be developed to reason about some specifiable system. This includes the areas of fault diagnosis, identification, and most planning applications. We consider the use of models and more particularly simulations to complement and enhance the power of expert systems. Four benefits of such an approach are:

1. Increasing the problem solving capability of the resulting expert system. This can be achieved by allowing the expert system to fall back on guided generate and test procedures using the model when the heuristics fail to locate a single solution. This will involve search but it will typically be limited to a small number of possibilities by the preceding activity of the expert system.

2. Increasing the confidence in the expert system's output. The use of statistical techniques to compare the output of the simulation emulating the fault and the observed fault data will allow an objective measure for the probability that the expert system's diagnosis is correct.

3. The inclusion of inductive learning, using the simulation to generate examples. If a simulation has been used to resolve or refine a diagnosis, the simulation's output can be used as the input to an inductive learning algorithm.

4. The use of simulation to substantially enhance explanation facilities [29]. The use of a simulation to illustrate an expert system's output is a powerful technique to "explain" the output in terms which are meaningful to a user.

This chapter also describes a simulation and modelling toolkit in order to illustrate the facilities and techniques which are now available for integrating the above simulation facilities into existing and future expert systems.

6.2 Why is Simulation becoming easier?

Until recently, simulation building techniques were still stuck within the classic waterfall diagram of design shown in Figure 6.1 [121,34].

Building a simulation, even if it utilises modern toolkits or systems, generally requires a great deal of work before the system will function in a meaningful manner. The use of dummy modules can be used to alleviate this problem but they often fail to help the designer to increase his understanding of the system.

A complication that faces simulation developers is common to all software enginners who wish to embrace modern prototyping and design techniques [15,124].

Prototyping is generally accepted as a necessary component in the design and development of engineering or processing systems but it has only recently become accepted as part of the design process in software engineering. Within software engineering, emphasis has been placed upon the fact that the prototype should be disposed of rather than developed into the final system [24].

While this need for disposal is apparent in the pilot chemical plant or prototype car, it is often not apparent in software systems where the interface or visible components match the users' impression of the target system.

This can lead to pressures being placed by management and end users upon the developers to "enhance" the prototype so that it can be utilised directly. Such enhancements are normally difficult to achieve because of poor or inappropriate design within the prototype system (which was, after all, developed to explore possibilities and not to be expanded into the target system).

This problem is largely responsible for the high development costs of simulations. The cost is incurred by virtue of the fact that without incremental development, design and requirement errors are not discovered early, and without prototyping, design decisions are often arbitrary.

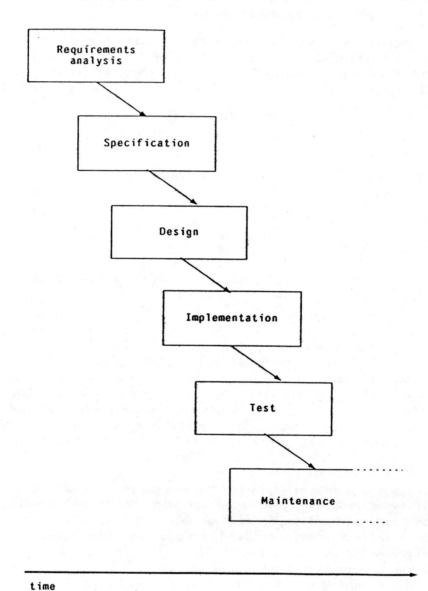

Figure 6.1: Waterfall design model

It is for this reason that the research group at AI Limited chose to develop an alternative simulation toolkit, called STEM [5], rather than buy an existing simulation toolkit off the shelf. The objective was to reduce effort in the development and modification of simulations to a point where they can be considered as a practical tool for general decision making concerning a wide variety of domains. This objective was attained by utilising the techniques developed for prototyping and development within AI.

6.3   A Description of STEM

This section describes STEM and provides the basis for the discussions in subsequent sections.

STEM arose from an internal requirement at AI Limited for a highly flexible general purpose simulation toolkit. Its roots are established in the early simulation systems such as SIMULA [43], and in more recent work covering areas such as exploratory and data flow programming [23,132]. The STEM system is quite small when compared to other recently developed simulation toolkits such as SimKit [2]. This is because STEM is designed to act as an extendible kernal. Many of the advantages of STEM arise from the integrated environment upon which it has been developed. This consists of the En-vos Software Development Environment (ESDE, previously known as the Xerox AI Environment) and the Lisp Objects Oriented Programming System (LOOPS [17]). The possibilities for user extension apply to all the features described below.

STEM may be viewed as a process interaction simulation package or as an event scheduling system [95,56]. The simulation is developed as a collection of data driven processes which exchange data at specifiable times down fixed channels. This mechanism was chosen for STEM because it is easy to understand and use.

A system is modelled using nodes, representing processing points, connected together by paths, representing the potential for data flow between nodes [61].

For example, a node could exist which combines two different inputs into a new single output is shown Figure 6.2.

The Lens source and the Bulb source are nodes which are combined to generate new car lenses and their bulbs respectively. The Combine process node combines the two inputs into one output, a complete lens unit, whilst the Unit sink disposes of the complete units from the simulation.

The Combine process node is data driven. The appearance of a bulb or lens on its input will give rise to it processing that input accordingly. If both components are available, the process will generate an output, the finished unit. This input, process, output model is generally true of STEM nodes.

The paths indicate that data may pass from Bulb source and Lens source to the Combine process node and that data may pass from the Combine process node to the Unit sink. The Combine process node could be connected to any number of producing nodes on its input (including the output of another combiner node).

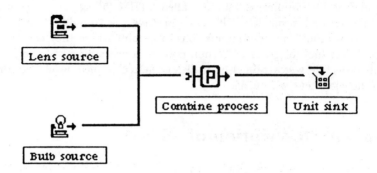

Figure 6.2: A simple STEM example

The sources represent entry points into the model. In many models, this involves the simple creation of data according to some predefined distribution but as STEM operates within ESDE, this can involve data arriving over ethernet, data from other software, data directly from the user, or data generated by other software within ESDE. The sink represents an exit point and can pass data on in a manner similar to the way sources receive data.

The developer builds models in STEM by graphically creating nodes and connecting them together by paths which indicate the potential data flow. Nodes may represent real world components or they may be logical constructions. A node can be a simple object or its behaviour may be defined in terms of a set of nodes which are already connected together.

The developer creates nodes by selecting them from libraries of node descriptions. He can then connect nodes together appropriately even when the descriptions are unfamiliar because each node has a set of associated gates which constrain and describe the connection potential for that node.

In the above example, the Combiner process node has two gates called componentIn and componentOut. The Lens and the Bulb sources have a single componentOut gate. When a user adds a path to either of the sources and selects the Combine process node, the system verifies that connection between these nodes is possible by examining the gates on the nodes. If there is only one possibility (which is usually the case), the connection is made immediately, otherwise the user will be presented with a list of the gates that could be used to make the connection. The gate description on a node has a protocol which indicates the direction(s) of the data flow and the way in which the data may be handled at either end of the path.

When STEM is running a model, the events can be of two types:

1. data transfer down a path between two nodes;

```
(EVENT datum gate time which wrapperClass)
(EVENT-TIME event)
(LATER howmuch)

(GET-ATTRIBUTE object attribute)
(ADD-TO-ATTRIBUTE object attribute value)

(QINSERT object) (QEMPTY?)
(QNEXT)
(QCONTENTS)

(CONNECTED-NODES gateName)
(CHOOSE-NODE gateName selectorOrClass messageArgs ..)
(GET-SENDER package)
```

Figure 6.3: Example EMUs

2. data transfer to the sending node (a local even).

Each of these is given an optional time tag which identifies the time at which the event is to occur.

In addition to specifying gates and behaviour, the descriptions of STEM nodes carry documentation on the node as a whole, the state variables for the node, the behaviour of the node, and the generic variables for the node. This documentation, together with the gate descriptions is always available to the modeller using single mouse clicks. When combined with the constraints on connection imposed by the gates, this provides an environment where the sharing of nodes between users is very simple.

Behavioural specification at the lowest level involves recourse to a programming language. The behaviour of each node is specified by LOOPS methods which are usually written in Lisp but which can be specified in Prolog [6], LOOPS rules, or as external calls to foreign software (using ethernet communications if required). The use of inheritance and existing libraries of nodes (which are being extended by users all the time) minimises the low level programming requirement. The programming environment is further simplified by the presence of EMUs (Event Manipulation Utilities). The EMUs are a set of Lisp functions and macros which provide a simple interface to the event mechanism. They also provide a set of macros which make it easy for inexperienced users to make effective use of STEM at the lowest level. Figure 6.3 shows some EMUs. All development and use of a simulation is mediated via two menus and a number of special windows called *maps*. The menus handle the control of the simulation and the general editing of the simulation. However, most operations are carried out on the map which is best viewed as a graphic editor and interface for the simulation.

Top down design and modelling is supported through the use of composite nodes (*CNodes*). A CNode is a special node whose behaviour is defined in terms of other nodes (which may also be CNodes). Each CNode has two representations. It may appear as an ordinary node on a map and it may appear as a model in its own right with a map describing its components and connection potential. CNodes also support bottom up construction, allowing progressively more complex nodes to be constructed from simpler ones.

For example, Figure 6.4 shows a top down view of an eight bit adder decomposed into its 1 bit and $\frac{1}{2}$ bit components. The eight bit adder is a CNode constructed from a number of full adders which are also CNodes. In this case the model has been extended down to the logic gate level of detail. This highlights the levels of abstraction that STEM supports rather than any particular suitability or design for logic circuit simulation.

In order to support a rapid development cycle, a model builder will normally start with a very simple top level view of his simulation using existing library nodes. The model is thus functional from a very early stage in its development. Refinement proceeds by either replacing particular nodes with alternatives (usually specialisations) or by creating a CNode out of the node and specifying the refined behaviour in terms of other nodes. In this way, new simulation models are often created by analogy. STEM supports the exploratory approach by allowing the builder to replace nodes (automatically reconnecting them wherever possible) or to specialise existing node descriptions very easily.

The model builder has a variety of facilities that can be used to verify and to validate the model:

- **Animation.** Transfer of data between nodes can be visually animated on the open maps allowing the observer to get a clear picture of how the system is behaving. This is used to get a quick feel for the model's behaviour and is often useful in enhancing understanding of the model under development. Thus animation provides visual feedback on the data flow while the simulation is running.

- **Monitoring.** The state variables associated with each node can be monitored in a variety of ways. This involves a continuous display of the values taken on by the monitored state variables. Monitors can be used to observe trends, record running averages, etc. They provide visual feedback on the underlying state of the nodes while the simulation is running.

- **Tracing.** Variables and events may be traced allowing the builder to see what events are occurring in what order and what their effects are while the simulation is running.

- **Logging.** This facility is used to record data for post run analysis. This is used to record data which can be used by the analyser to examine the event tree for the simulation or to provide a variety of graphs based upon data recorded during the simulation run.

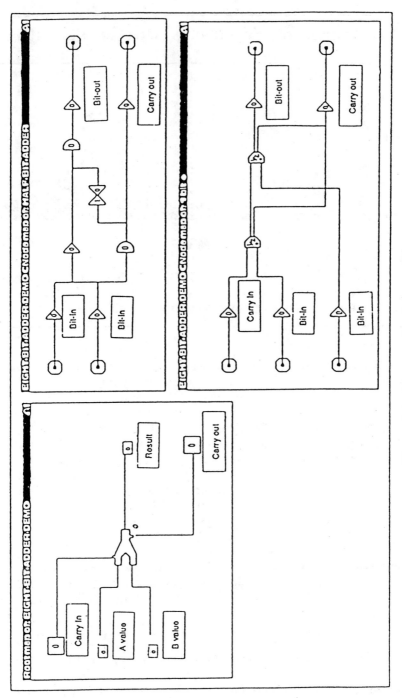

Figure 6.4: An example of composition

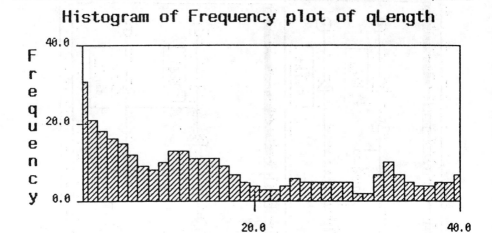

Figure 6.5: Example graph produced by the STEM analyser

- **Analysing.** An analyser examines logged data, allowing the user to produce
  a causal graph of the events which can be used to directly pursue the node
  or the source code which gave rise to the events. It can also produce a
  variety of graphs which may be included in documents prepared within the
  environment. For example, Figure 6.5 shows an incidence graph created by
  the STEM analyser using the results contained in a log file of the queue
  length on a router node.

The logging and monitoring facilities are completely independent of the model
code and structure. This avoids complexity in the model and allows the users to
vary what data is collected and how it is displayed or analysed.

All of these facilities are amenable to specialisations in the same way as nodes.
Thus a developer may produce analysers designed to present or analyse data in a
particular way.

Debugging facilities are provided by the surrounding ESDE. They provide the
capability for run time alteration of code, rewinding, and continuing after fixes or
alterations have been made.

6.4   Integrating Simulations and Expert Systems

This section considers the integration of simulation within an expert system. The
architectures are briefly illustrated using diagrams. The commercially available
ESDE and LOOPS environment provides a convenient common medium within

which both expert systems and simulations can easily be developed. The communication facilities and external interface can be used to interface simulations or expert systems to other existing systems.

6.4.1 Using a Model to Define Confidence Limits

Many expert systems have attained a significant level of expertise and a wide acceptance within the AI community but have never been used in anger. Systems such as MYCIN have not been widely used because it is not easy to be confident about its output. This issue has nothing to do with MYCIN's probabilistic reasoning but refers to the fact that the potential users of the system must understand and believe the output.

The use of a model to verify an expert system's output can provide a much higher level of confidence in the output because it shows to what extent the output accurately describes the observed information. Figure 6.6 shows how a model can be used to obtain the confidence limits.

6.4.2 Using a Model to Assist in Diagnosis

If the expert system fails to discriminate between several possibilities, the simulation can be used to model the small number of possibilities and the 'best match' can be selected. This increases the discriminating capability of the expert system without leading to excessively poor performance. Figure 6.7 summarises how a model can be used to discriminate between several possibilities.

If the expert system cannot provide a small candidate set of possible outputs, the simulation can be used as a normal generate and test mechanism but this would require powerful heuristic control in all but the simplest of cases if the problem is to be solved quickly. It should be remembered that such cases could reasonably be expected to require a long time to solve because they are outside the heuristic knowledge of the system. The same would be true of a human expert if presented with the problem.

6.4.3 Using a Model for Learning

An extension of using the model to assist in diagnosis is in using it to actually extend the set of heuristic rules to cover more cases, and possibly in reducing the rules so that the existing cases are covered more efficiently.

Several rule induction techniques have been developed but their effectiveness has been limited by the need for a large number of training examples. The advantage of a simulation system underlying the model is that the simulation output for a new fault provides a training example which can be used to extend the heuristic knowledge possessed by the expert system. Figure 6.8 shows how a model can provide training examples.

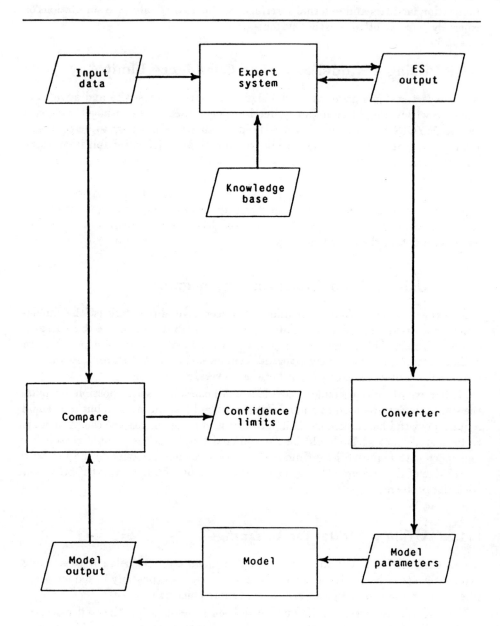

Figure 6.6: Using a model to give confidence limits

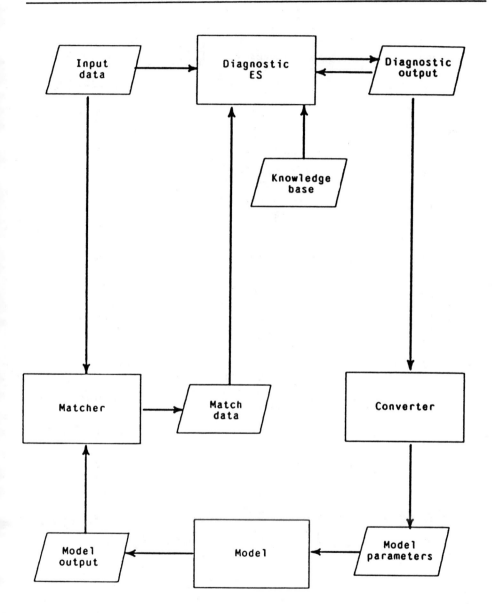

Figure 6.7: Using a model to assist in diagnosis

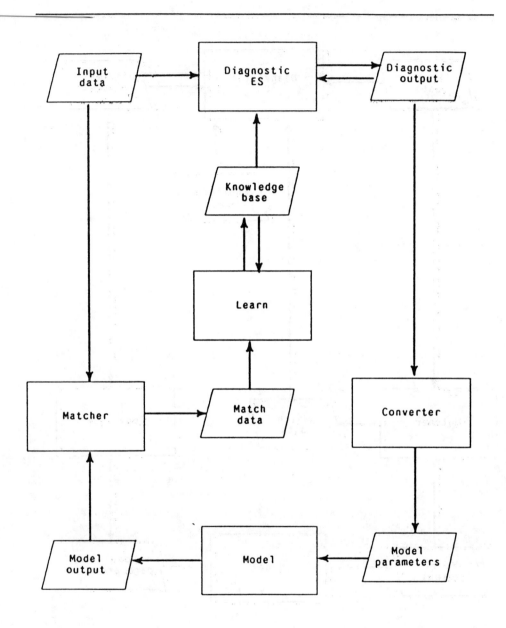

Figure 6.8: Using a model for learning

6.4.4 Using a Model to enhance Explanation Facilities

When expert systems arrived on the scene, they were provided with explanation facilities which were initially developed to allow knowledge engineers to debug the rules making up the knowledge base for the system. Two basic facilities were provided:

- **How.** As in "How did you arrive at that conclusion?" where the expert system would show a causal path from known or assumed information to the derived conclusion.

- **Why.** As in "Why do you want to know?" where the expert system would show to what use it will put the requested information once it is obtained.

While both these facilities are of significant utility for debugging and development purposes, they do not provide explanations which are meaningful to end users of the system.

Various strategies have been used to improve the explanation facilities for end users but they are limited because the information available to these systems does not form a suitable basis for an explanation in the majority of cases.

In order to understand why this is the case, the nature of a typical rule needs to be recognised: it is a set of heuristics which form a partial representation of some real search space.

A doctor may reason with rules similar to those used by MYCIN, but he uses the rules to arrive at a description of the problem for which he will prescribe a treatment. Any explanations that the doctor will offer are based upon the resulting description and upon his understanding of it in the context of the behaviour of the body, and not upon the rules which were used to arrive at the description.

When a diagnosis is made, the rules used may be quite obvious to the useer. It is not the rules that he wants explained but why the rules are applicable. This can only be provided if the system supports some underlying representation of the system being diagnosed.

The simulation can help firstly by providing a comparison between the model output and the observed data as shown in Figure 6.2. The level of match obtained gives a statistical comparison showing to what extent the expert system output is a plausible description of the system being observed. This does not justify the rules directly but it provides a convincing illustration that the conclusion arrived at is a reasonable explanation of the the observed information.

If the explanation facilities are based upon both the model and the rules, the power of the expert system as a learning tool is greatly enhanced. Users can achieve a real understanding of the system represented by experimenting directly with the simulation. The fact that the output of the simulation is similar to the output of the real system allows the user to experiment with the heuristic rules by introducing faults or combinations of faults into a simulation and treating it as if it were the real system. Thus the limitation of the heuristics can be explored and understood.

6.4.5   Using a Model as a Knowledge Elicitation Tool

When developing an expert system, the largest amount of effort is often devoted to the development of the knowledge base. The use of rules is very convenient in the early stages because it provides a working model which can be incrementally enhanced as failings are recognised. However, the rules do not visibly describe the system about which they are reasoning. This has prevented the significant utilisation of the knowledge bases for training purposes and can inhibit their development beyond "toy" systems.

If the rules are developed in parallel with a model of the system which can be driven in a simulation to observe its behaviour, the knowledge elicitation process can proceed more rapidly. The simulation provides a medium of communication between the expert and the knowledge engineer and serves to give the rules meaning. The problem with this approach in the past has been that the model requires a substantial development effort in its own right.

The advantage of systems such as STEM is that the model can be incrementally developed in parallel with the knowledge base. The system can initially be represented at a high level, executed ant its output compared to experimental observation or predicted results. The model can be refined progressively until it models reality to an acceptable level for the diagnosis of faults or for planning purposes.

Developing a simulation with an advanced toolkit such as STEM can often take place in the presence of an expert. Thus it forms a valuable knowledge elicitation tool — the expert sees the system he is describing in a natural and comprehensible diagram. The diagram can be animated to show the behaviour of the model it represents, even when it is under development, so errors of description and omission are discovered early avoiding high development costs. This can also lead to the elicitation of rules which would otherwise not have been uncovered.

6.5   Conclusion

Expert systems have not been as successful in their general application as was indicated by their early successes. This failure arises from their lack of capability to handle problems not explicitly recognised in their development and the difficulty of producing user confidence in their output. It also arises from the problems faced when extending simple knowledge bases into systems which can be used to solve real world problems.

Simulations integrated with expert systems provide: experimental verification of expert system output, limited handling of unknown problems, and the potential for learning.

The simulation itself provides; an experimental platform for learning about the system by users, verification of expert heuristics, experimentation with modifications to the system, and statistical collection of information concerning the system.

Until recently, the building of simulations has been a costly exercise but the feedback from AI programming has provided simulation toolkits which can be used to rapidly prototype and develop simulations which can easily be integrated with existing or proposed expert systems.

The current generation of expert systems have seen only a limited success because of the inherent failings of the technology when it is considered in isolation. The next generation of expert systems will be integrate with models which will provide "deep reasoning" capabilities in a manner described in this chapter. Such systems will be able to provide adequate explanations, and carry out limited learning within their particular domain.

Part III

Ecology

This part of the book describes the experience of using Prolog, and the P.R.O. shell to develop expert systems in the area of ecology.

Chapter 7 describes the use of Prolog to develop a tool which enables ecologists to build simulations. The designers give reasons for preferring Prolog to shells and toolkits. It gives an excellent account of the kind of problems encountered when designers attempt to bridge the gap between a user's model, and the system's model of a problem. In particular, it describes the deficiencies encountered when a Systems Dynamics formalism was adopted, and how these are being solved in a system based on sorted logic.

Chapter 8 describes three applications in ecology which were developed using the P.R.O. shell. It describes the main features of each application and then gives a summary of their common features. It will give the reader an indication of what is possible with a shell, and the kind of benefits that can be obtained by using expert systems.

Chapter 7

Helping Inexperienced Users to Construct Simulation Programs: An Overview of the ECO Project

Mike Uschold, Dave Robertson, Alan Bundy, Bob Muetzelfeldt

7.1 Introduction

In this chapter, we describe an applications driven research project. The application is the construction of simulation models in the domain of ecology. Conventional rule-based tools which are suitable for diagnostic expert systems were found to be insufficient for our task, which consists of building up a large structure (i.e. the model) during a session. This chapter is a revised and extended version of a paper by the same title published in the proceedings of Expert Systems 1987 [118].

In the remainder of this section we introduce the problem, identify requirements for solution, and discuss tool selection. Subsequently, we describe our first prototype system (ECO) in relation to our original objectives. We highlight some important inadequacies in the basic system. We then describe our current implementation (EL) indicating in some detail how we have tackled these problems.

7.1.1   The Problem

Ecological researchers are becoming increasingly reliant upon mathematical models as a means of concisely representing their understanding of ecological systems. Having constructed a model of a given system, it is possible to test the validity of the representation using computer simulation and analysis of results. Models which are deemed valid may be used to predict the behaviour of their corresponding real world system when subjected to a specific set of conditions. This capability is particularly necessary in the assessment of environmental impact of resource management decisions.

Ideally, it should be possible for any ecologist to fit his/her description of an ecological system into a modelling framework which allows it to be easily accessed and analysed by other researchers. Currently, there are various problems which prevent this:

1. Many ecologists do not have the mathematical, modelling, or programming skills needed to construct ecological models.

2. There has been little standardisation of modelling approaches. Individual modellers tend to write large, one-off, representations using their favourite modelling language and/or mathematical framework. These models are extremely difficult to analyse unless one is familiar with the formalisms involved. Model defects are thus liable to pass unnoticed by the ecological community.

3. Model parameters and relationships are scattered through a wide range of literature and are expressed in different formalisms (e.g. mathematical formulae ; Fortran subroutines). Therefore, a large amount of effort is wasted in defining model components which have already been used elsewhere.

7.1.2   Requirements

Ecologists need to be free to concentrate on investigating the dynamics of the systems which interest them, rather than wasting time learning esoteric programming techniques or deciphering obscure mathematical formalisms. Our research aim is to provide an ecological modelling system which can be used by ecologists with minimal mathematical or programming skills. Ideally, a user should be able to describe their problem in ecological terms; the system should act as an expert modeller asking for further information as required, advising on how to make modelling decisions. In order to address the problems listed above, we considered

Figure 7.1: Large Terminological Gap

that the following features were required in the system:

- A **task specification formalism** which is capable of representing a wide range of ecological simulation models. This helps provide a standard representation for different models, tackling problem 2 in section 7.1.1. A specification of a particular simulation model must itself be runnable, or able to be translated into a runnable program.

- A **front end** which interacts with the user in terms familiar to him/her, converting the user's ecological statements into the task specification formalism. This is needed to help overcome the technology barrier of problem 1 by making it easier for users formally to describe the program they require.

  This is a major problem, which proved to be a central focus of the project. How can the computer system help bridge the large gap between the ecological terms and concepts familiar to the ecologist (e.g. sheep graze on grass) and the terms and concepts of the eventual implementation language (e.g. Fortran)? In between these two extremes are modelling concepts which are at a higher level than the Fortran and at a lower level than the ecological descriptions (See Figure 7.1).

- A **data base and browsing mechanism** for storing and accessing ecological data and relationships. By providing this repository of information, users should find it easier to isolate model structures appropriate to their application (alleviating problem 3).

- An **automatic checker** of the consistency and ecological sense of the model. This also addresses problem 1 by preventing all syntactic and some semantic errors during the interactive specification phase.

- A **back end interpreter** to run the completed model and display the results. The specification may be run directly, or translated into runnable code.

The first ECO system, although prototypical, largely achieves these original requirements for a subset of ecological modelling. In Sections 7.2, we describe this system, discuss some of its deficiencies and how we have dealt with them in a later version.

7.1.3   Selecting a Tool

The available tools may be broadly grouped into three categories: programming languages (usually symbolic), programming environments, and shells. Their differences are best characterised by considering issues of generality (i.e. flexibility) and set up cost (i.e. how much effort to build prototypes). Programming languages are very general, highly flexible but require a great deal of set up cost and programming skill.

Shells are at the other extreme. They are highly specialised, suitable for only a small range of tasks. Shells are most useful when the nature of the problem is well understood, and furthermore, the structure of the knowledge being captured is similar to the knowledge representation structures offered by the shell. However, with shells, reasonable prototypes can often be built very quickly. Furthermore, less programming skill is required.

Environments are best described as being in between these two extremes on both counts. The key is that they provide a wide range of features. This gives added flexibility since they can be tailored to many different uses. Additionally, there is considerable savings in set up costs because the features are already programmed.

Before selecting a tool, it is important to identify the nature and relative importance of the system requirements. In any project there are many different things to take into account at varying levels of detail. Here, we discuss two fairly general issues which (for us) were the most important for the purpose of selecting a tool:

- The functional role of the system. The nature of our task is one of planning or design. The output (a computer program) is highly structured.

- How well understood is the problem? Neither ecology nor the art of modelling is well understood. Thus, flexibility was an important requirement.

Shells were ruled out on both counts. They are typically best suited for diagnostic tasks with much less structured output. Using a shell would be difficult, at best for our planning/design problem. Furthermore, they offer insufficient flexibility. Since we did not know exactly what we would require, we could not restrict ourselves to a shell.

The flexibility requirement suggests that we should use a programming language. However, would an environment also work? We believe the answer to be yes. In deciding, we must look more closely at the sorts of information that we need to represent and manipulate; and then look to see if any of the tools offered by environments are particularly well suited. If so, it may be worth sacrificing some of the flexibility of a language. This exercise was made difficult by the fact that the problem was ill understood; the research was exploratory. With the exception that an object-oriented environment would make it easy to represent plant/animal taxonomies, environments had nothing to offer that was particularly suited to our perceived needs. As an aside, environments are expensive and we did not have one available. Furthermore, there is the hidden cost of becoming familiar with an environment. This can be quite significant, usually requiring training costs etc. We chose Prolog, the language that the group was familiar with. Other symbolic languages would also have been suitable.

As it turned out, the conceptual work was always the bottleneck for our project, not the programming. The quick prototyping provided by Prolog was always more than adequate. In later phases of the project, we could well have moved to an environment if it was deemed suitable. The representation and inferencing techniques that we eventually settled on were based on sorted logic descibred in Section 7.3.2). As this is not a standard expert systems technique, no shell or environment provided for this to entice us away from Prolog.

7.2 Description of the First ECO System

7.2.1 Overview

ECO, ([138], [94]) is a computer program — written in Prolog — for constructing ecological models. A diagram illustrating the general architecture of the system appears in Figure 7.2. It relies upon a System Dynamics formalism [55] to express model structure. This formalism can be manipulated by users, via an interface package, to produce a Task Specification for the model they require. A knowledge base of ecological relationships is used by the system to perform some simple checks for ecological consistency in the developing Task Specification. When complete (as determined by the syntactical structure of the formalism), the Task Specification is automatically converted into a target language (e.g. Fortran) and the simulation may then be run. Recently, we have added the ability to run simulations directly in Prolog, using a special purpose interpreter. This bypasses the code generation phase but does not effect the core of our research — the interface between user and formal Task Specification. We now consider the main components of the system, stemming from our requirements described in section 7.1.2.

7.2.2 Task Specification Formalism

A task specification formalism, for our purposes, is a language for specifying simulation programs which embody models of ecological systems. The range of possible

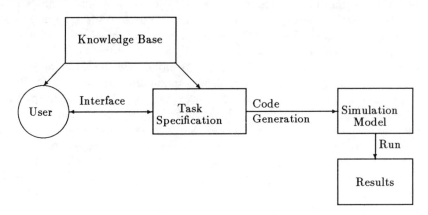

Figure 7.2: The original ECO system

models and programs is far to vast to capture in its entirety. As a starting point we limited ourselves to a special class of models, called System Dynamics models. This is a methodology which encompasses the technique of compartment modelling, commonly used in ecology to model the flow of materials such as energy, nutrients, and pollutants. As such, it is quite a powerful methodology capable of capturing a wide range of models. It also has the advantage of being based on relatively few simple concepts.

System Dynamics modelling makes use of a concise schematic representation which helps the ecologist think about the model without mathematical formulae. This representation was adapted and expanded to produce a task specification formalism which helps to bridge the gap between the user's view of the problem in ecological terms and the final Fortran simulation program. It did this by enabling the ecologist to think in the ecological terms of flow of materials, and expressing their models (via an interface package) into the flow-based specification formalism in a fairly straightforward manner. Gradually, through interacting with the system, the specification of the model was completed. The eventual Fortran code is generated automatically from this specification and is never seen by the user.

Figure 7.3 shows a diagrammatical representation of this formalism for a very simple model in which wolves are preying upon sheep. The rate of predation is a function of the current values for sheep and wolf compartments and a coefficient (e.g. directly proportional).

7.2.3   Interacting with the User

At the most general level, the ecologist describes a model in terms of objects (such as trees, sheep, wolves) and relationships between these objects (such as predation, photosynthesis, etc). Equations and parameters defining these objects and

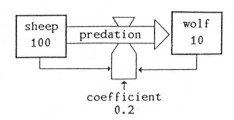

Figure 7.3: A System Dynamics Model

relationships can be selected by the user, with automatic connection of appropriate structures in the underlying task specification. The user is free to decide how to approach the task of model construction. For example, submodels can be constructed separately and linked together later or, alternatively, the user can specify all the objects and relationships at the general level before finally attaching equations and parameters.

In order that ecologists should readily accept the system, it is crucially important to have a friendly means of interaction. Initially, users were required to input ecological statements in stylised English (e.g "wolves eat sheep"). This statement is interpreted by the system to mean that there are two populations, wolves and sheep and that there is a process (eating) which causes biomass from the sheep population to "flow" to the wolf population. This allowed the user to decide how the model would be constructed but required that the user remember the syntax of each command. As a means of providing more guidance for users, an alternative menu based interaction system was implemented and, recently, computer graphics techniques are being tested as a more convenient way of eliciting input and displaying the developing model. This removes the necessity for remembering command syntax but provides no help with decisions about strategies for building the model (e.g. Should a deer population be represented as a single entity or as separate individuals?). Incorporating this sort of advice into the system is being tackled in current research. Currently, the user must make strategic decisions which are only checked for consistency by the system.

The issue of user interaction is closely related to the larger issue of conveniently bridging the terminological gap. We have devoted considerable effort to experimenting with various forms of user interaction. More details on this and other related issues can be found in [120].

7.2.4 Storing and Accessing Ecological Data

During the model building phase, the user has access to a base of ecological knowledge and data. Its primary function is to provide the user with the building blocks necessary for creating the model. This includes such things as ecological objects which may be contained in the models (e.g. animals, trees etc), taxonomic information relating classes of objects when possible (e.g. primates are mammals), mathematical relationships (with associated contexts indicating their appropriateness), and processes (e.g. grazing and evaporation) each with the appropriate types of objects which may participate (e.g. only animals may graze). This knowledge is used to perform semantic consistency checking as described below.

Ecologists need the capability to store data from field observations or laboratory studies and retrieve them in a flexible, efficient manner. Often, these observations are made in different contexts and ecologists want to store and retrieve information according to the circumstances in which it was first recorded. For example, an observation may be made that "A tree in plot 5 of the Glentrool plantation was 5 metres high in summer 1976". Another observation may state that "The rate of photosynthesis of sitka spruce is $10 mgCkg^{-1}day^{-1}$ in bright sunlight". We have utilised relationships between items in different observations to provide a structure for browsing through records based on such observations, progressively refining the user's description of the observation he/she wants to find. Ecologists who have used the system find the browsing mechanism easy to understand and operate. For a more detailed description of the ECO browser see [119].

7.2.5   Consistency Checking

As the user is building the specification for his/her model, it is continually checked for internal consistency. Two separate types of consistency checking are performed. First, there is a syntactic or mathematical consistency associated with the formalism (e.g. destructive circularity should not occur in the task specification; a parameter must have an initial value). Since these consistency rules are few in number and clearly defined, we can ensure that ECO never produces a model which cannot be run — the user is guaranteed to get something that works. Secondly, there is semantic consistency checking which helps maintain ecological sense in the specification. Ideally, we should like to guarantee that a final model will be ecologically sound and, furthermore, will accurately and appropriately describe the behaviour of the ecological system to meet the original goals of the user. This is well outside the capabilities of our current implementation. However, we do provide limited semantic checking capabilities. For example, if the user says that "sheep eat wolves" he/she is warned that this relationship may be the wrong way round. If the system does not recognise a particular object, it will make default assumptions on the basis of the context in which it appears. Thus if the user says "foo eats sheep", the system assumes that "foo" is an animal. All future uses of the object "foo" must be consistent with it being an animal. A more comprehensive attempt to define specific objects and relationships in terms of general ecological principles is described briefly in section 7.3.2. This should facilitate improved checking and explanation capabilities.

7.2.6 Running the Completed Model

Completed models can be passed to a code generation subsystem which translates the task specification into Fortran source code. Due to the constrained nature of our formalism for expressing models, this process was relatively straightforward. The interesting problems of automatic programming from specifications were avoided. The user can then compile this code, run it and revise the task specification if the program does not behave as expected. Currently, the onus is on the user to decide whether revisions to his/her task specification are necessary. Ideally, there would be a much closer association between the system for eliciting the model specification and the subsystem for running the model so that feedback on program execution can be related to the specification. As a first step towards integrating these systems a Prolog program for running simulations has been developed. This allows test simulations to be executed directly from the task specification (no intermediate translation phase) and provides for the possibility of automatically passing back information from the simulation to influence subsequent model refinement. Because our research effort is directed primarily at formally representing user's models rather than analysis of program execution, we have not yet concentrated on these execution issues.

7.2.7 Summary and Critique

The system can be used to construct a particular type of simulation model easily and efficiently, provided that the user knows what he/she wants to do. We tested this version of the system on undergraduate students of ecology and on various visitors to the department. These trials revealed several shortcomings of the original system. The most important of these are that:

- the task specification formalism is insufficiently expressive

- the system is too reliant upon the user to drive dialogue during model construction

- the modelling guidance provided by the system is insufficient for naive users.

7.3 A New Implementation: EcoLogic

In this section, we describe a new implementation EL. It is a culmination of our efforts and achievements in combating the three main problems in ECO (mentioned above). We first give a general overview of EL, listing its major features. The subsequent sections discuss each of the three problems from section 7.2.7 in detail, and the solutions as embodied in EL.

7.3.1 Overview of EL

EL is described fully in [116]. Some of its features are listed below:

- It constructs simulation programs written in Prolog. Such programs can represent many modelling relationships which would be difficult to implement in standard simulation formalisms, such as System Dynamics.

- It utilises the modularity inherent in the structure of Prolog programs to neatly divide the task of program construction into nested sets of goals and subgoals. This property enables us to provide a database of schemata (stereotypic model structures) which generate portions of program for solving given goals. We provide a mechanism for applying these schemata to construct a runnable simulation program.

- It does not operate directly as a program editor. Instead it extracts from the user a description of the ecological problem which requires simulation and uses this information to guide the construction of a program through the application of schemata. The problem description is constructed by selecting and editing ecological statements (expressed in a sorted logic) using a general purpose browsing and editing mechanism.

- It can actively help users to decide how to describe their ecological systems by suggesting new logical formulae (using an abduction mechanism) and automatically establishing any formulae which are implied from the current problem description (by deduction). This guidance is achieved using domain independent inference mechanisms which reference a knowledge base of ecological and modelling rules.

- It supports interaction with the user during all stages of program development. This gives it the flexibility to allow the user some free choice over the shape of the final program, rather than automatically churning out some "standard" result.

- The completed Prolog program can be run either as standard Prolog or, to improve efficiency, using a special purpose interpreter.

- Since the problem description and program schemata are represented explicitly and manipulated using clearly defined mechanisms, it is possible to reconstruct a previous program construction session from the final program, problem description and a record of answers to queries during schemata application. Users can browse through this reconstruction, obtaining information about the choices made during the original session.

7.3.2   Extending the Task Specification Formalism

The System Dynamics based task specification formalism used by ECO served two major purposes simultaneously:

1. It could unambiguously express a wide range of models (although limited to the System Dynamics framework). This is to do with the issue of the *range of models expressible*.

2. It enabled the ecologist to think of their problem in ecological terms, freeing them from the details of programming. This is largely due to the fact that it was based on a modelling paradigm familiar to many ecologists. Thus, the ecologists already were thinking in terms similar to those that the system understood. This is to do with the issue of *bridging the terminological gap*

Although satisfactory for a limited range of situations, the System Dynamics based Task Specification Formalism was ultimately found inadequate on both counts. We discuss these in turn.

Range of models expressible

Although the System Dynamics formalism was useful for constructing a wide range of simulation models, there were many things which it could simply not cope with. It could not easily be adapted to represent certain more complex computational structures (e.g. models with age class subdivisions or models in which structural components were created and destroyed, representing births and deaths).

The range of models expressible was extended to include these facilities. There are two issues to consider. One is the specification language itself. It needs either to be augmented, or completely redesigned. The second is the target language, which in ECO, was Fortran. To encode the fact that a population has age and sex classes in a high level specification language is not so difficult. The real problem is in generating sensible Fortran code to accommodate these features. We abandoned that route and decided instead to build Prolog programs. The task specification formalism used by the first ECO system was redesigned for EL. It is based on a sorted logic. Some examples of statements in this formalism are given in the discussion below on bridging the terminological gap.

Bridging the terminological gap

The successful bridging of the terminological gap for ECO users depended critically on the assumption that users were thinking of their problem in System Dynamics terms (i.e. materials flowing from place to place). The model is the description of the ecological system in these terms. Thus, ECO is essentially a convenient tool for specifying System Dynamics models. Note however, that users were forced to specify the model *directly*.

So long as the above assumption holds, the terminological gap is minimal. The problem arises when a user is **not** thinking of their problem in System Dynamics terms. For such individuals, ECO is of no use. In this situation, there is a considerable terminological gap which must be bridged. Users are thinking about their problem in terms of ecological objects and relationships; the system only understands System Dynamics terms. There are two aspects to the solution of this problem. First, a new *problem description* language must be designed which directly captures the terms that the user is thinking in. Secondly, the system must be equipped with modelling knowledge and reasoning mechanisms to help the user convert their problem description into the model (i.e., the solution). We

now address the issue of constructing a problem description language and defer
discussion of the latter issue to Section 7.3.4.

EL uses a formalism in which common ecological statements are represented
using a sorted logic. Some examples of typical ecological statements expressed in
the logic are:

"All wolves prey upon all sheep at all times."
$$\forall W \in wolf \ \forall S \in sheep \ \forall T \in time \cdot predation(W, S, T)$$

"If predation occurs at any instant in time, then there will be a
transfer of biomass from the prey to the predator at that time"
$$\forall A, B \in animal \ \forall T \in time \cdot$$
$$predation(A, B, T) \rightarrow biomass\_transfer(A, B, T)$$

The procedural structure of the simulation is supplied by introducing fragments
of simulation code (schemata), each being active only under certain conditions of
the user's description of the ecological system. This approach to program construction provides greater representational power in terms of the range of models
expressible, as well as increased ability to represent ecological statements in a form
close to that employed by users. It also provided a foundation for later work on
dialogue and guidance. A more detailed discussion of these issues appears in [117].

7.3.3   Flexible Dialogue Control

Many computer systems tend to force users into a rigidly structured dialogue,
designed to suit some "average" user. In ECO, the dialogue was primarily user
driven, with the system responding to the user's commands. Our experience shows
that different types of users require different balances between system and user
initiative during model construction. Expert users want freedom to define task
specification structure as they see fit. Novice users need to be guided through
the model construction process until they become accustomed to the system. A
flexible dialogue system is required, which allows users to take the initiative if they
want to but continually provides advice as to what it thinks would be a useful thing
to do at any time. To accommodate these needs, EL utilises graphics displays and
multiple windowing facilities to simultaneously display different possibilities for
interaction. There are two main features of this architecture.

First, there is a window in which users may, of their own volition, provide
information about model structures and their goals for the current model. This
has been implemented, based on a mechanism for selecting and editing sorted logic
statements, rendered into English text [117]. The left-hand window in Figure 7.4
shows a sample display in which the user has, using a browsing system, selected a
sentence (number 218) from the system's knowledge base:

> For all animal:1, animal:2 and time:
> animal:1 preys upon animal:2 at time.

The stylised English is generated from a formal logic statement represented internally. This makes it more easily understood by ecologists. The user has edited this sentence by restricting the sorts animal:1 and animal:2 to the more specific sorts wolf and sheep respectively. This forms the expression below which is then added to the problem description.

> For all wolf, sheep and time:
> wolf preys upon sheep at time.

To have added this sentence to the problem description means (in everyday English) that in the ecological system of interest, wolves prey on sheep.

The second major feature of the dialogue architecture is a suggestion box of system advice about model construction. Suggestions are generated by the system, allowing an entire model to be constructed simply by following the system's advice. This part of the system has been only partially implemented (see Section 7.3.4). A display from EL appears in the right-hand window of Figure 7.4. Here the system has used the expression added by the user (see above) in conjunction with the following rule from its knowledge base:

> For all animal:1, animal:2., and time:
> IF animal:1 preys on animal:2 at time
> THEN there exists some probability_value such that:
>   the probability of animal:1 kills animal:2 at time
>   is probability_value

to generate the following suggested sentence, rendered into stylised English by the system:

> For all wolf, sheep, and time:
>   there exists some probability_value such that:
>   the probability of wolf kills sheep at time
>   is probability_value

By referring to the appropriate identification number (in this case: 1), the user may get the system to implement this advice.

This architecture allows flexible changes of initiative during the session. It also helps alleviate the perennial problem of ordering the sequence of suggestions because the user is allowed to choose which to accept at any time. This is especially true when the number of suggestions at any time is fairly small. Further discussion of dialogue issues may be found in [120].

7.3.4 Guiding the Design of Specifications

Even with an expressive specification language, and a friendly dialogue system at their disposal, many users have difficulty in constructing program specifications. A major part of the problem is that there are many choices that have to be made. For example, the user may be unable to decide whether to represent a deer population as a single entity or as a number of individual objects and, if the latter option is

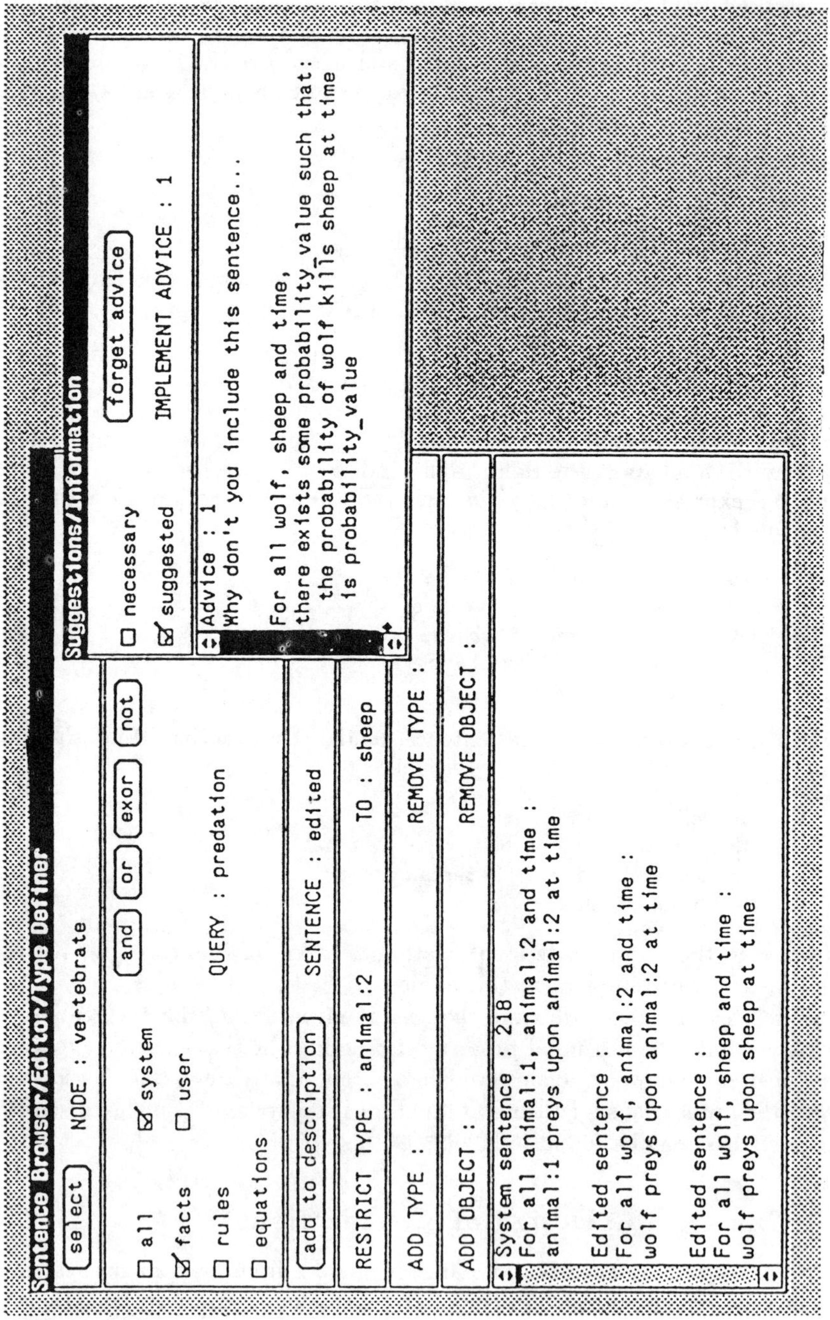

Figure 7.4: Mixed Initiative System - Sample Display

chosen, he/she may not know the appropriate structures to insert into the task specification. Novice modellers do not know how to idealise the objects in models so that they are consistent with the overall objectives of the model. Without this information, they may construct inelegant specifications or, worse, may leave out crucial structures. The objective is for the system to be an expert modelling consultant rather than 'merely' a convenient tool. A useful guidance component must be able to:

- identify what decisions need to be made

  e.g. how to represent an object

- identify what the choices are for a particular decision

  e.g. a population, or as individuals

- advise on selecting among these options

  e.g. If there are large numbers of individuals, it will generally be infeasible to represent each individual separately.

At the start of a session, advice may be provided by asking users to specify their modelling objectives or to provide some of the principal high level components of their model — for example, the fact that wolves prey on sheep. From this general description, the system may be able to select a modelling framework — a predator-prey schema, perhaps — and display this to the user as a suggested structure. If the structure is acceptable, it may be further elaborated, using additional schemata if necessary. For instance, a respiration subschema might be added to the predator (wolf) component of the predator-prey schema.

The guidance component of our system is the least developed. Having first designed and implemented a framework for modelling, we are now concentrating our efforts on the provision of sophisticated guidance. The guidance provided by EL is based on the design described above. It fits cleanly into the dialogue architecture described in Section 7.3.3 above. The system currently has a small set of rules for providing suggestions. Efforts are currently underway to acquire the knowledge required to be able to provide a wide range of advice on model building. The recommendations that the system makes must take into account the information that is currently available. This will include all that has been said about the ecological system. As an expert modelling consultant, the system should also take into account what the user's goals and/or objectives are for building the model in the first place. This information is captured in what we have called the problem description. Much effort has been devoted to developing a suitable problem description language. Part of this has already been described in Section 7.3.2. A significant effort is currently underway in extending this language to capture user's modelling goals which can then be used to guide the modelling process.

The area of providing suggestions is one where a conventional rule-based approach might have been possible. We did not choose to do this because they are typically lacking in any formal foundation which greatly jeopardises the reliability of the resulting system. It therefore becomes difficult to assess the status of inferences. See [30] for an extended discussion of the use of logic as a formal foundation for expert systems. See [116] for the details of how we use abduction and deduction and sorted logic to produce suggestions and draw conclusions.

7.4   Conclusion

We have given a brief overview of the ECO project. The fundamental aim of the project is to make ecological modelling more accessible to ecologists who are unskilled in modelling and/or programming. The domain of ecological modelling is particularly challenging because neither ecology nor modelling is well understood nor guided by firm principles. The goal is to produce a system which will enable an ecologist to describe their problem in ecological terminology. The system translates this problem description through further interaction with the ecologist and produces a correct simulation program which satisfies the user's objectives.

This project can be divided into two phases. Our initial work relied upon a simple System Dynamics formalism which represented users' ecological models in a mathematical framework. We chose this formalism for three reasons. First, ecologists were familiar with System Dynamics; second, we needed to start with some manageable subset of ecological models; finally for its simplicity, a surprising number and variety of models are representable using this framework. Users were assumed to be capable of constructing *solutions* to their ecological problems by (semi-)directly manipulating System Dynamics constructs. However, tests of the initial system revealed that all too frequently this assumption did not hold. In addition, they sometimes required more complex models than could be represented using System Dynamics. They wanted to describe their modelling *problem*, using terminology with which they were familiar, and receive guidance in converting this into a computable solution. These requirements provided the impetus for the second phase of development, which continues today. In the current system (EL) users can describe their modelling problem using ecological statements — represented in a sorted logic. Sorted logic permits a wider range of problems and solutions to be represented than was possible using System Dynamics. These statements can be used to isolate fragments of simulation code which, together, constitute a computable simulation model. We have also implemented relatively simple guidance mechanisms, and incorporated these into a "suggestion box" architecture. This allows the system to take control of dialogue at a user's request, thus elevating EL from the role of a passive assistant to that of an active participant in the modelling process.

Acknowledgements

This work was funded by SERC/Alvey grants GR/C/06226, GR/D/44294, and GR/E/00730. We are grateful to members of the Mathematical Reasoning Group in the Department of Artificial Intelligence at Edinburgh University for their practical advice and support during the course of this project.

Chapter 8

Three Ecological Applications in P.R.O

John Bradshaw, Jay O'Keeffe,
Nick Dean, Irene J. de Moore, Helen Purchase,
Dale Danilewitz, Denis Riordan, Micheal N. Bruton

8.1   Introduction

This chapter describes the development of three ecological expert systems which have been developed using th P.R.O. expert system shell. It shows that there are common advantages in developing the three systems and suggests that the same advantages can accrue in developing other ecological systems. It does not attempt to give detailed descriptions of the various projects; instead the projects are introduced and it is shown that the development of ecological expert systems holds some real benefits. The reader should consult the papers referenced for full details of the individual systems.

Aside from providing a useful tool, the development of an ecological knowledge base has some advantages in its own right. The need to articulate the knowledge precisely enough for inclusion into a knowledge base precludes the experts from hand waving and forces them to concentrate on the real issues. Often the result of this is to identify specific problem areas where more investigation is required as well as to provide a single, well defined source of knowledge around which experts can debate the issues in a pointed and deliberate style.

This chapter is organised in three major sections describing the three applications. The first of these, the RCS system [100], computes the conservation status of rivers in South Africa, provides a useful method of comparing different rivers and also has real applications in environmental assessment projects. The second section describes the FISHFARMER system [45,46], which has been developed to help fledgling fish farmers choose the right combination of species, site and culture method. It fills a void in the process of knowledge transfer from researcher to client as well as identifying many areas which require more investigation. The third section is devoted to a description of the PISCES system [107]. This system addresses the problem of introducing exotic aquaculture species into the region. It makes recommendations to the user and is designed as a tool to be used by the controlling bodies. The system contains all the information which needs to be investigated as well as providing a fair means of examination.

This chapter concludes with a short section which ties together the common benefits realised from the development of the three individual systems and attempts to show the advantages which can be gained from the development of ecological systems.

8.2   The RCS (River Conservation Status) System

8.2.1   Introduction

South Africa's river systems vary from practically pristine natural systems to heavily exploited and degraded drainage ditches. The Olifants river system of the Southwestern Cape flows through a mountainous catchment of unique vegetation and includes in its fauna eight fish species endemic to the system. In contrast, 150 km further south, the Black River flows in a concrete canal through Cape Town, with effluent from the cities main sewage works contributing up to 90% of the flow. Other aspects of conservation concern are embodied in the Olifants River of the Eastern Transvaal, one of the main drainage systems for the highly populated, industrialised and mining rich Witwatersrand area, which then flows through the Kruger National Park.

Conservation in South Africa has been dominated by the economic and popular appeal of the large animal populations in protected areas, so that until recently, consideration of aquatic conservation has been confined to hippos, crocodiles, and a few fish species. Nevertheless, streams in undeveloped catchments reflect unaltered natural conditions and could be preserved in this state. Perhaps the most important issue is that South Africa is an arid country where water is often the limiting resource for future development. Natural freshwater lakes are unknown, and groundwater reservoirs meager. Rivers in South Afrca are therefore under intense development pressure, and the case for conservation must be very strong to be given priority. A major problem has been that no coherent river conservation policy has been developed, and consequently it has been extremely difficult for government agencies, planners and engineers to understand and consider conservation priorities.

A need was therefore identified for a means of assessing the major conservation attributes of rivers, for communicating these in a conceptually simple manner to people who are not ecologists, and for investigating the likely consequences of proposed river development schemes on the conservation of rivers.

Some aspects of conservation are quantifiable, but others involve subjective value judgements. Expert systems are well suited for modeling and decision making with conservation problems. In the following subsections the methods used to develop an automated semi numerical model for the assessment of conservation status of South African rivers are described.

8.2.2 The Aims of the System, and Initial Specifications

The aims of the RCS project were to identify attributes of rivers which are important for their conservation, to establish their relative nature and scale of this importance, and then to quantify the conservation status of any particular river or section of river. 'Conservation status' is defined as a measure of the relative importance of the river for conservation, and the extent to which it has been disturbed from its natural state.

Given the required information about a river, the system must be able to provide:

- A relative value of the conservation status of the river.

- Relative values for different components of the river.

- 'Confidence limits' indicating how precisely the conservation status can be measured and indicating where more accurate information is required.

- A listing of the relative importance of each attribute in determining the status of the river.

- Opportunities for the user to manipulate the program to examine its assumptions and change parameters.

8.2.3 Knowledge Acquisition

The initial problem in the design of the system was to identify which attributes should be considered and then to specify how they affected the conservation status of a river. The following information was required:

- The attributes to be included.

- The weightings of attributes, where attributes are weighted according to their relative importance. A positive weighting indicates that an attribute is beneficial (such as indigenous fish), while a negative weighting indicates detrimental effects (e.g. sewage effluent).

- The value bounds and the five class bounds.

- The nature of their effect. Some attributes affect the final score in direct proportion to the presence of the attribute, while others only become significant if they are present in large quantities (e.g. effluent). Still other attributes are of most interest when only a small quantity is present, e.g. the difference between a river having 0 and 1 endemic fish is much more significant than the difference between 8 or 9 different endemic species in a river.

The information was gathered by a two phase questionnaire sent to all ecological workers and professional conservationists on river systems in South Africa. It also benefited from a workshop where the same experts were brought together to discuss the problems of river conservation. Here they were able to evaluate and criticise an early version of the system.

8.2.4   The Knowledge Base

The RCS system uses the index inference system supported by the P.R.O. system. The objective of the knowledge base is to identify which characteristics are important in the determination of the conservation status of the particular river. The computed index score is then based on the values of the attributes and their relative weightings.

Aside from identifying which attribute values are required to produce a conservation status value, the rule base also holds rules which modify general weighting values, and which may cause more detailed questions to be asked, in response to recognised features of individual rivers. For example, the size of a river will to some extent cause the individual occurrences of particular attributes to be more or less significant, e.g. the influence of a single dam on a very large river will be less than that of the same structure on a shorter river. Rules which alter the effect of some attributes depending on the status of other attributes are thus present in the RCS knowledge base.

Another class of rules ascertains whether regulatory structures in a river have beneficial as well as negative effects. Dams and weirs are normally negative features, but where they prevent the upstream migration of introduced exotics they are obviously beneficial.

8.2.5   The Results

The final answer is given in the form of a range. The size of this range gives a good indication about the information which the user has entered in response to the questions asked. For example, a maximum score of 76 and a minimum of 68 reflects a river of high conservation status, for which fairly accurate ecological information is available. A maximum score of 76 and a minimum of 45 indicates that the river may have a high conservation status, but more importantly that better information must be obtained before a meaningful judgement can be made.

The results for a particular river, or stretch of river, are presented in tabular form. The overall maximum and minimum score is given, followed by a breakdown (available on demand) for the biota, the catchment and the physical features of the river. Each attribute is listed with the answers provided by the user, the scores calculated from the answers and the weightings, and the research priority index calculated from the confidence status and the weighting. The relative magnitude of the scores for each attribute identifies the most important conservation attributes of the river.

To identify which attributes will most benefit from further investigation, a research priority index is calculated for each attribute. A high research priority index indicates that more precise information about that attribute will do most to reduce the divergence of the overall score.

As with all P.R.O. based systems there is the facility to change any answers or weightings for any attribute to produce an alternative set of results. The P.R.O. system also gives the user the opportunity to store the results on disc.

8.2.6 The Significance and Applications of the RCS System

The system was originally designed as a communication tool, to describe conservation priorities to managers, developers and planners in a consistent way, so that ecological factors can be taken into account in plans for river exploitation and development. The results are presented in a conceptually simple fashion, thus allowing the non specialist to appreciate the relative conservation status of different rivers.

For the ecologist/conservationist, the primary function of the system is the classification and mapping of rivers over an area. Within this function the system can act as a guide for a conservation agency, classifying rivers of different conservation status, and also clearly identifying areas where more information is needed.

A second important function of the system is its use as a model to evaluate the effects of planned changes. In this case the system uses information about the river in its present state, and then compares this with runs, using data or predictions on river conditions following the planned changes. This should provide a powerful tool for environmental impact assessment.

The construction, evaluation and testing of the system provided an extremely valuable function in itself. This process forced the contributors to examine their own assessment methods carefully. Many conservationists, for instance, make 'intuitive' judgements about the importance of particular sites. In fact, this 'intuition' comprises a complex net of interacting variables, which are evaluated in terms of an individual's experience and the available information about the site. To be forced to analyze these variables and their interrelationships often led to considerable insight, and also often helped to pinpoint areas of disagreement, so that, while arguments were not eliminated, they were at least channeled into specific resolvable problems.

8.2.7   Some shortcomings of the RCS System

The RCS system has now been developed to its limits within the present specifications. The on board explanatory facilities within the program are inadequate, and a comprehensive user's manual has been produced to overcome this problem.

A criticism applicable to many types of expert systems is the difficulty a user has in relying on an outcome without a thorough understanding of the program, and the pathways used to reach the outcome. In applying the RCS, it is important for the user to understand the calculation methods, the implications of different weightings, and the application of the various rules. The user manual provides detailed explanations of these and other processes, but requires some study for familiarization. There appears to be no way around the requirement for the user to do considerable work, but our defence would be to point out that a thorough realistic assessment of a river is a painstaking operation, the system is not trivial, and any attempts at an 'easy' method will result in a trivial answer.

8.2.8   Conclusions

In South Africa, the development of the RCS system has led to the identification of those aspects which are generally felt to be most important in conserving rivers, and has provided a fair consensus as to the relative importance of different attributes of rivers. The ability to present this consensus view to ecological laymen charged with management responsibilities in rivers gives them a more realistic opportunity to take conservation priorities into account at the planning stage. Managers, planners and developers are too often seen by conservationists as being insensitive to environmental issues, when in fact a major part of the problem is the inability of the conservationists to present a concise summary of their complex points of view. It is unreasonable to expect laymen to unravel the multivariate probabilities and diffuse intuitions of the conservation ethic. The RCS encapsulates the more important components of river conservation status.

As with the other ecological systems discussed here this system has acted as a focus for a number of interested experts. It serves not only as a practical, working system but also as a unified source of knowledge and perhaps even more importantly it has served to identify points of conflict between experts and thus to identify areas where further research is required.

8.3   FISHFARMER

8.3.1   Introduction

The lack of aquaculture expertise has been defined as one of the major constraints on the development of aquaculture in southern Africa [140]. It was decided to develop an expert system to assist potential aquaculturists in assessing the aquaculture potential of various fish species in relation to particular sites and culture methods.

Computers have played an increasingly important role in aquaculture in recent years, but their use has been limited to data storage (to aid in pond management) and the monitoring of oxygen levels and water flow. As far as is known, FISHFARMER represents the first use of expert system techniques as a means of assessing aquaculture potential. Great emphasis has been placed on the 'user friendliness' of the system.

8.3.2 Background

Fish culture has been practised for over 2000 years, but it is only recently that intensive aquaculture has developed into a commercial activity which is dependent upon advanced technology and scientific research. World output from aquaculture has increased by 40% between 1975 and 1984 [140].

Walmsley and Bruton [140] propose a number of steps that should be taken if the industry is to develop. These include the establishment of a lead agency to initiate marketing, coordinate research and to promote the transfer of technology.

As a means to this end, it was decided to develop an expert system to evaluate the aquaculture potential of a given organism, site or culture method. Such an expert system would provide the ability to assess the aquaculture potential of a particular site independently of human aquaculture experts. In addition, it was hoped that the development of the system would have two side effects. In the first instance, it would bring together information from a wide number of different sources, and secondly it would clearly identify 'holes' in the available knowledge.

8.3.3 The Requirements of the System

The requirements of the system were the following:

1. Given available data on the biological, physical, financial and infrastructural parameters pertaining to a potential site, the system should be able to:

   - Evaluate the site with regard to its suitability for fish culture.
   - If the site is suitable for fish culture, evaluate the species included in the knowledge base in relation to the environmental characteristics of the site.
   - Provide a confidence value with each recommendation.

2. The system should be 'user friendly' in that it must:

   - Explain (on demand) why a particular question is being asked.
   - Explain (on demand) the rationale of reasoning at any given point in the evaluation.
   - Explain (on demand) any technical terms and procedures associated with any of the questions.

- Allow manipulation of the system by the user to examine its assumptions and change parameters.

- Require a minimum of computer expertise for its use and comprehension.

It is envisaged that the system will be used by Nature Conservation officers, fish farming consultants, researchers and of course, anyone interested in assessing the aquaculture potential of a site.

8.3.4   Methodology

Species included in the Aquaculture Expert System

At present the expert system is capable of assessing the aquaculture potential of 14 species. These species were selected for inclusion in the system because they are either already cultured in South Africa, have been successfully cultured in other countries, are local species which are high priority candidates for aquaculture, or are local species which have good potential as cultured species. Most attention has been paid to those indigenous species which are most likely to be cultured. It was thus decided that most of the effort should be focused on those species which are regarded as having high aquaculture potential in South Africa.

Criteria for Assessment

The criteria used in the aquaculture expert system are summarised in Figure 8.1 below. These criteria were selected after a literature review and consultation with a number of local aquaculture experts.

Knowledge Acquisition

While information gleaned from the literature provided a useful foundation for the knowledge base, experts working in the field often provided a better understanding of the subject. Scientists at the JLB Smith Institute of Ichthyology and Department of Ichthyology and Fisheries Science provided much of the technical input. Zimbabwean farmers were also interviewed because of their practical experience in culturing a wide variety of species.

At regular intervals the expert system was demonstrated to experts both privately and at conferences and workshops. Extensive modifications to the knowledge base resulted from their comments and criticisms.

The knowledge obtained from the sources described was used both to develop the structure of the knowledge base, and to provide a 'help system', which enables the user to obtain clarification on why criteria used by the expert system are pertinent to the problem. The help system also supplies the user with a description of the principles and practice of fish culture so that the layman does not need to use the system in a 'knowledge vacuum'.

WATER QUALITY:

temperature	water depth
pH	hydrocarbons
alkalinity	chlorine
salinity	ammonia
turbidity	phosphorous
hardness	nitrogen
oxygen	nitrate
carbon dioxide	

SITE:

soil type	presence of predators
soil pH	ability to develop site
slope	access to water
water flow	

PRODUCTION STRATEGY:

artificial versus natural propagation
source of eggs/fry/fingerlings
extensive versus intensive production
supplementary versus processed feed
production units
fertilization and liming of ponds

FINANCE:

sufficient capital to realise
production strategy

Figure 8.1: Criteria used by FISHFARMER to assess aquaculture potential.

8.3.5 How the System works

FISHFARMER attempts to determine the optimum match between a particular site, water source, market, species, culture method and financial resources. The system uses information provided by the user in conjunction with that from its own knowledge base in order to make the correct match. The system queries the user in detail about the proposed site in order to determine whether the site, culture and species complement each other.

Good use has been made of the relative importance measure. Thus water temperature, being a particularly crucial environmental parameter, influences the system's decision far more than would the state of the site's access road for example, and so is given a higher rating. In addition to answering questions the user may ask for further background information about the questions being asked.

8.3.6   Overview and Evaluation

FISHFARMER is a user friendly system with an introduction explaining its workings and an extensive help system to aid the user who is unsure of the meaning of a question or technical term. It is capable of evaluating the aquaculture potential of a given site provided that it is given enough information.

The P.R.O. expert system shell (Chapter 5) is a simple shell and its workings can be easily and precisely explained. FISHFARMER does not therefore suffer from the 'black box' image that is commonly associated with more complex systems.

The development of the knowledge base, however, required an unsatisfactory reliance on information and data from beyond the southern Africa subcontinent. The extrapolation of techniques and results from other parts of the world to southern Africa is not ideal but was necessitated by the paucity of local information. The scarcity of such data is a reflection of the undeveloped state of aquaculture at present.

Given the broad nature of the subject, it was necessary to obtain information from more than one source. This information was often conflicting and thus difficult to model. This means that logical errors and human bias cannot be assumed to be absent from the knowledge base.

FISHFARMER is only capable of evaluating a 'generalised' site. To attempt to model all the different permutations of soil type, slope, water supply, site accessibility etc. would make unacceptable demands on the system. There is thus a limit to the amount of information which FISHFARMER is able to use. A human expert standing on the site would be able to detect certain features of the physical parameters, which FISHFARMER cannot do. Despite their flexibility (in contrast to other computer programs), even expert systems deal in absolutes to a certain extent and there are few absolutes in aquaculture. If one is prepared to spend enough money one can circumvent most of the 'rules of thumb' on which FISHFARMER is based.

8.3.7   Recommendations for further Aquaculture Research

One of the benefits of expert system design is that the articulation of available expertise often identifies areas in which our knowledge is sparse. This has certainly been true of the development of FISHFARMER. The major areas which require future work include:

- research emphasis on local species which are believed to have aquacultural potential. The knowledge base relies too heavily on overseas information on alien species;

- more attention to cage culture;

- research into the selection and breeding of good quality broodstock;

- the development of high quality, least cost feed;

- increased understanding of the problems of pond culture.

Finally, this project has highlighted that research should address problems which are restricting the potential of the industry. While this appears to be self evident, it would seem that researchers and funding agencies are often tempted to concentrate on the most interesting or elegant research problems which do not necessarily yield the information that a developing industry requires.

8.3.8 Concluding Remarks

The development of the FISHFARMER expert system does not lend itself to a single researcher working in isolation; the design and contents of the knowledge base constantly need to be challenged and discussed. This project has greatly benefited from the inputs of a wide variety of individuals: aquaculture researchers, computer scientists and commercial fish farmers.

The FISHFARMER project has proved to be a most useful exercise from a number of different points of view. It has consolidated information and knowledge from a wide range of sources and people. Many areas which require further in depth research have been identified and it has provided the user with a useful tool to assist in solving problems and developing sites.

8.4 PISCES - An Expert System to Assess the Impact of the Introduction of Alien Fish into South Africa

8.4.1 Introduction

PISCES is an expert system which is designed to assist legislators, conservationists and resource managers in determining the advisability of introducing alien (exotic) fish species into local waters. The expert system shell used is version 2.0 of the P.R.O. system [106]. Because of its flexibility and the fact that the source code is readily available and can be tailored to suit the needs of this particular application, the P.R.O. system was chosen in preference to other available shells which were investigated (Micro Expert, Exsys, Apes and Synapse). The fact that the knowledge base for P.R.O. is written in Prolog [39] provides increased flexibility for the knowledge engineer to include his own Prolog routines.

P.R.O. version 2.0 incorporates additional features required for this particular application. These include:

- the facility to request textual responses and direct numerical answers instead of being limited to character answers or numerical ranges;

- the ability to read in a file of data at the start of a session, refer to it where necessary using special "look up" commands in the knowledge base, and update it with information gathered during the consultation;

- a more efficient and effective screen layout;

- the use of menu driven questions during the consultation.

8.4.2 Reasons for Building the System

In a country which is attempting to move from third world to first world status there is tremendous development pressure on the natural environment. Part of this pressure is exerted by the introduction of exotic species. Southern Africa has already experienced the negative effects which such introductions sometimes precipitate. It is important therefore not to allow the importation of foreign species to become totally out of control. At the same time it is recognised that a compromise is necessary between the needs for the conservation of our natural environment and the needs for the development of the region. It is therefore important that the introduction of exotic species be strictly controlled within well defined lines.

The PISCES system is an attempt to develop a method which will arbitrate fairly between the conflicting needs of the two causes. The development of this computer system should enable the controlling authorities to act in the most informed manner to ensure that those species which are introduced are not likely to cause a deterioration in the ecosystems into which they are placed. Aside from providing the solid method for screening possible introductions this project will also highlight areas where more information is required.

8.4.3 Knowledge Acquisition

An outline already exists, of how exotics should be evaluated before they are either allowed or not allowed to be introduced. However this methodology is more a guideline to be followed by an expert and assumes that data from the whole region is available to him as well as substantial knowledge of his own. The emphasis of this project was therefore on the collation of this data and the precise articulation of the experts knowledge in order that an expert system, which would quickly and fairly perform this important task, could be built. It was assumed at the outset that this data would be readily available in the literature and amongst the experts who were interested in the project and that the rules would represent the view of as many experts as possible. Thus it was anticipated that the system would represent a consensus of expert opinion as well as contain a comprehensive database on the various regions and river systems in the subcontinent.

Essentially the system needs to be able to answer three questions satisfactorily before the proposed species is allowed to be introduced. These are:

- Will the species survive in the area for which it is intended?

- Will the species, if introduced, proliferate and invade the area?

- If it is invasive will this have any deleterious effects on the area?

The system therefore needs to know about all the different areas within the subcontinent and be able to match this information with the data on the proposed species.

The initial phase of the project involved setting out the questions which the system would have to ask and detailing the sort of information it would require to be able to interpret the answers intelligently. At this stage a working system was built which was demonstrated to a number of delegates who attended the Alternative Life History Conference in Grahamstown in 1987.

This prototype system showed that an acceptable knowledge base structure had been established and the icthyologists in the project were left to concentrate on collating the detailed data required and the articulation of further rules. It was anticipated that the information required for this system would have been generated by researchers working in a number of related research institutes, namely Ichthyology, Fresh Water Studies and Hydrology. It was soon found that this was in fact not the case and that the project itself would need to generate the information required. As with the other ecological systems developed, this project has benefited the scientific community by identifying and investigating areas where there is a paucity of information.

8.4.4 How the System Works

At the start of a consultation the user is asked for the name of the species, the reason for introduction and the proposed area for introduction. At the end of the session the results are stored together with the name, area and reason. If a user subsequently wishes to reexamine an old case the system will use this stored information.

Before entering the main part of the system the user must provide satisfactory responses to three non negotiable criteria, namely:

- the validity of the reason for introducing the species,

- the possible introduction of harmful diseases or parasites, and

- whether or not the species is endangered in its natural environment.

If any of these questions is not answered satisfactorily, the consultation terminates immediately, and the user is told that it is not advisable to introduce the species.

Once this initial hurdle is passed the system then sets about deciding whether or not there are any areas that are likely to be adversely affected by the introduction of the species. The first step is to eliminate immediately any areas where the species will definitely have no chance of survival and thus to identify the areas of concern. In determining these areas, the degree to which the different regions are interconnected and the reason for proposed introduction are taken into account. If the reason for introduction is the aquarium trade, where the spread of the species is unlikely to be tightly controlled, all the areas in the country are considered as it is possible that the species may escape anywhere. If the fish is to be introduced for any other reason (e.g. biological control or fish farming), the areas which are considered are the proposed area of introduction and the surrounding areas. These areas of concern are an indication of the areas where the species may have a chance of survival.

A species cannot have adverse effects if it does not thrive in the environment. Therefore, in order to further eliminate areas before considering any effects the species may have, the system needs to determine for each area of concern whether the species will become invasive. This decision is made by the comparison of the life history style of the proposed species with the system's assessment of the ecology of the area.

For each of the areas of invasion, the effects that the species will have on the environment needs to be determined. If it is predicted that there is even a single area that may be adversely affected by the species, the final conclusion of the system is that it is not advisable to introduce the species. Otherwise, PISCES will recommend that the species be allowed to be introduced. Associated with any recommendations is a certainty value. This certainty value is calculated using the weighted confidence factors which are given by the user in response to questions asked by the system. A low certainty value is an indication that more research needs to be done on the species and its possible effects before it can be seriously considered for introduction. At the end of each consultation, the user may change any of his answers, and see what effect these changes have on the final result.

8.4.5   Future Developments

As has already been stated there is plenty of data which has yet to be included in the system. As the project develops further, issues which are currently resolved by asking the users direct questions will be expanded into rules to allow the system to make more accurate recommendations based on a more detailed understanding of both the proposed species and the proposed location for introduction. The hierarchical structure of the knowledge base allows this style of development — indeed it positively encourages it!

It is also anticipated that in time a connection will be made between this system and the FISHFARMER system to provide a comprehensive system for farmers interested in culturing exotic species.

'Blacklists' and 'greylists' of species which will be likely candidates for the PISCES system have been drawn up. These lists are comprised of exotic species which are normally in demand in the aquaculture and the aquarium businesses. The lists along with questionnaires have been sent to a number of experts both within the country and in the USA, Australia and New Zealand for comment. It is expected that much relevant information will be generated from these two exercises. It is further anticipated that the use of the PISCES system will eventually provide 'black', 'grey' and 'white' lists of evaluated species for publication.

8.4.6 Conclusion

The PISCES system is the most recent ecological system to be implemented in the P.R.O. expert system shell and consequently is not as advanced as the RCS or the FISHFARMER projects. It has also been found, contrary to expectations, that much of the data which the system requires to become really useful is not readily available. What has been developed thus far is the basic skeleton of the system, further work will add body and resilience by adding to and refining the rules and questions currently in the knowledge base.

8.5 Conclusion

Several common themes can be found in all three of these expert systems:

- They show that the development of the knowledge base is in itself a useful exercise in that it identifies clearly areas where there is insufficient knowledge or areas where experts may disagree. During the development of the RCS system it was found that where experts thought they had some major disagreement it turned out that they perhaps only rated one characteristic more highly than another. Thus the debate was moved from a general argument on the conservation status of different rivers to a discussion on the relative importance of particular attributes.

- Because a number of different sources have had to be used and owing to the gaps in the available knowledge and the conflict between different sources, the knowledge bases have developed into a single reference for that particular subject. The main experts involved have become more the curators of an evolving reference source rather than the developers of a one off system.

- That it is possible to build ecological expert systems which can perform worthwhile tasks.

These projects have succeeded because the ecologists involved have been interested in developing expert systems as part of their own research. It has been important therefore for them to be able to manipulate the knowledge base directly. The conceptual simplicity and flexibility of the P.R.O. expert system shell has enabled them to concentrate on deciding what to include, rather than on how to include it.

We would encourage other ecologists to develop their own systems. It has been our experience, from these three projects, that the exercise yields an interesting, usable system and generates a tremendous amount of extremely productive interaction between interested parties. It has also led to the identification of many related research projects.

Acknowledgements

We are greatly indebted to Professor Tony Starfield of the University of Witwatersrand, who first stimulated the development of ecological expert systems at Rhodes. The RCS project was financially supported by the Nature Conservation Research Division of the FRD at the South African CSIR. The FISHFARMER and PISCES project were financially supported by the National Foundation for Aquaculture Research of the FRD at the South African CSIR. Thanks also to Karen Wrench for reading early drafts of this chapter.

Part IV
Marketing and Data Processing

In 1982, the United Kingdom government initiated a five year research programme into information technology called the Alvey programme. Part of the Alvey programme involved the formation of *community clubs* to explore the applicability of expert system techniques. This part of the book includes a description of two projects from two of the community clubs. It also includes a description of a system which uses a method of learning from examples.

Chapter 9 begins with an outline of community clubs, and then describes the use of Inference Art to develop an expert system for localising faults within a data communications network. It also compares the implementation with a second implementation carried out using a PC-based shell.

Chapter 10 describes an expert system, developed in Prolog, which helps market specialists to build quantitative models of their markets. The application illustrates the kind of features and flexibility for which a programming language is more suitable than a PC-based shell.

Chapter 11 describes the experience of using the ID3 algorithm to develop an expert system capable of assessing the competence of a UK company marketing to Japan. It illustrates the kind of problems one might encounter when using ID3. It also describes the results of comparing the system's assessment with an expert's assessment.

Chapter 9

Experience of Constructing a Fault Localisation Expert System Using an AI Toolkit

Robert Inder

9.1 Introduction

One of the most popular initiatives within the UK government's Alvey programme was the formation of *Community Clubs.* These were collaborative ventures exploring the applicability of AI techniques to general application areas, such as the water industry, planning and insurance. Most were formed around a nucleus of one or two contractors, and attracted between ten and twenty commercial organisations, each contributing approximately £10000, with a comparable amount provided by Alvey. In addition, most clubs allowed academics to become members by contributing not money, but effort or expertise.

Once a club was established, its funds were used to sponsor the contractors to carry out a few man-years of work, guided by a steering committee of club members. At the core of most clubs' activities was the production of demonstration

This article first appeared in the Proceedings of the 1st International Conference on Industrial and Engineering Applications of Artificial Intelligence and Expert Systems, (Tullahoma, Tennessee, 1988) published by ACM Press.

software, the design and code of which were subsequently made available to members. However, quite apart from receiving actual software, club members hoped to gain from the experience of constructing it. To this end, clubs carried out varying amounts of awareness activity, intended to offer members an insight into the issues and decisions involved in implementing the club's own software and in applying AI to the club's area of interest.

The work reported in this chapter was carried out as one part of the programme of activities of the Alvey Community Club for **D**ata **P**rocessing **E**xpert **S**ystems (DAPES). Initially, the Club's contractors were the National Computing Centre (NCC) and Expertech Ltd. However, the club subsequently developed an interest in the specialist AI toolkits, such as Intellicorp's **K**nowledge **E**ngineering **E**nvironment (KEE) and **A**utomated **R**easoning **T**ool (ART) from Inference Corporation of Los Angeles. They decided to incorporate at least some experience of these tools into the later stages of the club's activities, and arranged for NCC to subcontract the Artificial Intelligence Applications Institute (AIAI) at the University of Edinburgh who, through the **K**nowledge **R**epresentations **S**ystems **T**rials **L**aboratory (KRSTL), were in a position to offer access to these tools and expertise in their use.

The club identified the operation of wide-area data communications networks as an area of interest to most of its members, and focused on two specific tasks within it. One of the two, supporting the operation of a telephone "help desk", was tackled by Expertech. They used their own shell (Xi+), and worked by incremental development, possibly the most commonly advocated approach to constructing Expert Systems (see Hayes-Roth et. al. [66]). However, club members came predominantly from Data Processing departments, and were attracted by the benefits in maintainability and manageability said to result from separating the knowledge elicitation (KE) from the system implementation. They decided, therefore, that the second specific task, that of localising a fault within a data communications network, should be tackled by completing an explicit KE and documentation stage before implementation started. This would produce an *Intermediate Representation* (IR), an implementation-independent representation of all the expert's knowledge required for a particular task.

This approach was able to be combined with the desire to investigate the AI toolkits by carrying out the actual implementation stage twice, once using a PC-based shell and once using ART. Constraining two such different programming tools to do precisely the same task seemed unlikely to yield the most informative comparison of their capabilities. Instead, it was decided that each implementation team should make use of the information specified by the IR to tackle the problem in whatever way seemed most effective given the capabilities of the tools available to them.

The next section describes the KE stage and the IR. This is followed by a very brief description of operation of the system in section 9.3, while section 9.4 discusses the interaction between the facilities in ART and the design of the system. Finally, Section 9.5 offers some observations on the differences between the two implementations of the diagnosis system.

NAME	OBJECTS	ORGANISATION
Strategic	Plans, Repairs Meta-Rules	Process
Task	Goals, Tasks,	Task
Inference	Meta-classes Knowledge Sources	Inference
Domain	Concepts, Relations Structures	Axiomatic

Table 9.1: Levels of Abstraction in KADS

9.2 The Knowledge Elicitation Stage

At the start of the KE phase, a brief literature search for any documented methodologies for using intermediate representations was carried out, with disappointingly few results. Grover [62] offered the greatest number of pragmatically useful suggestions per page, while the work of Keravnou and Johnson [76], who illustrated their ideas on systemic grammar networks with an application to localising faults in electronic equipment, also seemed relevant. On balance, however, NCC felt that the Knowledge Acquisition Documentation and Structuring (KADS) system, developed by Esprit project 1098 (see Breuker et. al. [21]), had most to offer, and decided to adopt this approach.

The KADS approach is based around analysing the task into four levels of abstraction, illustrated in Table 9.1.

The *Domain* level records all the static information about the task to be tackled: in this case, the structure of the network, the types of data communication equipment that are used and their behaviour and the kinds of symptoms that are observed. At the *Inference* level the various domain entities are categorised into *meta-classes*, and the way these can be used to make various **kinds** of inferences when tackling problems is specified. The *Task* level is concerned with specifying the way inferences are organised. Finally, the *Strategic* level describes the way one can choose which goals and sub-tasks are needed to meet the overall objective. Such an analysis is called a *conceptual model*.

The information in this hierarchy becomes progressively less application specific as one moves to higher levels of abstraction. One of the key features claimed for the KADS approach is the possibility of abstracting away all reference to the domain from the upper three layers, creating what is termed an *interpretation model*. This can then be used as a starting point to guide the analysis of similar tasks in other domains.

The DAPES fault localisation system was to work with the data communications network operated by International Paint PLC. (IP), with the relevant expertise being supplied by their network controller. The KE was carried out primarily by Mike Newman of NCC, who visited the central site approximately two days per week over three months, during which time he established a good working relationship with IP's staff. He used primarily a mixture of focused and unstructured interviews, although he also used some card sorting techniques (see Kidd [77]), mainly for eliciting the equipment classifications. He decided against tape recording interviews because he felt that it would involve more effort in transcription and analysis than the project had available.

The result of this effort was a collection of eight documents, supplemented by working papers and extracts from IP's data processing manuals. The core of these was a specification of the diagnostic strategy of the expert, together with a description of the network configuration and a detailed hierarchical specification of the capabilities of each model of equipment it contained, including a decomposition into functional sub-units. There were also descriptions of the test procedures normally employed by IP staff when localising faults, and a specification of the backup network configurations used while faults are being rectified. Finally, there was a glossary and some sample cases, as suggested by Grover [62]. Together these documents contained far more information than was expected to be used by either system, but this was deliberate, as it gave the implementors some freedom to ensure interesting demonstration systems.

The club's desire to use an IR was based around its role in specifying the content of the knowledge base before implementation began. However, at an early stage in the KE process, Newman felt it worth commenting that he found the IR a great aid to further elicitation. Furthermore, the club gained from its tool independence. Not only did this make the two parallel implementations possible, it also allowed NCC to defer selecting which tool to use for the PC-based implementation until the KE was almost complete, and they could form a clear idea of what was required. On the other hand, Newman felt that by the middle of the KE process the expert's enthusiasm was flagging. One of the advantages claimed for the early construction of a prototype is its ability to catch the expert's imagination. One could argue that a prototype would have made life easier at this stage, and that the decision to try deferring all implementation for as long as possible was not without cost. Note that using a prototype in such a role brings no commitment to incrementally enhancing it into the final system; it could well be discarded once its lessons were learnt.

While Newman liked the general KADS approach, he comments ([96, p15]) that KADS:

> "attempts to analyse problem-solving knowledge in a domain-independent way, in order to bring out the **structure** of the knowledge as an aid to knowledge elicitation.
>
> This leads to a very esoteric descriptive style which can prove difficult to relate simply to what actually happens at the domain level."

Rather than grapple with the more obscure aspects of the KADS methodology, Newman decided that within the limited resources of the project he could best apply the spirit of their approach by ignoring the distinction between the *task* and *strategic* levels. Having done so, he found that the KADS interpretation model for "Diagnosis By Localisation" was a very useful basis to work from. He concluded that a simplification of that approach provided a good description of the expert's fault location strategy.

9.3   System Overview

9.3.1   What is ART?

In Chapter 4, we gave an extensive review of Inference ART. In this section we review its main features again.

Inference ART is one of the leading specialised tools for developing AI systems. It offers programmers a language that integrates mechanisms for a wide range of approaches to knowledge based programming. At its heart is a rule-based system supporting both forward and backward chaining. Rule firings are triggered by a very flexible and efficient pattern matcher and allow both inferencing and the invocation of arbitrary (Lisp) procedures. In addition, ART has facilities for describing objects, which ART terms *schemata*, in terms of attributes, values and relationships being inherited by members of classes. It also allows behaviours to be associated with objects (i.e. object-oriented programming) or with particular attributes of objects (i.e. access-oriented programming). Finally, ART has very sophisticated facilities for simultaneously and efficiently reasoning about many alternative, and typically contradictory, states of the world, although these facilities are not used in the system being described.

As well as providing these mechanisms for manipulating information, ART make it very easy to construct system interfaces using a mouse in conjunction with both menus and high-resolution graphics. All these facilities are integrated within a single programming system, available within a powerful mouse-based development environment that offers a comprehensive collection of sophisticated tools for browsing and monitoring program execution.

9.3.2   System Objectives

The objective of the ART implementation team was to construct a system which would highlight the benefits of constructing a system using a workstation and toolkit in preference to a PC-based shell. It seemed that this could best be achieved by producing a system which was obviously more easily generalised beyond the specific task (i.e. network) in hand. This translated into specific desires to work from the most concise specification of the network and to reason as much as possible from first principles, both about the process of diagnosis and about the operation of the network. In particular, the system was to operate from a detailed simulation, or model, of the operation of the network.

Users of such a system will always have access to information that it cannot process: verbal reports, general knowledge or even just "hunches". In addition, they may well be skilled at fault finding, although possibly lacking knowledge of the precise configuration of the network or the capabilities of specific devices. For these reasons, the toolkit implementation tried to go beyond suggesting how to localise the fault, and to provide in addition the most flexible assistance possible to users wishing to employ their own knowledge and diagnostic skill. This resulted in two main facilities. Firstly, the user interface will allow access to the system's knowledge about the structure and operation of the devices in the network, together with the results and implications of all the tests that have already been carried out. Secondly, the control structure used is flexible enough to allow users to volunteer information of any form that the system can deal with and have it taken into account in subsequent recommendations. In particular, the user can direct the course of the localisation process by electing to do tests other than those recommended by the system.

Finally, concern about the computational efficiency of the AI toolkits motivated the Institute to seek to extract at least some information on how ART would perform on a large problem.

9.3.3   What the system does

The system is intended to help computer operations staff to diagnose faults within a data communications network, typically in the absence of the organisation's networking experts. It does so by indicating, at each stage of the fault localisation process, which test appears to offer the best tradeoff between the effort of carrying it out and the information it will yield. The system also accepts and interprets test results and updates its recommendations in the light of this information.

The operation of the system is based around its representation of the network which indicates the makes and models of the various pieces of equipment and their interconnections. It begins operating on the basis of an initial complaint about a single device (a terminal or printer) which is reported to be out of contact with the mainframe. By tracing the path of a signal from this device to the computer, the system determines what other communications devices carry it. These become the initial suspect set: i.e. the fault is in one of these devices. The system also constructs and displays a diagram showing all the devices and interconnections involved in the operation of the device that has been reported non-operational (see Figure 9.3.3).

On the basis of the set of suspect devices, the system proceeds to generate the set of all the tests that it believes could be carried out. It then uses its model of the operation of the network to determine which devices would be involved in which test, and builds a menu of those that appear interesting — i.e. that involve a suspect device. For each of the interesting tests, the system works out their usefulness (see below) and from this and the cost of doing the tests it constructs a second menu of the tests that seem most attractive. Diagnosis proceeds by the user selecting a test from either of these menus, and the system asking for the result of carrying it out. The system analyses this information to extract evidence about the working status of devices and re-considers its idea of which ones could

157

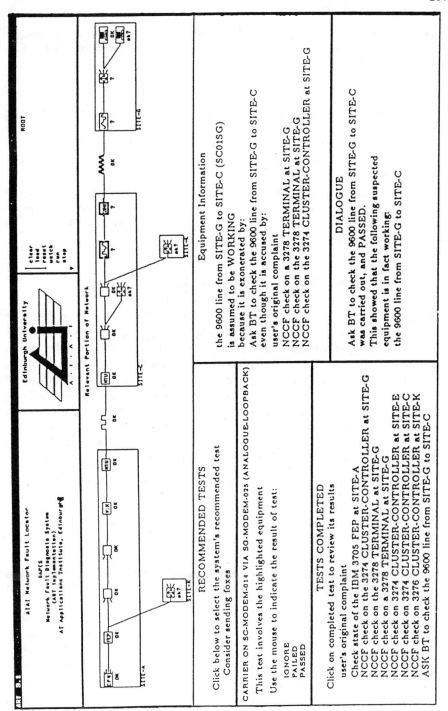

Figure 9.1: The network fault locator

be responsible for the difficulty. It then updates the menu of interesting tests, revises its test recommendation, and waits for the user to select another test.

9.3.4 The Code

The system contains 110 rules, of which 33 are a menu manipulation package, and a further 7 are used only for checking network specifications, leaving 70 that actually localise faults. There are approximately 260 schemata defined of which 120 describe specific devices and a further 80 specify the hierarchy of models. There are also 8 active values.

Note that the program was the first project undertaken by the development team using release 3 of ART, in which the object- and access- oriented facilities were introduced. Their relative unfamiliarity undoubtedly contributed to their relative usage within the system.

9.4 How the System Operates

The operation of the system is based on the simulation of the behaviour of the network, a process which requires a great deal of computation. However, the desire to explore ART's performance when manipulating high volumes of data suggested adopting a deliberately simplistic approach to the storage of the large information structures: the entire network description and all information about every device are simply stored within ART's schema system with minimal thought for efficiency (see Section 9.4.1). This approach obviously caused some concern that the performance of the resulting system would not be acceptable. This possibility was explored by the construction of a prototype, which was subsequently significantly re-structured to produce the system described below.

9.4.1 Data Structures

The information structures at the heart of the system are its model of the network and its representation of the hierarchy of device types. They are both represented using ART's schema mechanisms; though this was less a matter of making a design decision and more a matter of adopting the blatantly obvious approach. The schema system is designed precisely for describing the properties and inter-relations between devices and the sharing of information by members of classes.

Within the DAPES system, the top-level node in the hierarchy is equipment, which is broken down into components, which have a specific location at a single site, and lines, which don't. These are subdivided into classes of components (modems, processors etc.) and lines (digital, analogue). Class of equipment is an important level of classification for describing devices (hence it is where devices are associated with graphical icons for displaying network diagrams) and specifying tests and their applicability. The classes are in turn subdivided into particular models such as an IBM 3070 processor. This is the level in the hierarchy where the most detailed information is stored, such as what modes of operation a given device supports (e.g. loopback, self-test) and what ports it has and how they are classified. In addition, a complete specification would include further information on what indicators the device has (and what form they take), who manufactures it, how to operate it (i.e. to get it into any particular mode), etc.

This description suggests that each type of information is specified at a particular level of the hierarchy. While there is a level at which most information of each particular type is supplied, the system does in fact take advantage of the possibility of specifying inheritable *default* values which are over-ridden lower down the network where more specific values are available.

The network itself is also described using schemata, with each individual piece of equipment being represented by a schema. In this case, however, the implementation has not followed the most obvious route to its conclusion. If it had, each device would have been declared to be an instance-of a particular model — for example:

```
(instance-of terminal-02 IBM-3276)
```

and thus would have automatically inherited all the attributes applicable to such devices. This would be semantically sound, but the way ART handles inheritance would cause it to explicitly represent everything known about a model for each individual instance of that model. Since there are many instances of certain models, only very few of which will ever be involved in localising any one fault, this appears to waste a considerable amount of storage. Instead, devices are associated with their models by a user-defined (non-inheriting) relation model-is, which identifies the model of each device without replicating information.

Doing this means that the left hand side of any rule that uses model-related information has to be somewhat more complex. Instead of just referring to the property of the device thus:

```
(schema device-01 (possible-mode self-test))
```

it has to identify the model of the device, and then refer explicitly to the property of the model, thus:

```
(schema device-01
       (model-is ?model))
(schema ?model
       (possible-mode self-test))
```

This approach requires additional work from the pattern matcher. Since much of the information about a device (model) is only accessed occasionally (e.g. when the user explicitly asks about it), this is usually acceptable. In contrast, class membership information — the fact that a particular terminal is a terminal — is used a great deal. As a result, another user-defined relation was established, with its properties specified to cause ART to automatically recognise and indicate a device's membership of all appropriate classes.

These features mean that the description of a typical device resembles that of a IBM 3705 FEP (Front End Processor):

```
(defschema fe-fep-3705 "FEP handling CPU-B at Site-A"
    (model-is fep-3705)
    (current-mode normal)
    (site site-a))
```

Notice that the description of the device is very specific and very short, and as a result, easy to furnish when devices are added to the network or replaced. Most attribute/value pairs are self-explanatory, though some deserve comment. The device name (in the example, fe-fep-3705) is chosen for the convenience of the system builder; that is, the operation of the system would be the same if it were renamed G0034. As mentioned above, the model-is relation serves to tie a component to the system's information about such devices without duplicating it all. The current-mode of the device is used (with the system-supplied working-status) to control the propagation of a signal through the device (see below). It is explicitly specified to allow for those devices like switches where the correct functioning of the network depends on them being configured into one of a number of equally "normal" (i.e. likely) modes of operation.

In addition to describing the actual devices within the network, it is of course necessary to specify how they are inter-connected. This is done by providing a fact for each connection within the network specifying which port on which device is connected to which port on which other device. For example:

```
(linked (fe-fep-3705 processor-port-1)
        (fe-site-a-processor port-2))
(linked (fe-mux-01 port-0b)
        (fe-fep-3705 36))
(linked (fe-mux-01 port-0e)
        (fe-fep-3705 26))
```

These facts are not part of the schemata for the devices involved. Nor can they be ART relations between the devices, which would have allowed ART to automatically handle the symmetry of relations. The facts represent connections not simply between devices, but between specific **parts** of devices (i.e. ports), and this is more information than can be captured in a single ART relation. Relations could be used if ports were treated as independent entities. However, the system is not expected to do enough reasoning about ports to justify creating a schema for each port.

Note that the description of the links is minimal and objective. In particular, there is no indication which way it should be traversed to find any particular device type or point in the network. Such information greatly aids fault finding, but at the expense of generality, since it cannot be provided for many network configurations. The ART implementation was designed to work without requiring this information, albeit at the cost of considerable effort in both programming and run-time computation.

9.4.2 Network Modelling

Most of the system's reasoning concerns simulating the propagation of signals within the network, a process which involves modelling the behaviour of each device. This is done by rules which are sensitive to a device's class, mode of operation (e.g. normal vs. looped back) and assumed status (i.e. working or faulty). The rules could be made sensitive to the precise model of the equipment, rather than just its class, if this was found desirable. However, there could be some difficulty in mixing levels of specificity within any class of objects, since the rules for modelling the class would still apply to devices which were being simulated by model-specific rules — i.e. such devices would tend to be simulated twice.

If this were considered a serious problem, it would be possible to model the behaviour of devices using active values, which would naturally support the desired superceding of inherited behaviours. However, there is no obvious way in which an active value can make use of ART's logical dependency mechanism. This would not matter as long as all possible failures and system configurations were considered from the outset (which in fact they currently are). However, one may well want to handle possibilities like network re-configurations or unlikely faults, which only appear appropriate once localisation is under way. In this case the logical dependency mechanism would make a useful contribution to determining the effects of the newly hypothesised failure.

On balance, the ability to use logical dependencies seemed likely to outweigh the option to describe behaviour at more than one level of specificity, and device behaviour was implemented using rules. Performance implications of the decision were not considered.

Another significant design decision concerned the representation of signals. In the system as implemented, each signal being received or generated by a device is represented by a single data structure with fields for representing various aspects of the signal at that point. All signals have a type, which is either digital or carried[1] and a message or content. In addition, digital signals can have format (e.g. baud rate and protocol), addressing information (e.g. from a multiplexer), and while carried signals have carrier properties (source, frequency etc.) and information about the digital signal being carried. A number of constructor and accessor functions were written in Lisp, thereby allowing these information structures to be used without commitment to their format.

A drawback of this representation is that the continuity of the signal throughout the network is not apparent. An obvious alternative would be to create schemata for signals, with separate slots for each property. However, many devices substantially alter the form of a signal (e.g. modems convert it between analogue and digital), and this means that a number of schemata would have to be used to represent each signal. Since the system considers the propagation of a great many signals, this did not seem like a good idea.

---

[1] Since the system deals only with data communications, the only analogue signals considered are carrying a digital signal.

9.4.3   Specifying and Selecting Tests

The operation of the system involves recommending to the user the most effective test to carry out at each stage of localising the fault. To offer the user the greatest possible control over the way the task is tackled, this process is split into two: explicitly generating the range of tests that could be done, and evaluating them in terms of the difficulty or cost of doing them and the amount of information they will yield. Because a range of tests is generated, the user can direct the fault localisation process simply by selecting among them. For both tasks there was a desire to provide mechanisms which were as general as possible.

Generating Possible Tests

To generate possible tests, it is necessary to allow the expert to specify two things: the circumstances in which a class of test may be appropriate and the precise details of the specific test that should be considered. This requires a way of coupling possible actions (or assertions) with the conditions of their appropriateness, which is precisely what rule based systems are for. Since ART provides arguably the most sophisticated rule system currently available, it was natural to use it for this task.

Test generation is based around the notion of a family of tests being characterised by a rule which is able to recognise when specific instances of such tests are appropriate. The rule then constructs a schema which contains the details of the particular test to be carried out — i.e. which devices need to be put into which modes, which signals are involved and where one should look to determine the outcome of the test. The rest of the system is structured around working with these schemata, not just in the process of diagnosing the fault, but also to allow the user to select or examine the test. This information could also be used to generate detailed instructions for carrying out the test, and for calculating the difficulty/cost of doing so, a parameter which is currently estimated by the rule that proposes the test.

There is a significant addition to this basic mechanism. Certain kinds of testing activities can generate a great many specific tests. For instance, when one considers sending a test signal from a central point to a device in loopback (so-called "fox sending"), there can easily be twenty different points at which the signal could be looped back, each constituting a subtly different test. In such cases, the specific tests are not initially generated. Instead, the system works with the *generic* test, which is treated like a specific test in all respects, including allowing the user to select it and even considering recommending it on the basis of some notional utility (see below). When the user selects a generic test, the system generates the specific instances of the test which appear possible, and henceforth treats them as any other specific test.

Recommending Tests

Once a schema has been created for a specific test, the system will determine a number of its parameters. The first of these is the set of devices which are exercised by the test. Where the test involves setting a device into a particular mode, the schema describing that mode is consulted to see whether the device itself is actually tested. In addition, the rule specifying the test can associate it with a particular test signal, which it injects into the network model. The passage of this signal through the network is duly calculated, and the devices which are carrying it are known to be involved in the test.

Once the system has determined which devices are exercised by a specific test, it uses a reliability measure provided by the expert for each (class of) device in order to determine the total reliability involved. This is then used, together with the cost/difficulty measure associated with the test and the total reliability of the devices that are still under suspicion, to determine the *utility* of the test. The system's ideal test would involve half the cumulative reliability of the devices still under suspicion — i.e. be equally likely to succeed or fail. This is, in effect, trying to perform a binary chop on the set of suspect devices, with each device weighted according to its reliability. Note that the utility of a test relies on the total reliability of all the devices that are under suspicion, and thus has to be re-calculated whenever **any** device is classified as no longer suspect.

9.4.4 Interpreting Test Results

The system offers the user a menu of all the tests it knows about that it thinks are "interesting" — i.e. that involve a (currently) suspect device — and another of the test(s) with the best cost/utility tradeoff. It then waits for the user to select a test to be carried out, and asks for a result which it duly processes. If the test is successful, it is taken as evidence that every device involved in the test is working correctly. If the test fails, it is taken as evidence that the problem is with one of the devices involved. On the assumption (shared by the system and the network controller) that there is only one fault, this means that every suspect device which was **not** involved in the test is functioning correctly. For instance, suppose the system has narrowed the problem down to one of six devices, and the user reports that a test involving four of them has failed. The system takes this not only as showing that there is a problem with one of these four devices, but also, since it assumes that there is only one unknown malfunction in the system, as showing that the remaining two devices are no longer under suspicion.

9.4.5 User Interface

During the KE phase, it became apparent that almost every discussion of a network fault situation naturally (indeed almost inevitably) began with drawing a simple diagram of the components involved. Because the system deals with networks where there is at any one time only a single signal path connecting a terminal device to a computer, these diagrams were usually a single row of linked boxes representing devices, which thus became known as "kebab" diagrams. These were clearly very important for focusing thoughts about the situation, and offered a natural way of organising the interaction between the user and the computer. The icons themselves indicate the class of the associated device, so that the icons for modems and multiplexers are clearly different, and reflect the system's idea of their status. They also have a "bold" form which is used to highlight (sets of) devices, such as those involved in the test currently under consideration. Active Values (access-oriented programming) are used to trigger the redrawing of icons whenever appropriate.

The icons are also mouse sensitive, which allows the user to specify a particular device very quickly, without requiring keyboard skills and without needing to know any query language or device identification code convention. The current system is able to describe the device and justify its assumed status in terms of the results of tests. However, the intention is to allow different mouse clicks to request access to the system's information about the model of the device and its capabilities — e.g. physical description, modes of operation, indicators, etc. The flexibility of the ART mouse and menu mechanism means that it is easy to have this information continuously available throughout the diagnosis.

Throughout the fault localisation process, the user is offered dynamically updated menus of the tests that have been carried out. This allows the user to review the course of inference so far and the range of tests which (the system recognises) could conceivably be done. The system's test recommendations are also presented on a menu. This usually has only one entry, although sometimes the system's (currently crude) idea of test costing does not allow it to distinguish between the desirability of two tests. However, the user is always free to choose either the system-recommended test, or some other test from the list of interesting possibilities. Presenting the possible test procedures in this way has two major benefits: not only does it show the user the options open to him, but it also constrains him to suggesting tests which the system can understand.

9.4.6   Control

One of the most unusual aspects of the system, from a conventional programming point of view, is that there is no specification of the overall behaviour of the system. Instead a number of behaviours are specified in isolation, and it is left to the pattern matching capabilities of ART's rule engine to ensure that they are carried out whenever they are appropriate. With only one or two minor modifications intended to control execution, this approach has allowed the system to exhibit satisfactory behaviour. Moreover, the resulting architecture is both easily expanded and well able to respond to unexpected information or instructions from the user.

Most of the specified behaviours have already been mentioned earlier in this section:

- recognising the applicability of specific tests of a particular type (9.4.3);

- propagating signals through the network (9.4.2);

- determining what equipment a test involves and its likelihood of involving the fault and combining this with its estimated cost to determine which is currently most attractive (both 9.4.3);

- interpreting the result of a test in terms of changes to the set of suspect devices (9.4.4).

In addition, there are behaviours for determining what entries currently belong in each menu being displayed and ensuring it is up-to-date, and generating and positioning icons for any devices involved in the diagnosis. Some of these behaviours require only a single rule, while others require the coordinated interaction of several rules.

9.5 Evaluation

The finished ART system was demonstrated to club members on a SUN 3/260 workstation with 16 MByte of memory and 80 MByte of paging space. Under these conditions mouse response is effectively immediate and the longest pause for computation is approximately 30-45 seconds. This occurs when a generic test is selected and results in the generation of about twenty new tests, each involving long signal paths. At this point the system is running with between 5000 and 6000 ART facts.

The project makes a number of assumptions that greatly simplify the process of diagnosis. In common with IP's network controller, the system assumes that each device is either working correctly or not at all, and that there is only one undiagnosed fault present in the network at any time. It also takes advantage of the fact that all links within the network are bi-directional and constant — that is, unless the network is explicitly re-configured, every signal from A to B is always carried by the same devices as every signal from B to A. No account is taken of the possibility of intermittent faults or of tests being carried out badly or mis-reported.

Within these restrictions, the system is able to localise a fault to a specific network device, and will suggest sequences of tests which are in accord with the criteria suggested in the IR. Club members were impressed with the performance of the system, and (perhaps inevitably) with the interface in particular, especially since this had been achieved in only three man-months, and there is interest in further development.

9.5.1 Comparison with a Micro-based System

The PC-based system was the result of 20 man-weeks using Version 2.4 of KES.[2] As might be expected from the difference in costs of the development tools, the resulting system was clearly less powerful than the toolkit version in a number

---

[2] The Knowledge Engineering System (KES) from Software A & E is an expert system development tool runs on a range of PCs, minis and workstations.

of respects. However, these deficiences do not necessarily indicate any absolute limits of the development tools, but merely of what could be achieved with the effort available.

The most obvious omission from the KES system is the network diagram and mouse-based menu interface; its interface uses only text and keyboard. Moreover, in providing the interface they did, the NCC team were obliged to write some routines in 'C'. While the ability to readily incorporate such procedures is one of the features of KES, the drawbacks of a mixed-language system in terms of comprehensibility and maintainability should be born in mind.

The KES system does work from a description of the network in terms of interconnected devices of specified types. However, it requires the links between devices to be directional (see Section 9.4.1). Moreover, it has no conception of signal-flow, which will also limit its ability to deal with complex network topologies. These restrictions, together with the capacity limitations of their tools, restricted the PC implementors to tackling only a section of the network (25% of the devices, straightforwardly interconnected).

In contrast to the toolkit implementation, the PC-based system did offer guidance on carrying out some of the more complex tests, although it did so using mechanisms which were specific to the tests and devices concerned. It also dealt with sub-components, though this was achieved by defining the network in terms of them and thus represents no increase in actual functionality.

The PC-based system has nothing comparable to the ART system's *generic tests*, and has no generalised ability to determine the costs and implications of specific tests. These are facilities which together allow a wide range of general testing procedures to be represented both very concisely and independently of the specific network. The inability of the PC fault localisation system to represent signals seems likely to put it at a severe disadvantage when attempting to consider partial failures of devices.

9.6   Conclusions

The use of an explicit IR, and the concomitant separation of the KE and implementation stages, seems to have worked effectively. The exercise has demonstrated the possibility of constructing an expert system with virtually no direct access to the expert, although the expert's flagging enthusiasm seems a cause for concern. The general KADS approach made a definite contribution to the project, though, possibly due to its presentation, it proved difficult to follow in its entirety. The performance of ART held up reasonably well for a non-trivial problem, which is a pleasant discovery. Using ART clearly brought considerable gains in programmer productivity, having required less effort to produce a system with greater functionality and generality, although it does not seem meaningful to attempt to quantify this.

Acknowledgements

The work reported in this chapter owes much to the staff of NCC, and in particular Mike Newman, who carried out the KE and constructed the PC-based system. Thanks also to John Kingston, who did much of the ART programming. The work was funded by the members of the DAPES club, and AIAI staff made use of the KRSTL, which is supported by the Alvey programme, the Department of Trade and Industry and the Science and Engineering Research Council.

Chapter 10

EMEX:An Expert System for Market Analysis and Forecasting

Mark Lewis

10.1 Introduction

The EMEX system is a market analysis tool designed to assist market specialists to build quantitative models of their markets. The intended user is expected to have a good qualitative understanding of his/her market but not necessarily to have the model building skills to undertake the quantitative analysis of that market.

EMEX requires two forms of input. The first is the market specialist's expectation about the behaviour of the market, and the second is the historical data of the factors that influence the market.

The expectations are such things as which factors influence the market and what form that influence takes. For example, if we were considering soap powders, we might think that sales of soap powder depends upon the price we charge; that if price goes up, sales will drop, and that this response in sales will take several months to filter through. It is just this sort of information that EMEX will consider as it builds a model for the market.

Although guided by the user's expectations, the analysis that EMEX performs involves complex statistical operations on data. Therefore historical values must exist for each factor over a sufficient period of time.

The system will guide the user through all the stages of the model building process; from defining the factors, to proposing the first model, to refining the model, checking the models validity and finally interpreting the model in terms of the market.

The model that EMEX builds is a mathematical equation. This equation relates the factors the user is interested in, say sales of soap powder, to other factors, like the price. This equation in itself is not likely to be understood by the market specialist without knowledge of econometrics, so EMEX assesses the implications of the model in terms that would be meaningful.

The model will sharpen the user's understanding of his/her market, focusing on the key factors and perhaps identifying factors which have very little influence. The model can also be used to assess the sensitivity of the market to changes, and to make more detailed investigations into different scenarios. This can assist with the formulation of policies and marketing strategies by forecasting the effect of such decisions.

10.2   Model Building

Model building is a very complex and time consuming process. The techniques employed in EMEX are drawn from the work of econometrics and are applied to a given problem using the "rules of best practice" that have been developed by The Henley Centre for Forecasting.

The aim of econometric modelling is the identification and quantification of causal relationships within some economic system. It involves the application of statistical techniques to discover systematic and quantified relationships between movements in one variable, such as sales, and movements in a number of other variables, such as prices, advertising, real incomes and so on. The techniques enable movements in the variable being explained, in this example sales, to be related simultaneously to a number of variables, and not just to each one separately. Economic and market specific knowledge is frequently used to give an indication of the explanatory variables to include and to provide expectations against which to assess the model.

The method used in EMEX is known as testing downwards from the most general form. It may be characterised as follows:

> 'intended overparameterisation with data based simplification. Commencing from the most general model which seems reasonable (or possible) to maintain, sequential testing procedures are used to select a data coherent specialisation.'

Briefly the model building process consists of the following tasks:

1. **Define Economic System.**

   The user must declare which factor they wish to model and the other factors that are expected to influence it. Details about the relationships between these factors, such as direction, approximate magnitude, variability and speed of the effect, can be stated if they are known.

2. **Propose Equation.**

   The modelling strategy that EMEX uses is to build a very general model at the outset and then to refine this model to a simplified form, deliberately casting the net too wide and drawing it in around the identifiable relationships. The model is built in the light of the expectations set out in the previous task and on the basis of statistical analysis of the data for the factors.

3. **Refine Equation.**

   Having set up the very general form of the equation the next step is to perform statistical analysis of that model and so simplify it by removing those parts that are not supported by evidence.

4. **Validate Equation.**

   Having arrived at a simplified version of the model. EMEX then checks that the model is sound in a technical sense. Various tests are performed and any problems and their implications are reported.

5. **Interpret Equation**

   Finally, the mathematical model that has been built is interpreted in terms of the market. The relationships between the factors are analysed in terms of the effect of changes in the market. Using the soap powder example EMEX might tell us that a 1% increase in the price of soap powder would result in an immediate 0.873% decrease in sales which levels out to a 0.467% decrease in sales over some specified period of time.

In practice it is common for any or all of these tasks to have to be repeated or revised in some way. EMEX reflects this by breaking the model building tasks into exactly these stages. EMEX will try a respecification itself if problems are encountered with the model and the user can also re-invoke any stage. The user also has the ability to revise his/her expectations by changing responses to questions and then rerunning any of the tasks in the light of this change.

10.3 The EMEX System

The aim of the EMEX system is to guide the user through the stages of the model building task. Its role is that of an assistant. It is important that the user, as the expert in the market being modelled, exercises judgement over the results and suggestions that the system makes. The combination of the system's model building expertise and the user's market expertise together can provide a very powerful insight into the operation of the market.

Ease of use is an important consideration for such a package. The user and the system interact via a series of forms and menus. There are facilities to allow the user to browse through the details of the current consultation, to change previously entered information and at all times a help system can offer advice relevant to the current context.

EMEX is now in regular use and continues to undergo refinement. To date its performance has been judged by comparing the models it generates with the models produced by the experts, and on several occasions it has actually improved on a model originally built by the experts. Moreover, a model which might take an expert half a day to build is more likely to take around thirty minutes for EMEX, so great time savings can also be made.

10.4   Technical Background

The user interacts with the EMEX system, which in turn invokes a statistics package to perform the appropriate operations on the data. The user is therefore shielded from the statistics package. The expert system was written in Prolog-2 and interacts with the Fortran statistics package by passing command and result files via the operating system.

The knowledge in the system is represented primarily as frames and rules, though the consultation is controlled by a state transition network, which was required in order to represent the explicit procedural nature of some of the expert's knowledge. The knowledge is compiled into directly executable Prolog. This means that, at run time, inheritance amongst the frames and the firing of individual rules is performed directly by the Prolog interpreter rather than via a separately defined inference engine, greatly reducing the run-time overhead of using the knowledge.

The minimum hardware requirements under which EMEX will operate is an IBM XT with 640K memory. The recommended environment is an IBM XT, or a compatible or a 386 machine such as a Compaq.

10.4.1   The Past

The project to build EMEX had been conducted within the context of an Alvey Community Club. The clubs were an initiative by the government to encourage groups of British companies to jointly undertake high technology development. The club members were: Allied Vintners, ASDA Stores, British Telecom, Cadbury Schweppes, Co-operative Wholesale Society, Davidson Pearce, Electricity Council, ICI, J Walter Thompson, Jaguar Cars, Leeds Permanent Building Society, Proctor & Gamble, Shell International, and United Biscuits.

The joint contractors were The Henley Centre for Forecasting, responsible for supplying the model building expertise, and Expert Systems International, responsible for the knowledge engineering and technical development.

The EMEX Club was founded in November 1985, and was brought to a successful close in September 1987. The cost of building EMEX was £250,000.

10.5   The Future

It is in the nature of expertise, and therefore expert systems, that both can be constantly improved. In order to ensure that such developments can continue and that an appropriate level of support can be given to users, the system is being made available on an annual subscription basis.

The old club members, given the success of the project, are keen to continue with a new commercial club, because they wish to retain a forum at which to exchange experiences of using the system and in order to influence future enhancements.

Any organisation may apply to subscribe to the EMEX system. Each subscriber, for an annual payment of around £12,000 is entitled to the following benefits for the subscription year:

- use of the EMEX software;

- telephone support;

- training in the operation of EMEX;

- quarterly subscriber meetings/workshops;

- at least two updates to the software.

During each year new releases of EMEX will be distributed to all subscribers and meetings will be held at which recent developments will be explained and subscribers will have an opportunity to suggest directions in which the product may be enhanced.

Chapter 11

Assessing the Competence of a UK Company Marketing to Japan

Sunil Vadera, Nigel Holden, Vivienne B. Ambrosiadou

11.1 Introduction and Background

Japan is predicted to become the world's leader in industrial science by the end of this century [81]. Even if this particular prediction does not actually come true, it is indubitably the case that 'the competitive decisions and actions (of western businessmen) require a more complete understanding of the Japanese kaisha (company)' [7] than ever before. Such understanding is not only a prerequisite for anticipating Japanese firms as competitors who have global leadership in industries hitherto dominated by Western companies; it is equally vital for firms wishing to improve their marketing performance in Japan, where 'the peculiar nature of the ...distribution system makes it uncommonly hard for foreign manufacturers to sell their goods' [37].

According to a former President of the American Chamber of Commerce in Japan, Western firms need to undertake 'extensive study of Japanese psychology and the structure of Japanese society'. This, he claims, 'is absolutely essential to fruitful dealings with the Japanese' [150]. Beyond that, Western firms must be able to apply this knowledge actively, thus developing that all-important capacity 'to communicate (themselves) and (their) business objectives within Japan's own terms of reference' [98].

The knowledge and insight needed for this 'enchanced' capacity for communication with the Japanese require in turn an interpretative sensitivity towards the responses and motivation of the Japanese people at the personal and corporate levels of interaction. This combination of knowledge and insight into Japanese society, involving as it does a corresponding awareness of the Japanese language as 'that which defines the Japanese more distinctly than any other feature in their culture' [114], is both in short supply and unevenly distributed among firms.

The fact is that firms wishing to do business with Japan, specifically those concerned with developing strategies for penetrating the Japanese market, potentially require the sort of knowledge that is associated with several experts on specific aspects of Japanese life and society: sociologists, historians, anthropologists, linguists, management specialists, cross-cultural trainers, to name but a few.

Businessmen are in fact hard-pressed to know which aspect of the now vast English-language literature on Japan to consult for insights into their own specific business problems. Indeed, we may safely assume that the range of knowledge about Japan that may assist firms in enhancing the quality of their decision-making is:

- is not systematically consulted by firms;

- not available in a form that is convenient for firms to consult;

- not structured so as to enable firms to seek guidance on points of relevance to their decision making needs.

As a first step in aiding a company, we develop a system capable of assessing a U.K. company's competence in marketing to Japan.

Section 11.2 describes the model of competence on which the assessment is based. Section 11.3 describes the implementation of the system. Section 11.4 compares the systems assessment with that of the expert, and also describes some improvements to the system.

11.2   Description of Model

The system exploits a qualitative model developed by Holden [68,67], on the basis of extensive interviews and empirical investigations in the U.K. and Japan. Specifically, the model not only integrates facets of communication behaviour characterising interactions between U.K. and Japanese industrial firms; it can also evaluate firms' capacity to communicate. This capacity is termed *communication competence*.

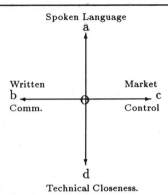

Figure 11.1: Model of communication competence

The model dimensions aspects of interactive behaviour along four axes (Figure 11.1) pertaining to :

- the role of spoken English and Japanese;

- the Japanese written language as a noise/information source; and repository of of technical information;

- control over relationships in the market;

- achievement of technical closeness.

The idea behind axis a-o is that the use of language, whether English or Japanese, in interactions is associated with a lesser or greater capacity to generate goodwill, secure cooperation and effect interorganisational bonding. This axis does, however, take account of the highly complex nature of the language barrier and communication gap that faces the Japanese in their cross-cultural encounters [69,114,150].

Axis b-o concerns firms capacity to exploit the Japanese language as a repository of technological information and to overcome the effects of the Japanese language as a noise source in Japan i.e. to read or decode written Japanese to enhance personal mobility in Japan to reduce one's sense of alienation.

Axis c-o reflects facets of firms' capacity to control the progress of relationships with Japanese partners and to create and exploit appropriate means of feedback from the Japanese market.

The fourth axis, d-o, relates to the degree of technical closeness that industrial firms are able to achieve in the Japanese market.

All the axes take account of key facets of Japanese national psychology such as complex attitudes towards foreigners, the powerful sense of 'uniqueness', the tendency to see business relationships as fulfilling sociological as well as economic functions.

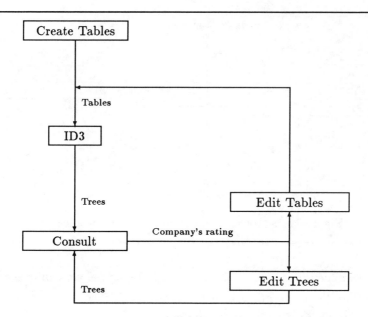

Figure 11.2: Outline of the approach

11.3   Implementation

11.3.1   Use of ID3

The major requirement of this system was that it should be easy to adapt it to match a particular experts assessment. This requirement led us to choose Quinlan's ID3 [109,111] algorithm as a basis of our implementation. As described in Chapter 1, ID3 takes a table of examples as input and produces a decision tree which is consistent with the examples. The benefits we expected from ID3 were:

- **Creation**. An expert could easily provide examples.

- **Evolution**. An expert could change the behaviour of the system by adding, deleting, and changing examples.

- **Relevance**. Only relevant attributes would be used.

- **Discovery**. The decision tree produced may have relationships which the expert is not aware of.

Figure 11.2 gives an outline of the approach that we use. In keeping with the model described above, the expert was asked to create four representative tables; one for each axis. For each table, the expert had to:

- enumerate the factors that may affect the competence;

	Spoken Lang.	Written Comm.	Market Control	Technical Closeness
No Examples	47	36	28	25
Possible Attributes	11	12	9	9
Attributes used by ID3	6	7	5	6
Maximum Depth	4	4	4	4

Table 11.1: Number of attributes used by ID3

- decide upon the possible values of each factor;

- decide upon the possible values of the competence.

Enumerating the factors proved to be easy for the expert. However, the choice of values for the factors and the competence was more difficult. For example, do we choose the range of values: ($good, average, fair, poor$) or ($very\ good, bad$) ? If the expert chooses a narrow range, he encounters situations where he can not distinguish between two examples which he knows are different. If he chooses a wider range, he has to provide redundant examples. When the range is changed, the expert has to re-examine the existing examples. In general, it is more mechanical to convert a range to a narrower one than it is to convert it to a wider one. For example, we can use an editor's substitution command to implement an expert's wish to compress ($fair, poor$) to (bad) in all the examples. We decided to choose the following range of values for all the tables:

Competence : ($very\ good, good, fair, poor, bad$)
factors : ($high, medium, low$)

ID3 was then used to produce a tree from each table. Table 11.1 lists the number of examples, the number of attributes enumerated by the expert, the number of attributes selected by ID3, and the maximum depth of each tree.

11.3.2 Consultation

The initial consultation is carried out by traversing each decision tree in sequence, obtaining a rating for each axis, and producing an assessment graph. The user can then amend the answers and observe the effect of this on their marketing competence. Of course, amending an answer may result in some further questions. Figure 11.3 shows a typical consultation (for conciseness, we omit the menus).

11.3.3 Code

In order to give us greater control (and to save a little money), we decided to code ID3 in Prologix [13] on a Prime rather than purchase a commercial implementation.

After one consultation a user's answers are (where adjeng means the ability to adjust English, monjaptech means ability to monitor the Japanese technical literature, whilst the other attributes should be self explanatory):

Attribute	Value	Attribute	Value	Attribute	Value
acquiring	med	adjeng	med	decode	high
integration	high	involvement	high	monjaptech	high
work-know-jap	high				

User changes some of the answers:

Attribute	Value	Attribute	Value	Attribute	Value
acquiring	med	adjeng	med	decode	high
integration	**low**	involvement	**med**	monjaptech	**low**
work-know-jap	**low**				

User selects graph colour before continuing consultation:

> Spoken Language
>
> > Question id: foreign
> > Q2) proficiency in speaking one or more foreign language?med
>
> Assessment of Spoken Language is :good
>
> Market Control
>
> Assessment of Market Control is:fair
>
> Technical Closeness
> > Question id: educate
> > Q6) ability to educate Japanese partners?med
>
> Assessment of Technical Closeness is:fair
>
> Written Communication
>
> Assessment of Written Communication is:fair

The System now produces the graph in Figure 11.4 where the outer graph is result of the first consultation, and the inner graph is the result after the changes.

Figure 11.3: A consultation

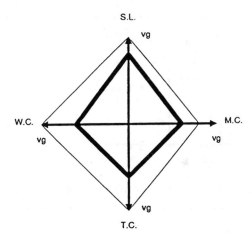

Figure 11.4: Graph after consultation

The decision trees were represented as in Doores,Reiblien and Vadera [47], so that we could use their tree editor.

11.4 System's Ratings = Expert's Rating ?

11.4.1 The Tests

As Figure 11.2 suggests, the system can evolve to match a particular expert's rating of a company. However, how far is our first attempt from the expert ? To discover an answer to this question, we generated 50 random examples for each axis and asked the expert to produce a rating for each example. We also asked the expert to circle those values whose attributes influenced the decision. These were then compared with the systems ratings of the examples.

In this section we present the results of this comparison. Of course, one cannot generalise these results. However, we hope that the reader will become more aware of the kind of differences that can occur.

The graphs in Figure 11.5 to 11.8 presents the results for each axis. As a measure of disagreement, we use:

$$ordinal(system's\ assessment) - ordinal(expert's\ assessment)$$

where $ordinal(bad)$ is 0, the $ordinal(poor)$ is 1, ..., $ordinal(very\ good)$ is 4.

The average disagreements together with the standard errors (see [36] if you are not familiar with this statistic) show that the system is unlikely to differ from the expert by more than one ordinal. However, the graphs display some interesting differences between the expert and the system. We summarise the features:

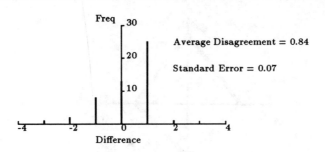

Figure 11.5: Disagreement graph for spoken language

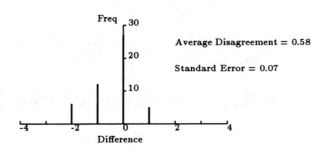

Figure 11.6: Disagreement graph for written communication

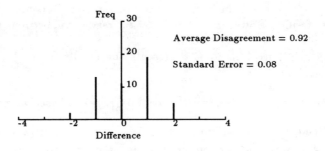

Figure 11.7: Disagreement graph for market control

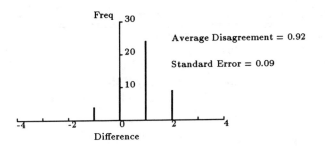

Figure 11.8: Disagreement graph for technical closeness

- **Spoken language.** The peak difference of one on the graph suggests that the system has a tendency to overrate the competence of a company with respect to our expert along this axis.

- **Written communication.** The graph suggests that decisions correspond very closely to the expert's, and that there is no clear bias along this axis.

- **Market control.** The graph suggests that on some occasions the system overrates a company's competence, and on other occasions it underestimates a company's competence.

- **Technical closeness.** Like the spoken language graph, this suggests that the system overrates a company's competence along this axis.

11.4.2 A Flaw: Inconsistent examples

As the above graphs indicate, there are a few cases where the system may indicate a *poor* competence when the expert would indicate a *good* competence! In general, this is bound to occur because ID3 produces a decision tree capable of producing decisions for cases not included in the training set. Indeed, the decision tree would be useless if it could not do this. However, when we examined the disagreements, it became clear that the system and the expert were producing assessments even when the example contained inconsistent information. What appeared to be happening was that the system and the expert were basing their decisions on a consistent subset of the example. The consistent subset used by each was different and therefore resulted in different assessments. We first give an example of this, and then describe two possible approaches which can be used to counter this problem.

Attribute	Value	Attribute	Value
English	med	Foreign	high
Awareness	low	Simple Japanese	low
Civilties	low	Adjustability	low
Effort	med	Everyday Comm.	low
Telephone	high	Work knowledge of Japanese	low
Business Japanese	high		

Table 11.2: Example situation for spoken language

Example

Consider the situation given in Table 11.2 for the spoken language axis: This example has inconsistent information. A company which has little working knowledge of Japanese is very unlikely to have a *high* capability in business Japanese. For this example, our expert decided (for some reason) to give more weight to the *high* in business Japanese than the *low*'s elsewhere and gave a rating of *fair*. The system chose the *low* in adjustability and then the *low* in working knowledge of Japanese to rate the company as *bad* !

11.4.3   Handling Inconsistencies

Two possible approaches to detecting such inconsistent situations are:

- Include information about inconsistent situations in the tables. This can be done by allowing an additional outcome to denote 'inconsistent' situations. ID3 will then produce a decision tree which checks for inconsistencies.

- Augment the decision trees with the relationships between the attributes. Use the relationships to deduce the expected values of those attributes which are not used to obtain a rating. Compare these with the actual values of the attributes.

The first approach will, at the expense of more questions, detect most inconsistencies. It does not help much in identifying consistent subsets; particularly since the most likely cause of an inconsistency is an error. The second approach is only appropriate when the relationships between the attributes are much clearer than their influence on the outcome. For our application, we do not expect different experts to disagree about relationships between attributes. We therefore prefer the second approach. The system generates an assessment based on a consistent subset and displays the expected values of the other attributes. The user can detect any inconsistencies, alter answers and obtain an assessment for an alternative consistent subset. We implemented this scheme by representing the relationships by rules, and using a forward chaining control.

11.5 Conclusion

We have described an application of ID3. We compared the system's assessments with that of the expert. The greatest differences occurred in situations which contained inconsistent information. The system used a different consistent subset from the expert to arrive at a rating. We described an approach that we used to resolve this problem. Generating suitable explanations from decision trees remains a problem. Converting them to rules and identifying necessary conditions [41] does not produce adequate explanations. In our type of application, where the values of attributes and results are ordered, we can detect whether an attribute has a good or bad effect on the outcome. However, this observation has not lead to suitable explanations. If one wants better explanations, then other approaches should be tried [136, for example].

Acknowledgements

We we would like to thank Alastair Kelly and his colleagues of ICL Manufacturing for their interest in the development of this system and for sponsoring further development.

Part V

Industry

One of the most challenging uses of expert systems is in the area of process control. In addition to the usual problems encountered by most expert system application, expert control systems must tackle the complexities introduced by time, and safety constraints.

Chapter 12 describes Ferranti's evaluation of the applicability of expert systems in the process control industry. The chapter describes the design of a fault diagnosis system which receives information on the condition of a plant from a Process Management System. It then outlines a prototype implementation of the fault diagnosis system using ART.

Chapter 13 discusses the problems associated with representing safety constraints, and the problems of performing simulations to show how an initiating event could lead to a potential hazard. The authors describe their experience of using a toolkit, called Knowledge Craft, to provide a partial simulation tool which helps to check safety constraints. An important feature of their implementation is the use of schemata, inheritance, and demons.

Chapter 12

A KBS Approach to Fault Diagnosis in a Process Plant

David R. Bedford

12.1 Introduction

As a result of Ferranti's long involvement in the process control industry and use of new technologies with this field, an evaluation of the applicability of the knowledge based systems in the process control industry has been undertaken. This evaluation took the form of an implementation of a model-based fault diagnosis system which received information on the condition of the plant via Ferranti's Process Management System (PMS) and was written using the high-level expert system development environment, Inference ART.

12.2 Aims

The major aim of the investigation was to prove that the technology of expert systems has a part to play in providing solutions to the outstanding problems of the process industry. Two requirements were immediately identified. Firstly, any system had to be capable of working on-line. Although this is not a strict criteria for all possible areas of application (for example, plant simulation) it was felt an inability to reason with "live" data would be too restrictive. Secondly, any system had to be capable of "real-time" performance, where real-time means response rates in terms of seconds rather than of minutes. Again, this is not an essential requirement for all applications. However, faster response times will make any system more desirable (provided such a system comes up with sensible conclusions). Due to the nature of Ferranti's business, a further requirement was also identified. Any development should be via techniques that could be generalised, since Ferranti Computer Systems Limited, as a service company, would be looking to apply these techniques to a number of different process plants. Based on these requirements a prototype problem was selected. Any development should be via techniques that could be generalised, since Ferranti Computer Systems Limited, as a service company, would be looking to apply these techniques to a number of different process plants. Based on these requirements a prototype problem was selected.

12.3   Prototype Problem

12.3.1   Selection

The problem selection process began with a review of current projects and of current research. Many potential areas were identified, such as fault diagnosis, alarm filtering, plant scheduling and plant optimization. It was hoped that this review would identify problems encountered on other projects and indicate, from areas of current research, possible solutions. Two problem areas stood out; that of obtaining the knowledge for the system and that of validating the knowledge once coded into the system. The main thrust of expert system research was focusing on the use of 'deep' knowledge as opposed to 'shallow' knowledge. In the case of a process plant for example, this would require a description of the structure and function of the plant (deep knowledge), as opposed to a set of rules of thumb obtained from experienced operators and engineers (shallow knowledge). It was felt that the more 'deep' knowledge approach would go some way towards solving the identified problem areas; structured information should prove easier to obtain and to subsequently validate. Also, such an approach should lend itself to generalisation, thus satisfying one of the initial requirements. In particular, research being carried out at the University of Tokyo ([71], and [125]) and the Massachusetts Institute of Technology ([82]) into 'deep' knowledge process fault diagnosis seemed to provide a strong basis for a practical large-scale fault diagnosis system. Fault diagnosis would, in most situations, have to satisfy the two main requirements of the investigation; that of being on-line and of execution in real-time.

12.3.2   Design

There are basically two ways to view the diagnostic problem. In the first view past experience plays the dominant role. Experienced failure situations are coded as heuristic rules, together perhaps with some predictive or statistical knowledge, all obtained from a human expert in a particular diagnostic domain. This could, in some sense, be considered the traditional expert system approach. The second view, and the view taken here, is diagnosis from first principles. The knowledge required is a functional model of some system and some measurement of that system. If the measurements conflict with the functional model then there is a diagnostic problem. That is, it is required to determine which part of the system, if it is assumed to be in fault, explains the discrepancies in the measurements of the system.

In the case of the process plant the knowledge available to describe structure and function can be conveniently broken into 4 parts:

1. Plant topology; that is, a description of the connectivity of plant items.

2. Plant items; that is, the characteristics of individual items contained within a plant, encompassing both their functional properties and their fault modes. For example, a pipe propagates flow and can either be blocked or be leaking.

3. General laws of physics and chemistry; that is, a description of the plant in terms of the physical and chemical laws that the plant obeys. For example, the principle of conservation of mass.

4. Plant operational information; that is, a description of the plant control strategy, as well as the current operating conditions of the plant.

This knowledge can be further classified into two types, plant-dependent and plant-independent. Topology and operational information is plant dependent. The description of plant items and the laws of physics and chemistry represent the plant independent information. By such a classification, and by minimising the plant specific information, generalised methods can be formulated.

In describing the structure of a particular plant the first two items, topology and plant items are used. A knowledge of the connectivity combined with knowledge of each individual item within the plant, provides a comprehensive description of plant structure.

Function is described via the second pair of items, physics and chemistry and operational information. The method of description is qualitative physics, which attempts to model the plant in terms of a model of the general physical and chemical relationships in the plant rather than by rigorous mathematical modelling of the process. Two methods are used. The first, known as governing equations, uses closed-loop relationships between variables; the second utilises a cause and effect model.

Governing Equations

This model utilises the laws of physics and chemistry governing the plant that represent signature relations between plant variables. That is, equations of measured variables that, if observations indicate an imbalance, imply a closed set of possible faults on a particular plant. For example, conservation of mass will be applicable to most plants. This model requires the instances of conservation of

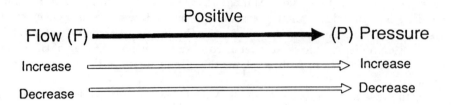

Figure 12.1: A positive causal relationship from flow to pressure

mass that give significantly reduced implications, should there be an imbalance. For example, to take the input from feeder tanks and the output of product and by-product would not significantly reduce diagnosis. However, taking input and output on a reaction chamber would.

The diagnostic analysis in this method involves evaluating which of the governing equations have been violated, and which have not, according to the current set of measurements on the plant. By analysing which faults have been proposed and which have not, it is possible to produce a significantly reduced diagnosis of the current state of the plant.

Cause/Effect

This model utilises the cause and effect relationships between plant variables. For example, consider a pressure point P, and a flow into that point F. If there is an increase in flow F (perhaps caused by a valve stuck open) then there will be a subsequent increase in pressure P. Conversely, if there is a decrease in flow F (perhaps caused by a valve jammed closed) then there will be a subsequent decrease in pressure P. The causal relationship from flow F to pressure P is said to be positive (see Figure 12.1). Now consider the case where pressure P is the cause and flow F is the effect. If there is an increase in pressure P, (perhaps caused by a blocked pipe) then there will be a back effect of a decrease in flow F. Conversely, if there there is a decrease in pressure P (perhaps caused by a leaking pipe) then there will be a back effect of an increase in flow F. The causal relationship from pressure P to flow F is said to be negative. (See Figure 12.2).

By representing a plant via such causal relationships, and establishing which of these relationships are valid for the current sensor measurement pattern, it is possible to establish which of the plant variables, if disturbed, could be possible causal origins of that measurement pattern.

Each plant variable has an implied set of faults should it be disturbed. By identifying causal origin candidates and combining their implied fault sets, the method yields a set of faults that should they exist on the plant are possible

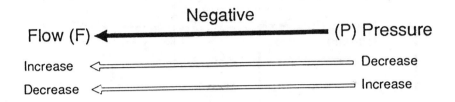

Figure 12.2: Negative causal relationship from flow to pressure

explanations of the current measurement pattern.

Combination

Providing that each method is individually evaluated, the diagnostic sets produced by each of these methods can be combined to produce a greatly reduced diagnosis of the current plant state. Figure 12.3 illustrates the full model.

12.4 Implementation

A prototype fault diagnosis system has been implemented using the previously defined design. Development work was done using high-level Expert System development environment ART using a TI Explorer (and later on a Symbolics 3640). Following is a description of that implementation.

Plant Representation

The plant representation is derived from two sources; topology and plant items. The plant topology can be obtained from the original design drawings. Availability of such design drawings on a CAD system would make possible the automation of this task. Plant items can be generally described thus providing an ability to produce an expandable computer-based library. When combined, these provide a full description of plant structure.

Governing Equations

Two expert tasks were identified for this method; the identification of the instances of the laws of physics and chemistry that can usefully applied, and the implied faults should they become inconsistent with plant measurements. An expert system utility has been written that attempts to apply such concepts as conservation of mass in order to identify instances that could provide reduced fault candidates.

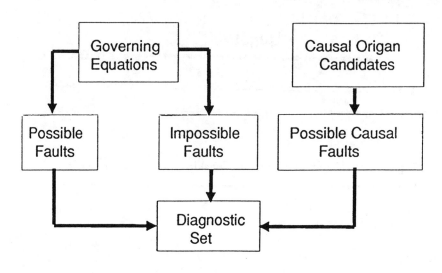

Figure 12.3: The full model

Given the description of the structure of the plant, this utility generates rules that represent the specific instances of each physical and chemical law within the plant. Since the description of structure contains knowledge of plant fault states (via the description of plant items), the utility also generates the set of faults implied, should one of the law instances be violated. Since the utility itself is rule-based, it can be easily expanded, providing an adaptable generalised method for the creation of the governing equations knowledge base for the fault diagnosis system.

Cause/Effect

This method has two major requirements. Firstly, a representation of the plant in terms of the causal relationships and secondly a search strategy, to identify possible origins, that executes in real-time. The causal relationships, described in principle earlier, can be simply represented and can be deduced from the description of plant structure. The problem is the search. The most obvious way to implement the search is using the measured values as start points, and propagate along consistent causal pathways, recognising redundancy, logical inconsistency, and finally possible causal origins. It became clear that this strategy was inadequate if real-time performance was to be obtained. Again, an off-line utility provided the answer. This utility firstly represents each of the causal relationships as a predicate. It then performs an exhaustive search that identifies for each plant variable, the complex combination of predicates that define when a particular plant variable is a possible cause of the measurement pattern currently observed on the plant. The rule base produced provides an efficient on-line causal search that can execute within real-time environments.

Functional Unit Partitions

At a prototype level the method is extremely efficient. However, there is a possibility of linear degradation of performance as the prototype system is expanded to perform diagnostics on a full-scale plant. In order to overcome this problem, a plant is divided into what can be termed *functional units*. Functional units can be thought of as perhaps a sub-plant that performs a particular function as part of the whole process. Such functional units are represented as separate diagnostic 'knowledge' sources. That is, each has its own implementation of the methods described. This allows each functional unit to be treated as a separate entity thus enabling localised diagnostics. There is however a problem. Disturbances may be observed across separate functional units. By implementing the knowledge sources via ART's viewpoint mechanism, the knowledge of two or more functional units may be combined to perform a fuller diagnosis. An intersting side-effect of this partitioning is that disturbance in separate functional units may be concurrently, but separately, considered thus giving some ability for multiple fault diagnosis.

12.5 System Architecture

In defining a system architecture for an on-line expert system, the implications of retrofitting to existing computer control systems must be considered. The view of an expert system as an add-on rather than an intrinsic part of the control system is unlikely to change in the near future. The practical consequence of this view is that the information available on the control system is likely to be the only information available to an expert system. Also, since it is unlikely the system has any significant capacity available, as much as possible of the extra computing required must be done elsewhere. For the method described the architecture envisaged is shown in Figure 12.4.

12.6 Interfaces Issues

12.6.1 Machine/Machine

The system architecture requires the fault diagnosis system to have an interface into a process management system. For the prototype system a link was engineered to the Ferranti Process Management System (PMS). The expert system has access into the PMS database, obtains the information required and performs a diagnosis. Currently, the governing equations are evaluated on the PMS; only the results are passed to the fault diagnosis system.

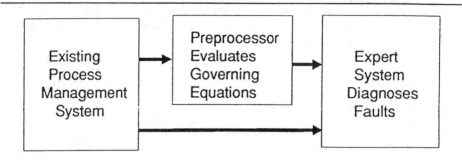

Figure 12.4: System architecture

However, since it is envisaged that this task will be performed on a preprocessor, the protocol will need modification. In essence, each functional unit has a
defined memory area on the PMS. The expert system continually scans this area
for sensor disturbance. On detection, the information for that functional unit is
taken into the expert system, and the required governing equations are evaluated
via a call to the preprocessor. The preprocessor then accesses the PMS and passes
its results to the expert system. This protocol enables efficient inferencing without
overburdening the PMS.

12.6.2   Man/Machine

Once the fault diagnosis system has come to some conclusion, the operator must be
advised. The type of information that can be easily provided is a short description
of the diagnosis together with the appropriate parts of the operator manual which
gives details of the required actions should the diagnosis presented be considered
valid by the operator. Justifying a diagnosis is more difficult. A full trace of
the rules fired is clearly unsatisfactory. The operator would find such information
difficult to understand and time consuming to analyse. Since the implementation
is based on well-structured information, the presentation of a more easily under-
standable justification is possible. The operator is provided with information on
governing equations violated and not violated, together with possible origins of
fault. This should provide the operator with enough information to give him
confidence in the diagnosis without overloading him with detail.

12.7   Testing

Testing took place via a simulation, on the PMS, of the fault states of the piece of
plant modelled. Because of the structured nature of the knowledge, and because
the knowledge base produced has defined boundaries, rigorous testing is possible.
This will most likely be via the Inference ART test harness developed at Ferranti,

and an exhaustive simulation of possible plant states on the PMS.

12.8 Conclusion

The structured method described has gone some way towards solving the 2 major problems identified initially; knowledge acquisition and knowledge base validation. However, practical considerations will effectively make such a structured approach a first step towards a full diagnostic system. The expertise this approach captures is that of a plant designer and a process engineer. Commissioning and 'start-up' of a plant involves tuning of this expertise by the operators. The advantage of the expert system approach is that this operator tuning can be added in via heuristics. The final proof of the validity of the approach taken will be the implementation of a system on a real process plant. However, the investigation has led Ferranti Computer Systems Limited to the belief that Expert System technology has a significant role to play in providing solutions to the outstanding problems of the process industry.

Addendum

These model-based techniques have now been applied as part of a fault diagnosis expert system on an operational industrial plant. It is one of the largest on-line industrial expert systems operational in the U.K. Further information can be obtained from the author.

Chapter 13

Representing Safety Constraints Upon Chemical Plant Designs

Anthony Waters, Paul Wai Hing Chung, Jack Ponton

13.1 Introduction

A design synthesis task can sometimes be formulated as a constraint satisfaction problem and tackled by the use of planning techniques such as *means-ends analysis* and *generate and test* (e.g. [57] & [128]). This is only possible, however, for the sub-tasks of design that are concerned with selecting and sequencing actions or pieces of equipment, rather than the sub-tasks that examine the validity of those selections. The problem is that the latter type of task involves a predictive element when applied to complex and uncertain real world problems such as chemical plant design. This means that rather than being able to define exact constraints to differentiate between a valid and invalid solution we are forced to rely upon prediction to assess whether or not a design will fulfill its intended function.

This problem becomes even more difficult when we use constraints not only to define what a design should do but also to define what it must not do under any circumstances. Checking these types of constraints is really a separate task that involves asking "What happens if?" questions about the design. Nevertheless, it is a task that should be conducted in parallel with that of synthesising the design in order to integrate safety and economics throughout the design process. This paper is concerned with a tool to facilitate this.

We see from the above discussion that there are several possible uses of the word "constraint". For the purposes of this work it has been useful to divide constraints into the following two types:

- *Tautological constraints* such as physical and chemical laws.

- *Safety constraints* which disallow certain scenarios or regions of operation.

The first of these is not usually checked but rather used in a generative mode to produce new data from old data or other new data. This has been the approach taken in work dealing with *constraint propagation* such as that done on qualitative simulation (e.g. [44]). We call these constraints tautological because they should always be satisfied, subject to the validity of the assumptions upon which they are based. Nevertheless, it may sometimes be worthwhile checking a constraint of this type because a violation will signify an error of reasoning or abstraction. In contrast, a safety constraint such as "Don't let tanks explode" is rarely, if ever, used in a generative mode but rather is used to check for physically possible but highly undesirable situations.

Previous work on computer aids for hazard assessment have been concerned with either the *top-down* or the *bottom-up* approach. The first of these usually involves the construction of an AND/OR tree called a *fault-tree*. This begins with a top, undesirable event, such as explosion, and progresses downwards through AND/OR gates and sets of intermediate events to sets of *primary events*, each set of which could cause the top, undesirable event. The work of interest for this approach is therefore that which has been concerned with "automatic fault-tree synthesis" (e.g. [11], [84] & [135]). In contrast the bottom-up approach involves considering initiating events and trying to simulate whether or not they can lead to a hazard. This has been formalised in the Hazard and Operability (HAZOP) Study (see [79]) which involves a design team asking a series of "what happens if" questions about the design in a systematic manner. Waters and Ponton [141] have explored the application of qualitative simulation methods to this currently labour intensive task but found that such methods were too combinatorial for the high dimensionality problems found in process plant design. There has been little other work aimed at providing computer support for HAZOP studies. The approach taken in the work described in this paper is largely bottom-up but top-down techniques are expected to play some part in future work. The top-down/bottom-up distinction is more fully discussed by Lees [86].

In most of the above work the primary reason for trying to provide computer support is so that hazard assessment can be performed faster and more reliably than at present; which in turn would allow hazard assessment techniques to be used at earlier stages of design than is currently possible. In addition, advances in AI and database technology mean that the whole role of computers in design is perhaps changing as engineers look towards the provision of integrated, interactive environments within which they can perform complete designs (e.g. [19] & [72]).

These two goals have been the motivations behind our work, which is aimed at providing a tool that could be used to check safety continually within such a design environment. To do this the designers must be able to build and maintain a picture of the design as it progresses, to represent constraints pertaining to that picture and to have some help in testing the validity of those constraints. Thus, instead of trying to provide a fully automated expert system to carry out hazard studies in a stand alone manner we are trying to provide an interactive tool that can not only be used to access general safety expertise but also to represent and use expertise about a particular design.

13.2   Safety Constraints and Partial Simulation

Our work has primarily been concerned with the problems of representing safety constraints and of providing partial simulation tools to help check them. The word "partial" is used here to emphasise that the aim is not to provide a simulation tool that is complete in any qualitative or quantitative way but rather one that allows a user to maintain simple dependencies between pieces of design data. For example, the user should be able to write a rule that sets the flow through a valve to zero whenever the valve position is set to closed. In addition, the user should be able to write another rule that updates the flow whenever the valve is opened again. This latter case is more difficult, however, because we might have to check against blockages elsewhere in the plant. The user may therefore decide to forego this option and perform only a "partial" simulation.

13.2.1   Constraint Checking Versus Simulation

The level of detail of a constraint determines the effort that must be extended to check it but also has direct bearing upon how specific it is to a particular company or design. Consider the general constraint "Don't operate below the minimum design temperature" which could apply to any piece of equipment. If it is left at this level then each time that we wish to check it for a particular design we must first calculate what the minimum design temperatures are for the pieces of equipment involved. This requires reference to the mechanical designs and is wasteful because such designs will change a lot less often than this constraint needs to be checked. We would therefore benefit by replacing this very general constraint with more specific constraints such as "Don't let the temperature in tank-1 fall below -10 °C".

We can see how this reasoning can be extended by considering the example flowsheet in Figure 13.2 which is based on the propane export plant problem given in Kletz [78]. This flowsheet contains a heating-circuit which raises the temperature of the propane from -20 °C to 10 °C in order to protect the downstream equipment against brittle fracture. This occurs at -10 °C which leads to the constraint shown on the figure. Now, consider trying to ascertain the effect of steam failure in exch-2 (a heat exchanger). With the constraint represented as it is in this figure we need to model the cooling of exch-2 and the heating circuit, followed by the cooling of exch-1 and stream-3. We must then show that this cooling continues until the temperature of stream-3 drops to the critical value of -10 °C and the constraint is violated.

We might decide, however, that the structure of the design is fairly fixed hence the heating circuit will remain the only significant source of heat for stream-3. We could then cut down the simulation that is needed to prove the existence of a dangerous scenario by replacing the original constraint with the more specific constraint "Don't let the heating circuit fail". Or we could go a step further and replace that with "Don't let the steam fail" and "Don't let the flow of ethylene glycol round the loop fail" etc. At each stage we make the simulation easier but our constraints become more specific to the current design. Ideally a design team should be allowed to choose its own level for this specificity, at any stage in design. Consequently, our constraint representation tool must be easily specialised to a particular company, design team or even a particular design. This can be done in a tidy manner by using an object-centred design representation which allows constraints to be attached to objects at any levels in the inheritance hierarchies. This was one of our motivations in using an AI toolkit, such as Knowledge Craft, for this work.

13.2.2   Representing Safety Constraints

Some of the constraints that we will need to represent will be fairly simple, others will be more complex. Below are some possible classifications:

1. Constraints which involve a single attribute of a single object e.g. "The temperature in conduit-3 must be greater than -10 °C".

2. Constraints which describe a forbidden combination of values of different attributes of a single object e.g. "Don't allow fuel flow to burner while the air flow is zero".

3. Constraints which involve the comparison, perhaps arithmetic, of values of different attributes of a single object e.g. "The operating pressure of any piece of equipment must be less than its maximum designed pressure".

4. Constraints which compare values of attributes from different objects e.g. "The maximum designed pressure of a vessel must be greater than the set-point of any relief valve which relieves it".

5. Constraints which are the inverse of ones that have already been attached e.g. the inverse of that in (4) is "The set-point of a relief valve must be less than the maximum designed pressure of any vessel which it relieves".

Of these, constraints of types 4 & 5 are the most complex because they require us to first identify the other objects involved before we can compare attribute values to check the constraint. Again, this strongly suggests the use of object-centred

programming and the facilities that such an approach usually provides to represent
the relationships between objects.

We see that the constraints that we may need to represent can be quite complex. This suggests that a constraint description tool should meet the following
requirements:

- Constraints must be easy to see and cross-reference. For example, we should
  be able to ask to see "all the constraints concerned with pumps". This may
  have a bearing upon how we choose to store and represent the constraints.

- Constraints should be easy to write and use so that the "automatic safety
  checklist" that we are trying to provide is easily specialised to the needs of
  a particular design team.

- The constraint languages must be flexible enough to say complex things.

- Some constraints should be checked automatically, others only on request.
  It should be possible to enable and disable automatic checking at any level
  of detail. The types of things that we might want to demand are "Automatically check all constraints on tanks" and "Switch off automatic checking of
  constraints on tank-1".

In addition, the following issues are important:

1. How do we know when a constraint might need checking?

2. To what level of detail should we check the constraint?

3. What action should be taken if there is insufficient information to check the
   constraint?

4. What action should be taken if we find a constraint violation?

In the work reported here constraints are written in "simplified Lisp" and
attached to objects in the design representation. The constraints can then be
inherited and applied to objects lower down in the various hierarchies. The constraints can refer to attributes of the object to which they are being applied or
to attributes of objects that are related to it. We consider that a constraint may
need rechecking when any of these attributes change, which is implemented by
the attachment of demons to the relevant attribute slots. We provide methods to
attach such demons automatically, hence issue 1 has been tackled in this work.
However, issues 2, 3 & 4 have not yet been properly considered; the only action
taken on finding a constraint violation is to print a warning.

13.2.3 Writing Simulation Rules

Simulation rules should be manifestations of physical and chemical laws which can
be used in a generative mode to maintain simple dependencies between pieces of
design data. In this context it is useful to draw the following distinctions between

types of design data:

- Data that can be changed as a result of operator action and may therefore be changed as a result of simulating operator action e.g. temperatures, pressures, the running status of a pump ("running" or "stopped").

- Data that is fixed by design and so cannot change during a simulation e.g. design limits, pipe sizes, equipment connections.

Only data of the first type should be changed by the action part of a rule but both types of data can effect the validity of a constraint.

There are several other issues to address with respect to the use of simulation rules:

- Is there any danger of circularity in the rules such that propagation never ceases? This could arise where there are feedback loops in the digraph (influence graph) of the process. Such loops are caused by recycle loops of material, energy or control information.

- What action should be taken if there is insufficient information to perform the test part of a rule?

- What strategy should we use to decide which of conflicting rules should fire and in what order?

- If the rules are incomplete, and whilst they are firing, the design may be in an inconsistent state e.g. a valve is marked as closed but the flow through it has not yet been set to zero. Is this a problem? Should we forbid constraint checking at such times?

The strategy for selecting between conflicting rules and for establishing a firing order could be important because rules may interact by making additions and deletions to the knowledge base. A possible strategy might be to take the OPS approach and use recency and an MEA strategy which institutes goal-directed rule firing by always using the most recent information first [26]. In our work, however, the selection and ordering of simulation rules is instead governed by rule partitioning and by the control of inheritance. This gives us more explicit control over the firing of rules than if we had used CRL-OPS to implement the simulation. This is at the expense of having to provide a Lisp-like language to write the rules and the relevant demons to fire them.

13.3   Current Implementation

The current implementation classifies objects as belonging to one of the four hierarchies described below. These hierarchies structure the background knowledge that is to be generally applied to classes of design. Objects within a hierarchy are usually connected by *is-a* links, along which most of the inheritance takes place.

In contrast, the topology of a particular design is described by the use of other relations which are primarily used to represent connectivity rather than to carry inheritance.

13.3.1 Problem Representation

Schemata Hierarchies

The following are the four hierarchies that have proven to be useful:

- The *process-subsystem* hierarchy which contains physical objects and functional subsystems (see Figure 13.1).

- The *process-data* hierarchy which contains schemata representing streams, process-variables and some equipment parameters.

- The *flow-system* hierarchy which contains schemata describing unit topologies (e.g. single-input-single-output or "siso"). It also contains simulation rules describing the behaviour of temperature and flow through such topologies. Most of the schemata in the process-subsystem hierarchy will inherit from at least one schema in the flow-system hierarchy.

- The *utility-object* hierarchy which is used to group together miscellaneous utility objects such as those used to hold very general methods or those used as global storage areas (i.e as an alternative to Lisp global variables),

Part of the process-subsystem hierarchy is shown in Figure 13.1 from which we see that some of the schemata represent whole subsystems, such as control-loops, rather than just individual units, such as pumps. Such abstraction can support reasoning by allowing us to write constraints and simulation rules that cover large sections of plant and by allowing us to make analogies to standard design cases. It can also cause problems, however, because the objects on a plant cannot necessarily be exclusively assigned to one subsystem or another. For example, a pump may be part of a fluid delivery system as well as being within a control or trip loop. This could potentially cause problems in deciding what is effected by what but can be coped with by the use of relations. In particular, the fact that inverse links are created gives us a better chance of keeping dependencies consistent and propagating updates correctly.

Relations also make it easy to expand our topological plant representation to represent process variables, such as temperatures and pressures at particular points in the flowsheet, as actual schemata rather than just as slot values. This is done in the process-data hierarchy which contains the *process-variable* schema. This schema has a slot, called *variable-value*, which is inherited by all schemata used to represent process variables and used to hold the value of such variables. The advantage of this is that the process-variables can be used as information links to propagate disturbances between units on a plant. This is more desirable than trying to propagate directly because we do not need to check for connections from

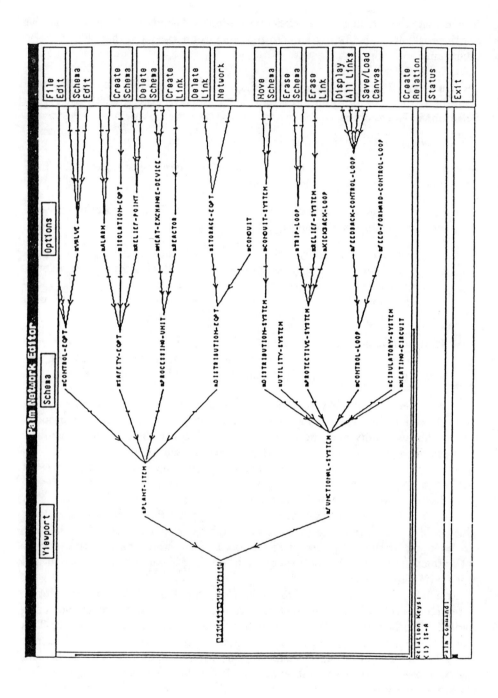

Figure 13.1: The process-subsystem hierarchy

a given unit to units of every other type but only from that unit to the more limited set of process-variable types. In addition, we can institute automatic propagation by placing a demon on the generic variable-value slot. This simulation demon can then fire when the value of any process-variable changes.

This approach elegantly captures the idea that process variables and the streams containing them are information pathways on a plant. Unfortunately, however, it does increase the number of schemata required to represent a given design and the work needed to retrieve information. For example, if we want to find the temperature into a tank we must first find the schema representing the temperature and then retrieve the value in the variable-value slot. Again, this is facilitated by the use of relations to connect the two schemata. In contrast, to find the maximum designed temperature for a tank we simply access the relevant slot in the tank schema. This difference comes back to the data distinction already described in Section 13.2.3. The temperature into a tank can be changed during a simulation and so must be represented as a separate schema so that propagation can take place. In contrast, the maximum designed temperature is fixed by mechanical design and can only be read, not changed, during a simulation. Consequently, we never need to propagate a change to the latter which means that it can be simply represented as a slot value in the schema representing the tank.

Lisp and CRL

Together, Lisp and Knowledge Craft's CRL module provide a powerful and flexible language that can be used to represent constraints and to write simulation rules. However, the following issues arise:

- The relevant information, such as schema names, is not always available when we want to write a constraint but only becomes available when we want to check it.

- Lisp can be tedious to write and read if it is heavily nested or there are too many arguments involved.

These problems have been resolved by allowing the user to write constraints and simulation rules in a form that is Lisp-like but much simplified. These forms are then translated into executable code, and the relevant arguments inserted, when the constraint is to be checked or the rule to be fired. For example, we allow a constraint such as:

operating-pressure < max-design-pressure

to be stored as a slot value of the following form:

(< op-press max-press)

where op-press and max-press will be defined as dummy-variables and will get substituted for the slot values that are relevant to the schema to which the constraint is applied. The important thing to note here is that the use of Lisp-like syntax allows the user to write constraints of unrestricted complexity by mixing Lisp functions, such as "<", with certain pre-defined functions or dummy variables that instruct the constraint checker to insert slot values, find related objects etc. Thus we are able to write general constraints which can have most of the functionality of Lisp but avoid the need for clumsy lambda expressions and tedious repetitions of arguments. The rationale for this approach is that to say complex things you need a language rather than a restricted set of options. Given this, it seems appropriate to use an existing language such as Lisp rather than creating yet another syntax to be learned. Of course it would be possible to provide a more user-friendly interface for the naive user who wants to avoid such complexity and flexibility.

13.3.2　Methods and Demons Provided

Methods concerned with Constraints

The following methods are provided for the specification and checking of constraints:

- A method to check a list of constraints for a given object. The constraints are stored in slots (which may be inherited rather than local). They are referenced by the slot name. In addition the method can be given the argument all, in which case it will check all the constraints that can be inherited by the object concerned.

- A method called attach-safety-constraint-demons that allows a user to institute automatic constraint checking for any constraints at any level in the hierarchy. Again this can take a list of constraints or the atom 'all as its argument. The method works by examining the constraints concerned, one at a time, picking out slots that are involved in them and attaching the relevant demons to these slots. The demons make use of the constraint checking method mentioned above so consistency is ensured.

- A method called detach-safety-constraint-demons which detaches demons that were attached by the last described method and so turns-off automatic checking.

These methods can be applied to objects at any level in the hierarchy so some degree of specialisation has been achieved. For example, we can check constraints for any pump or just for a particular instance of pump instance. There are, however, some difficulties in identifying all the slots that are involved in a constraint. We anticipate that these problems will be resolved in future work.

Demons for Simulation

Simulation rules are stored and represented in a manner analogous to that used for constraints. The consideration of rules is activated by a demon on the variable-value slot of a "process-variable" i.e. a demon which fires whenever the value of a process-variable changes. When this happens all the plant units and systems effected by the variable are identified by the use of relations. We then find the sets of simulation rules that apply to these objects and fire the first valid rule from each set. As with constraint checking the list of rules to be considered is effected by the control of inheritance. The rules are divided into sets to give us greater control. Circularity is avoided because the process-variable change currently being considered is checked against a list of those already being dealt with. Changes are removed from that list when they have been explored fully; termination occurs when the list is empty.

The problems with temporary inconsistency remain. In particular we have not provided a feature to temporarily disable automatic checking during a simulation run. In fact, doing so is extremely easy but not necessarily desirable because there may be some situations where we need to check constraints as a simulation is proceeding rather than storing the call until a later time. This is likely to be the case when modelling scenarios in which the sequence of events is very important (see the example below).

13.3.3 Illustrative Examples

In this subsection we will discuss two example problems and how successful the system currently is at solving them. For the first example let's refer back to the propane-export plant in Figure 13.2.

After the problem has been described to the system and some additional schemata automatically generated the representation of heat-exchanger exch-2 might appear as:

```
{{ exch-2
        instance: heat-exchange-device
        has-he-cold-side: cold-side-2
        has-he-hot-side: hot-side-2 }}
```

This is a simplified schema representation in which exch-2 is the schema name; instance, has-he-cold-side and has-he-hot-side are the slot names and the elements after the colons are the slot values. This syntax will be used for the rest of this subsection.

All the slots in the exch-2 schema are, in fact, relations which means that the slot values are schemata in which the inverse links are created. For example, there will exist a schema called cold-side-2 which will have a slot that represents the inverse relation to has-he-cold-side (e.g. has-he-cold-side+inv) and contains the value exch-2. Similarly, some of the slots in such new schemata may be further relations which introduce yet more schemata. Consequently we get a succession of schemata that lead down to the thermodynamic variables that represent the actual process conditions:

```
{{ temp-4
        instance: stream-temperature
        variable-value: 5 ;; for example.
        is-temperature-for-stream: intens-4 }}
```

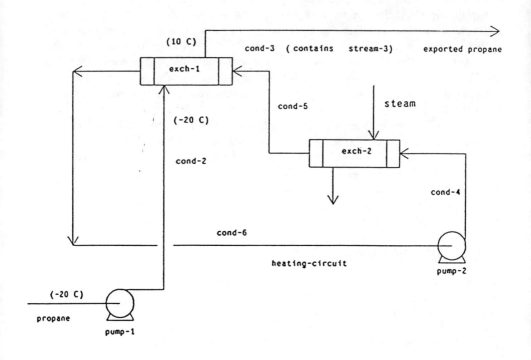

Constraint:"Don't export propane at a temperature below $-10°C$"

Figure 13.2: Normal operating state of a propane export plant

We see from this that the internal plant representation is quite a complicated network of schemata that are tied together by the use of relations. This can cause problems but is necessary to allow efficient and tidy propagation and abstraction (as already described). The problems arise because we often have to step through several schemata to connect a unit with one of its thermodynamic variables. They can be coped with, however, by the use of the CRL path grammar which provides a flexible tool for defining the transitivities of the relations used.

When the network of schemata has been set-up as above then they automatically inherit the background constraints, simulation rules and methods that are appropriate to them. Also we can include additional, specific constraints or rules if it seems necessary. Consider the specific constraint shown on Figure 13.2:

"Don't export propane at a temperature below -10 $°C$."

This can be rephrased as:

"Don't allow the temperature of stream-3 to be less than or equal to -10 while the flow is still greater-than zero".

There is no general constraint to represent this so we must define a new design specific constraint such as:

(not (and (or (< stream-temp -10) (= stream-temp -10)) (> flow 0)))

which must be attached to the schema representing cond-3. We have then represented the constraint adequately.

Now we can try to use the constraint and simulation tools to do some modelling of the flowsheet behaviour. As a particular example we shall discuss how the tool is able to show that switching-off pump-2 on Figure 13.2 will lead to a constraint violation because the flow of heating fluid is lost.

The pump-2 schema is related to a process-variable schema which defines its status as being "running" or "stopped". We can therefore 'switch' the pump off by putting the value "stopped" into the variable-value slot in that schema. This could result in propagation taking place because this slot has the simulation demon attached to it (see Section 13.3.2).

Pump-2 can inherit from several schemata which means that there are several sets of simulation rules to consider. The tests for these rules are examined and one of the valid rules is chosen for firing. The syntax of these is rules is (test action), i.e. a two-part Lisp list, but for the purposes of these examples we shall use English text to describe the rules. The rule which fires is:

IF the status of the pump has just become set to stopped
THEN set the flow into the pump to zero
    AND set the flow out of the pump to zero.

Suppose that the mass-flow into pump-2 is represented by the schema mass-flow-6. When the first action part of the rule proceeds this will then become:

{{ mass-flow-6
        instance: total-mass-flow
        variable-value: 0
        ...plus other slots }}

The simulation demon attached to the variable-value slot now fires again and ascertains that mass-flow-6 can effect several schemata, one of which is exch-1. This object will inherit rules that describe the interaction between the hot and cold sides of an exchanger and so can cause the propagation to leave the loop. For example, a rule such as the following may fire:

IF the flow on the hot-side of the exchanger is zero
THEN set the cold outlet temperature equal to the cold inlet temperature.

In our case this would set the temperature of stream-3 to the inlet propane temperature of -20 °C. This violates the design specific constraint because the flow of stream-3 is still greater than 0 but its temperature is less than -10. If the system had been instructed to check this constraint automatically then this violation would be picked-up immediately and a warning issued. Propagation would then continue around the flowsheet until no further effects could be found.

Now that we have considered the example flowsheet in Figure 13.2 in some detail, let's consider a new example that makes it slightly more complicated. The original constraint for the last example suggests that the flow of stream-3 should be shut-off if the temperature of that stream falls towards -10 °C. This can be achieved by installing a trip-system as shown on Figure 13.3. This time a constraint violation should not occur if pump-2 fails because the trip fires when the temperature has fallen to the still safe value of 0 Degrees Centigrade. Can we model this?

The trip-loop is represented as a system with several components which are tied together by relations. The trip behaviour is represented by the rule:

> IF the trip-loop has status reset
>   AND the measured variable is less than or equal to the trip set point
> THEN perform the trip action
>   AND set the trip-loop status to tripped-out.

In our example the trip action is to set the value of the stem-position of valve v-1 to 0 (i.e. to close v-1). This should, in turn, cause a valve rule to fire and set the flow in cond-3 to 0.

Most of the propagation for this scenario has already been described for the previous example so let's just take it from where the temperature of stream-3 has been set to -20 Degrees Centigrade. At this point two things may happen. The first is that our trip-loop rule can fire because the temperature is less than the trip-set-point. This immediately sets the flow in cond-3 to be zero so that the constraint will be seen to be satisfied if it is subsequently checked. In that case we would have correctly modelled the behaviour of the system. Unfortunately, the second thing that could occur is that the safety constraint is automatically checked **before** the trip-loop rule is fired in which case the constraint would appear to have been violated and our modelling would be flawed. Both of these are possible because they both involve demons which fire on the value of the temperature of stream-3. The deciding factor therefore appears to be the order in which the demons will fire.

Thus we have a problem which can arise if we are not careful about the order in which multiple demons are fired. In fact, this description hides the real problem which is that we fail to model time and sequence properly. In particular we need to show how the failure of pump-2 leads to a **gradual** cooling of the heating-circuit and the consequent firing of the trip-system when the temperature of stream-3 has only dropped to 0 °C (not -20!). Some of the work on qualitative simulation will be relevant here (e.g. [83]) but Waters and Ponton [141] have identified some serious combinatorial problems with such approaches. Consequently this is, as yet, an unresolved problem.

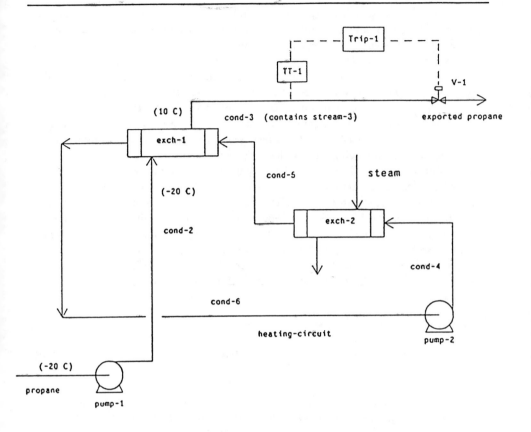

Constraint: "Don't export propane at s temperature below −10°C"

Trip-1 shuts off flow if temperature of exported propane exceeds 0°C

Figure 13.3: Propane export plant with trip protection

13.4   Summary

This chapter has discussed the use of Knowledge Craft to build a tool to represent and check safety constraints upon chemical plant designs. The tool must be extremely flexible so that it can be used throughout the design process, at a level of detail appropriate to the stage in design. In addition, it must be easily specialised by a design team to their own particular needs. This dictates that constraints should be transparent, easy to attach and easy to remove.

So far the tool is in two parts. The first provides a Lisp like language that is used to write constraints at any level of detail. The second is a similar language that is used to write partial simulation rules that can be used to maintain simple dependencies between design data. Together, these tools allow us to show how an initiating event can lead to a constraint violation for a simple problem, but they currently fail on more complex problems that require the proper modelling of time or sequence. Nevertheless, the approach has been shown to be flexible in the level of detail that can be used for these two tools. Indeed, it has been shown that we can trade one against the other to strike a balance between using a complex simulation algorithm to check very general constraints and using a simpler simulation algorithm to check more design specific constraints.

The object-orientated nature of Knowledge Craft has allowed constraints and simulation rules to be attached to the schema with which they are concerned. This aids transparency and cross-referencing since the user can see everything pertaining to a particular object in one place. Inheritance has allowed the use of abstraction throughout the system, thus enhancing efficiency and consistency. This has also been helped by the use of relations to support multiple viewpoints of an object. Finally, demons have been used to allow a user to institute automatic constraint checking, where desired, and to perform automatic simulation.

Acknowledgements

This work has so far been carried out at the Department of Chemical Engineering, Edinburgh University and during a four month period at the Artificial Intelligence Applications Institute, Edinburgh (under the SERC funded "Support for Engineers Scheme"). The authors gratefully acknowledge the support of SERC in making the trial use of Knowledge Craft possible via the above mentioned scheme. They would also like to thank ICI plc Engineering Department for their continued support in this work.

Part VI

Medical Education

Traditional computer based learning systems have tended to be static and therefore less effective. Expert system methods can be used to develop more flexible, and more sensitive environments for learning. This part of the book describes two computer based learning environments in the area of medical education.

Chapter 14 describes how a knowledge based approach can improve upon existing methods of teaching school children about nutrition. It describes how the APES shell can be used to provide a 'microworld' in which school children can learn by investigation.

Chapter 15 describes the development a system that is used for teaching medical students, and general practitioners about diagnosing and managing diabetes. The effect of improper teaching in such an area could, of course, have fatal consequences. Thus even though the representation of the knowledge in the system described is simple, its accuracy is imperative. The key feature of this chapter is the careful, and systematic manner in which the knowledge was obtained. It describes how, despite this care, differences between the system and the medical consultant did occur. Readers will also benefit by comparing the approach to knowledge acquisition used here with the KADS methodology described in Chapter 9.

Chapter 14

An Expert System for Nutrition Education

Peter Chalk

14.1 Introduction

Interaction with a knowledge base can be good for your health! This was the
starting point for an attempt at constructing an environment for exploration by
pupils, students, teachers and experts.

Part of this environment is an expert system which is being developed to provide advice on the nutritional properties of food and the needs of a healthy diet.
This requires an underlying knowledge base, which itself includes a very large
bank of data. A powerful learning environment or microworld is then capable
of interrogation, amendment and of supporting computer aided learning (CAL)
applications and short programs. Such short programs might be written by the
student or teacher to represent a cooking process or composition of a diet for
analysis.

A key feature of the project is the construction of a database, a *database
management system* (DBMS) and a set of rules for presentation to and use by
the user. To keep the initial development simple a non-probablistic, backward
chaining production rule system was chosen for implementation: Micro-Prolog
Professional and APES (Augmented Prolog for Expert Systems) produced by Logic
Programming Associates. Additional reasons for choosing this system were that

it was available for microcomputers already in use in schools and that powerful learning packages had already been successfully built, particularly by the *Exeter Project* under Jon Nichol at Exeter University. Application packages based on Micro-Prolog have been well received by History teachers, as described in [97].

The involvement of experts in knowledge engineering is a two way process. As they construct the knowledge base, so too they learn how to structure their knowledge and make explicit the underlying rules of behaviour. Furthermore, in the field of education this process can be harnessed to improve and extend the learning abilities of students. In this chapter we demonstrate some ways in which this can occur, citing examples which, though trivial, highlight key aspects, from the writing of production rules and Prolog programming to interaction with an expert system shell.

14.2   Trends in Nutrition Education

As in many other subject areas and with the advent of the GCSE and its course-work oriented approach, nutrition education demands a problem solving, practical style of learning. The Nuffield course [3], for example, promotes investigations and tasks in which pupils can apply their knowledge, utilising skills in organising data, planning and testing hypotheses and reasoning logically. In addition, the need to put the knowledge into a social and cultural context can be met by Prolog which allows concepts as well as data to be manipulated.

Nutrition education already makes extensive use of powerful information retrieval and analysis programs, such as NuPack and Balance your Diet [1]. A typical lesson may consist of pupils entering their list of foods eaten into the computer which then returns an analysis of how much of each nutrient has been supplied. These figures are compared to the recommended daily allowance of nutrients for that type of person. The pupil can then determine how healthy their diet is, which foods supply which nutrients, and how to make up for any deficiency. This computer based method of teaching about nutrition is being used successfully throughout Britain.

So why change it? The drawbacks to this traditional approach include inflexibility, no advice giving function and the lack of ability to explain results or how they were obtained. There is no way of taking advantage of students manipulating the knowledge structures themselves or programming processes. In other words, there is no facility for the computer to 'learn' new information or for allowing the student to input acquired knowledge and use it to help solve a problem. The packages use an imposed and narrowly structured method of information retrieval which could be greatly improved and extended by the use of relational database techniques, for which Prolog is highly suitable. Information retrieval using an expert system shell also adds the advantage of making explanations available to the pupil about how the computer performed its analysis. In a "query the user" mode a dialogue can be set up and the computer can elicit further information from the pupil. This could be set up deliberately by the teacher and the dialogue recorded for diagnosis or assessment. Furthermore, once the data structures become familiar to the pupil she can even start to write small programs to represent the processes learnt during the lesson. A similar approach in a Biology lesson is described in [40] thus:

> "The database was fully queried, a food chain was sketched out...Much verbal communication was generated. The database was analysed successfully and synthesised by writing into heirachical tree form."

14.3   Intelligent Teaching or Learning systems?

Advocates of artificial intelligence (AI) techniques in education have, broadly speaking, followed two paths. One group is exploring *intelligent teaching systems* where the aim is to provide a complete automated coaching system, adaptive to the needs of the individual student. This has been well documented in [127].

The other path of development has been in the building of what can best be described as *learning environments* or *microworlds*, particularly using the Logo programming language (a derivative of the AI language Lisp) but increasingly in Prolog too, as evidenced in [134]. This paper, published in 1985, mentions the beginnings of work on Prolog based microworlds. Since then, expert system shells have emerged as accessible tools in education, described by Ennals and Cotterell in [52] thus:

> "Non-numerical knowledge will have greater attention, with students able to manipulate, experiment with and interrogate structures. For each rule or connection there will be a corresponding explanation available to the student. A complex piece of reasoning can be traced and examined. Models can be tested. Large databases can be consulted, and pilot expert systems constructed to organise and explain problems in science."

The authors go on to suggest that, with formal thinking and problem solving given increasing importance in most curriculum areas, all students in further education should undergo a course, including topic areas such as "concepts of knowledge and information, procedural and declarative thinking and programming and an introduction to expert systems". Projects based on this approach, using Prolog and/or expert system shells, have been introduced now at further, secondary and even primary levels of education: see [33] for a survey.

All systems surveyed used a variety of approaches to constructing an intelligent learning environment. Four separately identifiable but complementary areas were adopted for the nutrition education project:

1. To create, maintain and interrogate a knowledge base using Prolog. This is to be based on an extensible relational type of database containing data about the nutrient content of foods, recommended daily allowances of nutrients, sets of rules about dietary health and social/cultural aspects of food.

2. To use this knowledge base to provide advice, information, analysis and explanation about healthy eating using the APES expert system shell. APES was chosen for its availability and for its flexibility, especially for its ability to incorporate a database and the complex rules needed for its manipulation. See [87] for a complete explanation of this.

3. To encourage and support the writing of small programs by students themselves using powerful higher level exported predicates from the knowledge base as a microworld of accessible commands. Such a program might represent the effects of cooking on the nutrient values of a particular food, using rules like 'food low in nutrient if food boiled'.

4. To build application modules for use by the student which use the knowledge base in some way. For example, a shopping game has been suggested in which the aim is to maximise the nutrient value for money.

Already, an adventure game shell, called The Plan [22], written in and using Prolog syntax for the input of rules, has been utilised to demonstrate the power of rule based, declarative programming. The adventure game concept lends itself easily to the description of procedural tasks. We have used it to simulate cooking procedures in a kitchen, modelling processes using rules such as 'action heat fat if cooker lit and fat in pan on cooker'. The action could not be 'fired' unless the conditions (cooker lit etc) were true. The need for such a complex rule would arise in a straightforward way during an exercise in home economics. A teacher carrying out research as part of a teaching diploma, in [102], listed the activities engaged in during the use of The Plan as 'analysing, communicating, planning, applying knowledge, being systematic, problem solving and posing, reasoning, listening, selecting data, understanding relationships and structure, learning about symbolic representation, acquiring good working habits, being imaginative, independent, cooperative and confident'. This could well be a list of the attributes of a knowledge engineer!

There are many similarities between such software and an expert system. To make all such environments more meaningful and powerful, the next stage is to link them to the nutrition knowledge base.

14.4   Constructing the Knowledge Base

The heart of the system is a database, similar to a relational database, containing basic information ("facts") about foods and nutrients. It is extensible and other data can be added as necessary. The first stage involved prototyping this database in the form of Prolog clauses, although the main file of some 20,000 data items (22 nutrients for each of 800 foods) would eventually have to be held as an indexed disc file due to internal memory limitations.

This food file, available with NuPack from the ILEA Home Economics Science Centre, is stored in the prototype knowledge base as the Prolog clause content, with the following structure:

content(*food-name, typical-portion, category, nutrient-amount-list*)

An example entry, in 'raw' Micro-Prolog syntax, would be:

```
((content allbran 30 1
    (5 43 15 27 26 15 273 74 12 100 8 0 0 2 49 0 0 2 2 0 0 0)))
```

This requires other clauses for interpretation. In fact, the clause states that allbran is served in a typical Portion of 30g, is in food group 1 (cereals) and contains the list of nutrient amounts per 100g. The order for the nutrients and the units of measurement is as follows:

```
((nutrients (fat carbo sugar starch fibre protein energy calcium
        iron folic-acid zinc vit-a vit-bl ribof nicotinic-acid
        vit-c vit-d vit-e water vit-b6 vit-b12 alcohol)))
```

```
((units (g g g g g g kcal mg mg ug mg ug mg mg mg mg ug mg g mg ug g)))
```

This means, for example, that 100 grammes of allbran contain 43g of carbohydrate and 100 microgrammes of folic acid. Already, some semantic problems arise. How do we choose meaningful names for the foods and for the nutrients? What about synonyms? What happens to these figures if the food is cooked? Although these questions were highlighted for future concern, it was decided to continue the prototype in one particular direction: that is, how to decide if a particular food provides sufficient nutrients for a specific person or requirement. To make this decision, the *recommended daily allowance* (rda) is needed, which for an average adult woman is:

```
((rda (109 253 0 0 40 54 2166 500 12 0 0 750 0.9 1.3 15 30 2.5 0 0 0 0 0)))
```

Hence the average adult woman requires 253g of carbohydrate per day. These clauses (content, nutrients, units and rda) are forms of primitive data — facts — which can be supplemented by others, such as food additive details, prices of foods etc, according to the application and the advice of nutritionists and teachers.

To extract information in a useful form, a DBMS is necessary, consisting of two levels. A low level module, hidden from the user, of complex but efficient rules, is needed for manipulating the primitive data relations described above, for handling the list data structures and so on. A visible higher level microworld consists of exportable relations, capable of being handled and interrogated by a student or for incorporation into small programs. Another reason for choosing the APES shell is that two such modules or sets of rules can be written, one of which can be hidden from the user and the other available for the 'Query the user' mode and for explanations. This usefully cuts down the depth to which explanations can sometimes go, which often confuses the user.

For an example of a set of low level rules, consider the requirement mentioned earlier for making available the value of a particular nutrient in a given food, fibre in allbran for instance. During the knowledge elicitation phase, it was established that one method for deciding this value is to measure the proportion of the recommended daily allowance of the nutrient required which is supplied by a typical

portion of the food. These values can then be set at high, medium or low. The
value clause can then be used by rules at a higher level which have only one or two
arguments, ie unary or binary relations.

The structure of the value clause demonstrates how complex the low level rules
may be:

```
((value food _nutrient _level)
      (required nutrient _amount)
      (composed _food _portion _nutrient _proportion)
      (TIMES 100 _temp _portion)
      (TIMES _temp _proportion _weight)
      (set-level _weight _amount _level))
```

This calculates the weight of a nutrient in a typical portion and calls set-level to
compare this weight with the required amount (rda) and to assign the level to
be either low, medium or high. The clauses required and composed are needed to
extract the relevant recommended daily allowance for the nutrient and the relevant
data from the content clause described above, respectively. These rules demand the
use of list handling and recursive techniques. The value rule above has been written
in raw Micro-Prolog: in-built primitives are written in capitals (e.g. TIMES) and
variables are preceded by the underline symbol (e.g. _food for the food name).

It would be unlikely that anyone other than a trained Prolog programmer
could manipulate such rules meaningfully. Moreover, different application programs might require this basic information, but in a variety of forms. What we
have so far, then, is an underlying database available for a variety of purposes.

To illustrate these points, consider a rule for returning a list of foods high in a
particular nutrient. Two arguments are needed, the food name and the nutrient
name, which would be instantiated, and it would need to invoke the value clause
with level set at high, i.e.:

```
_food high-in _nutrient if value (_food _nutrient high)
```

This demonstrates the way that the APES shell strips the brackets (only off unary
and binary relations completely) and the need for two levels of DBMS rules. The
high-in clause is much easier to understand, read and manipulate than the value
clause which, because it contains more than two arguments, appears in list form
(with brackets). The example of use of the high-in clause by small programs given
below emphasises this point.

14.5   Interfacing, Interaction and Programming

Having established a range of exportable primitives such as high-in it then became
possible to develop a number of application areas: a mini expert system, a support
environment for small programs and the initial design of some application CAL
(computer aided learning) programs.

To illustrate one form of interaction, consider the construction of a small program, which can also be viewed as the beginnings of an expert system. The aim is

to advise the student of an appropriate diet for someone with a particular medical condition. The objective (or goal), then, is to produce lists of foods the person should and should not eat, clauses we have called should-eat and stop-eat respectively, for example:

> _person should-eat _food
>   IF _person problem-with _condition AND _food good-for _condition

This clause is now written in the syntax used by the APES interface. Binary (or unary) relations obviate the need for brackets. The logical symbols IF and AND clarify the meaning and the reading of the rule and, as demonstrated below, it is also possible to make it read as a more presentable 'sentence'. The subgoal problem-with can be satisfied by querying the user for her 'condition' (e.g. constipation) and good-for is satisfied by writing a rule to find those foods with a high level of fibre content, i.e.:

> _food good-for constipation IF _food high-in _fibre

A whole set of entries for good-for can be researched by the student, or entered by an expert or teacher; similarly for, say, stop-eat and bad-for. The students small program now consists of five simple rules and can be entered into APES and tested, with explanations available to and interaction expected from the student.

For example, in response to the query by Peter (instantiating _person),

> Which _food: Peter should-eat food?

APES will respond by asking the user (using a read-as template as explained below to increase readability):

> Peter has a problem with?

The user or student now has to either type in the condition or, if the menu option has been programmed, select one (or more) possible conditions from a menu. At this point, in the prototype expert system, further questions are asked of the user to establish which list of rda amounts to use (such as the 'adult woman' example above). Once established, APES will return the first of the foods satisfying the rules, say allbran. The user can now proceed into the explanation by asking how the answer was found, continuing 'down' through as many levels as the user wants, until the concealed DBMS rules are reached. For the teacher, then, this provides a control over how 'deep' the student should go and if an explanation of how the computer calculated that allbran is high in fibre is required, this can be made available by declaring the relevant clauses interactive.

An advantage of this feedback and interaction when programming using an expert system shell is that the student (or expert!) can gradually build up the knowledge base, testing clauses as they are added, using the explanation to diagnose and correct any errors in their program. In some respects this is analogous to one of the stated reasons for the language Logo being popular in schools: that the feedback, in the form of graphic images, encourages the pupils to correct errors and independently set goals during the building of their programs. As in

Layer	Clauses
Hidden database of 'facts'	content, nutrients, rda, units...
Hidden DBMS rules	value, set-level, composed, required..
Exported DBMS relations	low-in, high-in...
Student's program	should-eat, stop-eat, problem-with, good-for, bad-for, ...

Table 14.1: A four-layer model

Logo, shells usually provide the facility for keeping track of the interaction and for storing any new facts or rules added by the user. A print-out serves as a useful record of the interaction, perhaps for perusal by the teacher and any useful data or programs added during the session can be permanently incorporated into the knowledge base/expert system if desired.

A four-layer model, shown in Table 14.1, illustrates the structure of the simplified knowledge base described so far.

It is likely that this four layer model will apply to many other application areas which need to access large banks of data. Indeed, systems now exist which combine a Prolog front-end with an underlying relational database.

It should be noted that, in discussions with nutritionists and teachers, it was pointed out that good-for and other clause names are value-laden. In practice, other forms of words can be used. For the purposes of this discussion, the above program suffices to explain the bare bones of a typical attempt by a student to research, explain, structure and program a knowledge base. The next stage for a more serious program or expert system is to re-cast the clauses into a more readable form. Additional information can be associated with clauses and displayed when a rule is invoked or on request from the user.

Several facilities are available in APES to provide a more user friendly interface to the knowledge base. For instance, read-as and which templates improve the readability of clauses, as with problem-with which can be expanded to 'has a problem with', as mentioned above. Expected responses can be supplied using an in-menu clause to simplify and limit users' replies. This can avoid users having laboriously to type out an answer which may be spelt wrongly — an additional problem which can also be overcome through the use of synonyms or some tricky programming techniques, parsing and so on.

There are, in addition, facilities in APES to limit the range and number of answers input by the user, data validation in other words. Advanced programmers, of course, can add to the facilities or even amend the underlying APES code which is written in Micro-Prolog and fairly "transparent" to the programmer.

Further small programs, extensions to the expert system or even CAL application modules can be built on top of the knowledge base. The change in nutrient values of fresh and cooked food can be modelled. Prices of foods can be obtained and used to calculate the cost of a healthy diet. The relationship between the amount of fat in a food and the energy supplied is an important topic. These and many more objectives of nutrition education can be achieved through experimenting with the microworld supplied by the knowledge base. The interaction meets many of the criteria expected of scientific discovery learning, the formulation and testing of hypotheses, the revealing of underlying structures and processes and the implementation and testing of ideas. The educational process and the knowledge engineering life cycle have many similarities!

14.6   Issues Raised by the Application

A wide range of expert system shells and AI languages is becoming available; even in education, specialist shells are being developed. How does one choose which system to adopt? For this application we needed a shell which could work with our own database module, a language which supports complex list handling and external files as well as possessing a syntax that is reasonably accessible to nutritionists, teachers and students. APES suited these purposes: it is flexible, extensible and available. The main drawback to this relatively open environment, however, is that the interface is not as user friendly as some shells.

The database itself can be hidden from the ordinary user in two major ways. For large applications the best strategy is to externalise very large files that cannot be held in memory and use the indexed method of record retrieval available with Micro-Prolog for reasonably fast access. The rules for extracting and manipulating the data can be held in a closed APES module loaded in with APES itself and an integral part of it. For prototyping, however, it should be sufficient to code part of the file as Prolog clauses and make the low level DBMS rules non-interactive, i.e. hidden from the user. APES allows for tailoring the environment to suit the application.

Prototyping the knowledge base was relatively straightforward. Both bottom up and top down methods were needed. Once the basic data needs were identified, efficient rules for presenting meaningful information were written. At the same time, the applications which would use this information were sketched out by teachers and experts. The skill lay in matching the needs of the application with the potential of the database. Differences arose over what programmers considered to be the simple choice of clause names: to nutritionists and health experts, words such as high-in and good-for as in "foods high in fibre are good for constipation" cause all sorts of problems which were not immediately apparent to us! One lesson learnt here was that the experts need to be more familiar with what the system can do in order to define the language to be presented to the user.

APES is not ideally suited to education. The interface is too complex, some of its language too advanced and, in any case, specialised applications do require specialised front-ends. Expert system shells, aimed at the needs of education, have been developed, with Micro-Prolog as the host language, at Kingston College. There is still a problem, though, that simplified shells for education restrict the complexity of the microworld available to pupils. Other avenues being explored for greater ease of use include object oriented languages and environments but it is still early days yet.

Another difficulty encountered was lack of teacher familiarity with declarative programming and the lack of suitable software systems in schools. There will need to be an investment in training in fifth generation computing before we even begin to discover the potential for interaction with knowledge bases and writing small "expert system" programs. Ten years of similar investment in Logo is only just beginning to show research results, though not all positive. Nonetheless, the small amount of work we have done with teachers, pupils, students and health educationalists convinces us that there is potential in educational applications of expert systems.

Chapter 15

DIABETES: An Expert System for Education in Diabetes Management

Vivienne B. Ambrosiadou

15.1 Introduction

Research in the development of computer based programs in diabetes has mainly focused on patient education and management. Maze et al [88] give an overview of the state of art in the computer aided instruction of diabetic patients, while Wise et al [146,145] evaluate various man-machine interfacing methods in the effectiveness of such systems for patient education. Artificial Intelligence techniques have also been employed for the education of the diabetic patient [90]. For example [90] consider the calculation of appropriate insulin doses.

Relatively little emphasis has been given to the education of general practitioners and medical associated staff on the diagnosis and management of diabetes.

This chapter presents an expert system which belongs to a number of knowledge based systems [9,10] developed for the education of medical students and non-specialist professionals on the management of diabetes.

Although diagnosis of diabetes is based on routine clinical tests, the development of long term complications involving the eyes, kidneys, peripheral nerves and feet, and their treatment still pose a challenge to the medical community [16,142].

There are two types of diabetes [73]:

- Type 1, or *Insulin Dependent Diabetes Mellitus* (IDDM). It has an abrupt onset at young age and the patient needs daily insulin administration for the maintenance of life.

- Type 2, or *NonInsulin Dependent Diabetes Mellitus* (NIDDM) can be present in middle age or elderly patients and may be controlled by dietary manipulation and oral hypoglycaemic agents (tablets for blood glucose monitoring) or insulin injections [65].

Long term complications can develop in both types of diabetic patients [142]. The major complications are: retinopathy which results in blindness of 50% of diabetic patients, if untreated. Nephropathy which affects 40% of Type 1 diabetic patients and is increasingly recognised in Type 2. It causes deterioration and finally failure of renal function and is linked with retinopathy. Neuropathy which occurs in at least 25% of patients, results in loss of sensation, leading to painless ulceration. Finally, vascular disease which is linked with neuropathy might lead to heart attacks. In all of the above complications, early recognition and treatment of symptoms can prevent either the onset of complications or deterioration of the symptoms.

Since the incidence of diabetes is increasing throughout the western world and because of the afore mentioned reasons, the importance of the education of medical related staff in diabetes and major complications can now be appreciated.

The knowledge based systems that have so far been developed [9,10] can be used effectively for the education of medical staff on diagnosis and treatment of the two types of diabetes and their complications, however, they deal with only a very limited number of patient cases. Obviously a more general system incorporating a variety of symptoms and patient cases, as well as differing methods of treatment, gives a more integrated and explicit view of diabetes and is therefore desirable.

The advantages offered by this more advanced tool are summarised as follows:

- Experimentation with a large number of patient cases.

- Interaction of complications. Symptoms are either common to certain complications, or treatment for one can affect the development of another.

- Different approaches to patient management and treatment like insulin administration, dietary control and home monitoring are included.

In this chapter, we present an expert system in a prototype form attempting to capture the above mentioned features. The system aided the feasibility analysis for the potential and usefulness of such advanced tools for education as well as clinical decision making.

The following two sections present the knowledge acquisition and representation phases of the development of the DIABETES system. Also the various modules of the expert system prototype are briefly described. The fourth section gives some results of an analysis of the reliability of the system. Finally, in the fifth section, we summarise some lessons learned from the system development.

Concept Sorting

Structured Interview

Teach Back

Protocol Analysis

Case Analysis

Inference Network

Prototyping

Figure 15.1: The process of knowledge acquisition

15.2 Knowledge Acquisition

Although there are a wealth of knowledge acquisition techniques, this is still a major challenge to any knowledge engineer. Some of the methods used are the following: case analysis, concept sorting, influence diagram, interviewing, teach back approach, protocol analysis, prototyping, induction and others. A single one or a combination of any of the above methods might seem appropriate to the knowledge engineer. Obviously there are advantages and disadvantages of using any of the above mentioned approaches. For example, protocol analysis involves observing the expert at work. He is then able to explain problems as well as his thinking process. However, there are two problems associated with this: first, the expert gets distracted, and second, it is not certain whether the knowledge engineer can follow his line of reasoning. Rapid prototyping produces a system that the expert can test very quickly. However, surface information is only included, since there might not be a good understanding about the underlying mechanisms of associations between symptoms, clinical tests and treatment.

The various phases of the knowledge acquisition procedure that we followed are shown in Figure 15.1.

At first, general knowledge about diabetes was collected from medical books, papers and reports, and by attending relevant conferences. An elementary concept sorting could then take place where the various stages of diabetes management were identified and diabetic patients were grouped according to types and complications.

A number of hospitals were then contacted. At Manchester Royal Infirmary (MRI) there was a well organised group in diabetes. A computerised program in the dietetics side of diabetes treatment using optimisation techniques was already in progress. There was keen interest on behalf of the experts for the development of computer aided systems in diabetes education. Therefore, the group at MRI was chosen for collaboration.

Following this, interviews were conducted with the experts. A teach back approach was followed, where rephrasing and repeating the expert's answers confirmed a correct understanding of the main issues involved.

Protocol analysis was another important aspect of the knowledge acquisition process. Attending clinics and observing the experts as real patients were interviewed and diagnosed, helped to identify gaps in the knowledge. In a talk through type of questioning the expert tried to explain the importance of certain symptoms. Details of the patient history amenable to diagnosis and treatment were suggested. He also commented on difficulties in the decision making process.

The experts were then encouraged to produce historical patient cases tackling particular problem areas which are of interest.

There were two kinds of historical cases. First, aspects of diagnosis and treatment of Type 1 and Type 2 diabetes were covered. Second, patients with major complications were dealt with. Each historical case consists of consecutive visits of the patient to the clinic, where the history of the patient and the outcome of treatment are reported. The history is comprised of age, symptoms, insulin dosage and physical reaction to previous treatment. Each visit to the hospital has its own unique history.

15.2.1   Diagnosis of Diabetes

Once patient cases were available, inference networks were produced for the extraction of rules [101]. An inference network contains system attributes and rules presented in diagram form. The attributes comprise the factual knowledge about the domain, while rules describe relationships between attributes.

For example, in the context of diabetes diagnosis, attributes can be the patient's age, symptoms, urine test values, etc.

The initial inference network, as shown in Figure 15.2, was the basis for this module of the expert system. This formed a model of the experts' knowledge and helped them identify and explain their decision making process in a more specific manner. When they were presented with this, they commented on the various aspects of patient management and an alteration of the network became necessary. This resulted in a new diagram on which the expert system was designed. More specific rules were also developed.

There were two types of changes suggested by the experts:

- Medical changes. Certain rules were either corrected or added in order to capture the decision making process of diagnosis and patient management correctly.

- Technical changes. It was established that a procedural flow or a decision tree representation would be the best way to represent the steps of clinical decision making to the user. This would, of course, depend to a certain extent on the information exchange between the patient and the doctor.

For example, relative to the medical changes, it was pointed out that in addition to Random Blood Glucose (RBG), Oral Glucose Tolerance (OGT) and Thyroid Function (TF) tests, a Fasting Blood Glucose (FBG) test is necessary. In addition to the rule advising when the patient should not have a TF test, another rule determines when it is appropriate for him to have such a test (refer to Figure 15.2). This depends on the negative result of a urine test which is also added to the network, since it is in almost all cases the first one to apply. The TF test also depends on symptoms such as abrupt weight loss and thirst. A number of rules were constructed to show when an FBG test should be suggested. For example, if the values of the RBG test results lie in the range of 7 to 10.5, an FBG test is advised. Depending on the FBG values, the patient is either reexamined for symptoms, or diabetes is positively diagnosed.

With respect to the technical changes, patient history with symptoms should first be presented to the user. Second, a number of tests that are applicable should be presented, for the user to choose from. This process then continues with diagnosis of complications and branches to the various aspects of treatment.

15.2.2   Treatment of Diabetes

There are three main types of treatment:

1. *Insulin management with Home Blood Glucose Monitoring* (HBGM);

2. *Dietary control*;

3. *Prescription of oral agents.*

The last two forms of treatment usually refer to Type 2 diabetic patients and these are just outlined in the current version of the system. Dietary control is a very complex issue and there is controversy amongst experts as to whether it is prone to computerised treatment.

Insulin administration with Home Blood Glucose Monitoring is considered in depth in this module of the expert system. The objective here, is to achieve optimisation of blood sugar control.

A diabetic patient is characterised by hyperglycaemia which means high sugar level in the blood. This results in polyphagia, polyaria, thirst and other symptoms which are the same as the ones used in the diagnosis of diabetes module. When treatment with insulin is prescribed, careful consideration of the dosage is important so that the patient will not suffer the hypoglycaemic effects of an overdose, some of which are: tremor, sweating, drowsiness, light headedness, confused state of mind and loss of consciousness.

For insulin management, multiple element regimes of insulin are prescribed, to cover the four periods of food intake during the day, namely breakfast, lunch, tea and bedtime snack.

The three types of insulin are short, intermediate and long acting. The following are the four most common kinds of insulin regimes.

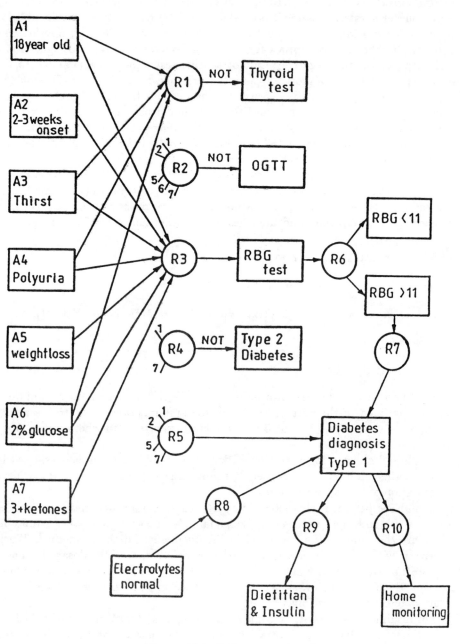

Figure 15.2: Inference network

First, intermediate acting insulin given twice daily at breakfast and tea. The first dosage, in the morning, will take care of the raised blood glucose after lunch, while the second will normalise the raised blood glucose after bedtime snack and into the night.

Second, a mixture of short and intermediate acting insulins, given twice daily before breakfast and tea. Note here that the short acting insulins before meals normalises the resulting raised blood glucose after meals.

On the above regimes, the average insulin requirements are 4060 units a day, with 2/3 of the dose given before breakfast and the remaining 1/3 before tea.

Third, a mixture of short and intermediate acting insulins given before breakfast, short acting before tea and intermediate acting before bed. The effect of this regime is attributed to the combined effect of the individual insulins as given in the two previous regimes.

Finally, short acting insulin given three times daily before breakfast, lunch and tea and long acting before bed. The effect of long acting insulin given at bedtime provides for the patient's basic requirements throughout the day and results in better insulin control and flexibility at the expense of increased number of injections. The long acting insulin covers the 50% (+10%) of the total daily requirement.

To assess the patient's glycaemic control and therefore the effect of the prescribed insulin dosage, blood glucose monitoring is essential. Usually this is performed at home, by taking blood glucose tests before meals. When nocturnal hypoglycaemia is suspected, a 3.00 am blood glucose test could be necessary.

There are certain difficulties in assessing glycaemic control. First, the blood glucose profile of a patient is a dynamic process and therefore measurements taken at particular time instants do not show the real profile. Complications arise when blood glucose changes rapidly when the test is taken. It is then possible that the patient complains of 'hypo' symptoms even though the blood glucose value is high above normal. Such a complication is the *Somogyi effect*, which describes the situation when a high fasting blood glucose is not indicative of insulin deficiency but could be the result of post hypoglycaemic hyperglycaemia. Therefore, the high fasting blood glucose is due to a rebound consequence after the patient has suffered severe hypoglycaemia.

There is very little in the insulin management literature concerning insulin adjustment. This might be because insulin requirements vary considerably between patients and there is a large number of factors to be considered. Some of these are the patient's degree of insulin resistance, his rate of insulin absorption, his food intake, his daily exercise and others. Also, insulin adjustment is heuristic in nature. There is no sufficient theoretical reasoning to support the administration of insulin. We can, therefore, appreciate the importance of an expert system to aid education as well as help doctors and nurses in this area.

In the next part, the knowledge representation scheme adopted as well as the hardware chosen are briefly described.

15.3   Knowledge Representation

There are a variety of knowledge representation techniques, including production rules, formal logic, semantic networks, frames and scripts.

The rule based representation is by far the most popular formalism and it has been extensively used in medical applications (e.g. MYCIN). It offers advantages such as modular and incremental development, modifiability of rules and the fact that it can support the system's transparency explaining the reasoning process of the system. Therefore, this technique was selected to represent knowledge in the development of the expert system for diagnosis and management of diabetes.

The knowledge that needs to be represented comprises:

- *hard data*, that is, test results, insulin damage, symptoms;

- *soft information* based on opinions and judgement of different experts in diabetes.

There are a number of ways for describing the uncertain nature of judgemental knowledge. Some of these are the incorporation of probabilities, the Bayesian rule, fuzzy set theory or the Dempster Shafer theory of evidence (as described in Chapter 1). We use an informal approach which uses operators like 'nearly', and 'likely' to represent uncertainty. Such an approach could, perhaps, be formalised to correspond to the logic based approach mentioned in Chapter 1.

In the next section we briefly describe the way in which the knowledge has been encoded.

15.3.1   Knowledge implementation

Rather than using a shell, the Prolog language was chosen for developing the expert system. This offers increased flexibility, easy modification and extension, low cost and choice of a desirable user interface. Due to its declarative feature, Prolog lends itself to an expert system environment which demands the programming of symbolic, as opposed to numerical computation. It is goal oriented as opposed to data driven. Although forward chaining is a natural representation of reasoning in medical diagnosis, Prolog despite being goal oriented, could be structured to suit our requirement.

Turbo Prolog was chosen which runs on IBM PC/compatible microcomputers of 384K RAM. Although Turbo Prolog is not likely to correspond to any forthcoming standard Prolog, it offers facilities such as fast execution due to its own compiler, interactive editor for fast development, use of declarative variables to permit secure development and execution control, standard predicates supporting graphics, windows, DOS strings and file operations.

15.3.2   The Expert System DIABETES

Any expert system consists of the following components:

- Knowledge acquisition system;

- Knowledge base;

- Inference engine;

- User interface.

The knowledge acquisition has been done manually in this case. It was extracted from medical books, journals and from historical patient cases, as has been already been explained in Section 15.2.

Different pop-up menus enable the user to select age, symptoms, urine test values, choice of test to perform, blood glucose values and others. Depending on the user responses, the outcome is either diagnosis of diabetes and type or he is asked to reexamine the patient. Following that, he either enters the treatment section or an investigation of complications. There are three types of treatment. These are, insulin management, dietary control and oral agent intake. The flow of information is thus represented to the user in blocks which are shown schematically in Figure 15.3.

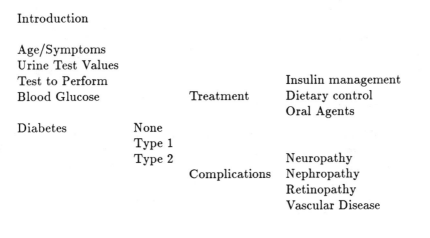

Introduction

Age/Symptoms
Urine Test Values
Test to Perform   Insulin management
Blood Glucose   Treatment   Dietary control
                                                   Oral Agents

Diabetes   None
                      Type 1
                      Type 2   Neuropathy
                      Complications   Nephropathy
                                                    Retinopathy
                                                    Vascular Disease

Figure 15.3: The Expert System DIABETES

The Knowledge Base

The knowledge base consists of Turbo Prolog rules and facts. Information is stored as objects. Objects and their variables are listed in the predicate section. Variables are also listed in the domain section. When using lists the variables are defined in the domains. The clauses section contains rules and facts that are needed to solve the problem. Each relation in each clause must have a corresponding predicate definition in the predicate section. The only exceptions are the built-in predicates that are an integral part of Turbo Prolog.

The Inference Engine

The problem solving strategy is one of top-down refinement, that is backward reasoning from its main goal through subgoals, utilising Turbo Prolog's interpreter.

The User Interface

The user interface caters for smooth communication between the user and the system and it also provides the user with insight into the problem solving process carried out by the inference engine. The screen display is controlled using certain predicates. Windows are always used to make the screen more attractive. Pop-up menus from the Turbo Prolog Toolbox have proved very useful. A status line is also included, informing the user how to interact with the program through the keyboard.

Graphics are also used to display curves for insulin action (isophane and soluble) versus time. This can be a useful aid in describing the different insulin types when they are used in treatment.

15.4   Tests

Even with the thorough procedure of knowledge acquisition, as presented in Section 15.2, it was difficult to incorporate all aspects of decision making during the program development. This might be because, as the experts put it, there are no general rules in medicine.

A careful testing of the system in consultation with the doctors was necessary in order to assess its performance under normal and extreme situations. General associations and the mechanisms behind them could be identified. That was part of 'deepening' the system's knowledge. We present two example situations which resulted in improvements to the knowledge base of the insulin management module of the expert system.

Example: Patient case - regime 2

Mixture of short and intermediate insulin twice daily, before breakfast and before tea.

The blood glucose profile is:

> fasting blood glucose: 32
> prelunch blood glucose: 25
> pretea blood glucose: 21
> prebed blood glucose: 3

3.00 am blood glucose: 5

The insulin dose adjustment advised by the expert system is:

Increase lst short acting   from 8 to l3
Increase lst intermediate   from 8 to l2
Decrease 2nd short acting from 4 to 2
Increase 2nd intermediate from 4 to 5

Also the following comment is given.

Follow up consultation in 3 months.

Expert's reaction

The expert suggested that he would see the patient next week, since he has three very high blood glucose values.

In general, when two or more blood glucose values are higher than 20 then rapid follow up was suggested. Therefore a new rule was added to the four general regimes of the program.

Example: Patient case - regime 4

Two short acting during the day and a mixtue of short and long acting in the evening.

The blood glucose profile input by the user is:

fasting blood glucose: 5
prelunch blood glucose: 7
pretea blood glucose: 8
prebed blood glucose: 12
3.00 am blood glucose: 12

The insulin dose adjustment is: increase 3rd short acting from 9 to ll.

Expert's reaction

The expert explains that because fasting blood glucose is normal and prebed blood glucose is high at 12 and blood glucose at 3.00 am has not gone up but stays at the same value, it is enough to increase the tea insulin. Given that prebed blood glucose would now be brought down to normal, this is likely to normalise the 3.00 am blood glucose as well.

Therefore, a new rule was added to take into account the interrelationship of the prebed and 3.00 am blood glucose values.

15.5   Conclusions

The expert system **DIABETES** has been presented, that is used for tutoring and teaching medical students, general practitioners and medical related staff on diabetes diagnosis and management. Major complications of diabetes are dealt with as well as treatment using insulin administration. The basic idea of the system is to present the user with a general tool for experimenting with a large number of patient cases by the choice of symptom and history from a menu driven interface. It is shown how a system based on production rules can be an effective decision making tool in such a complex area of medicine as diabetes.

Acknowledgements

The author acknowledges the enthusiastic collaboration of Dr Andrew Boulton, Senior Lecturer and Consultant at Manchester Royal Infirmary and the valuable contribution of her students, Miss Jane Liem, Mr Dan Weydahl and Mr Alkesh Dudakia.

Appendix A

Expert System Development Tools

Ian Filby, Nang Chan, Paul Chung

A.1   Tools

1. Acquaint (formerly known as Daisy)

A frame-based system consisting of two components: Kaint, the Knowledge Acquisition Interface module, and Qaint, the Query answering interface.

Machines: PC. Coded in muLisp.

Cost: £2000.

Features: Supports forward and backward chaining, frames, certainty factors, and fuzzy comparisons. Access to muLisp. There is a simpler version called Acquaint-Light.

Distributor: Lithp Systems BV.

Readers should, of course, consult the distributors for the **current** prices.

2. Advisor-2

A rule-based shell.

Machines: PC. Coded in Prolog.

Cost: £500.

Features: Forward chaining,. Interfaces tp Lotus 123, dBaseIII, GEM Graphics, and C.

Distributor: Expert Systems International.

Further refs: See Chapter 3 of this book.

3. APES

Machines: VAX, PC. Coded in micro-Prolog

Cost: $400 for PC version, $6000 for VAX version.

Features: Backward chainer with window-based interface.

Distributor: Logic Programming Associates.

4. Arity/Expert Development Package

An expert development system which runs on top of Arity/Prolog. Supports both rule-based and frame-based knowledge representation.

Machines: IBM PC, XT, AT and compatibles, MS-DOS, 512K memory (640K highly recommended), hard disk, requires Arity/Prolog Interpreter, or Interpreter & Compiler. Coded in Arity/Prolog.

Cost: $300 for Arity/Expert and $300 for Arity/Prolog Interpreter. No run time licence required.

Features: Knowledge Rep. — taxonomy of frames (multiple inheritance) and rules, 4 MBytes for storage of (5000 - 20000) rules. Inference Method — backward chaining; three strategies for calculating certainty factors; can specify control information to guide selection of goals and reporting of conclusions, or use default control settings. Interfaces to — Arity/Prolog, Microsoft C, Microsoft Pascal, Microsoft Fortran, C, Lotus 1-2-3, Lotus Symphony, dBase II. Other facilities — rule tracing, debugging facilities, "how" and "why" explanation options.

Developer: : Arity.

Distributor: Bonsai.

5. ART

A hybrid toolkit for developing knowledge-based systems. Biased towards a forward chaining rule-based approach to solving problems.

Machines: SUN, Symbolics, TI Explorer, VAX (VMS).

Cost: £17500 - £26500. Educational discounts.

Features: Knowledge rep — facts, schemata (frames), rules, viewpoints (contexts), relationships, inheritance. Inference — forward chaining, backward chaining, truth maintenace, hypothetical reasoning using viewpoints.

Developer: : Inference Corporation.

Distributor: Ferranti Computer Systems Ltd.

Further refs: See Chapter 4 of this book.

6. Auto-Intelligence

An interactive system for knowledge acquisition. The system identifies the structure of the expert's knowledge, explores the concepts of these areas and uses induction techniques to extend and generalise the knowledge.

Machines: PC/AT/XT MS-Dos 2.* and PC-Dos 2.*, Sun (Unix). Coded in Intelligence/Compiler.

Cost: $1000.

Features: Knowledge rep — uses induction from examples, and exact and inexact rules. Inference method — knowledge acquisition system, which also executes the generated rules.

Distributor: IntelligenceWare.

Further refs: News/Review in Expert Systems, November 1987.

7. CRESS

A simple backward chaining expert system shell with MYCIN-like uncertainty handling.

Machines: Any machine which supports Edinburgh Prolog or C-Prolog.

Cost: £100 distribution cost for the Prolog source code.

Features: Similar to Teknowledge's M.1 shell.

Developer: : Dr. Peter Ross, Department of AI, University of Edinburgh.

Distributor: AIAI.

8. Crystal

Machines: PC/XT/AT with 256KB Coded in C.

Cost: £1000. £200 per run time licence (or £2000 annual fee).

Features: Knowledge rep — production rules. Inference method — forward and backward chaining, supports uncertainty. Interfaces to — dBase III, Lotus 1-2-3, Symphony, Dos, ASCII, C, and interactive video.

Distributor: Intelligent Environments.

9. Edinburgh Blackboard Shell

A system written in Edinburgh Prolog for constructing rule-based systems with a blackboard architecture.

Machines: Any machine which supports Edinburgh Prolog, C-Prolog, Poplog Prolog, or Arity Prolog. Coded in Edinburgh Prolog.

Cost: £100 distribution cost for the Prolog source code.

Features: Access to Prolog, user definable certainty factor tests, user definable strategies for rule selection, built in facility for maintaining consistency of facts.

Developer: : Department of AI, University of Edinburgh.

Distributor: AIAI.

10. ESP Advisor

Text animation package. The system acts in a forward chaining manner to present text, and backward chains on rules.

Machines: VAX (VMS), PC. Coded in Prolog-2

Cost: £600 on PC. Educational discounts. (£100?). £4000 on VAX.

Features: Knowledge rep — English-like language. Inference method — forward and backward chaining. Interfaces to — Prolog-2 (optional).

Distributor: Expert Systems International.

11. ESP Frame Engine

Machines: IBM PC/AT with 640K. Coded in Prolog-2.

Cost: £1000 on PC/AT. Educational discounts.

Features: Knowledge rep — frames, inference commands. Inference method — forward and backward chaining, demons, inheritance.

Distributor: Expert Systems International.

12. EST (Expert Systems Toolkit)

Machines: PC (Pascal).

Cost: $500.

Features: Forward & backward chaining. Interfaces to — Lotus 1-2-3 and Symphony.

Distributor: Mind Path Product Corp.

13. Experkit

Machines: IBM PC/AT, Macintosh (512K), Macintosh II, other machines supporting Le-Lisp. Coded in Le-Lisp V15.2.

Cost: PC version £1000.

Features: Has two levels of interface — First level for naive users, a ready built interface. Second level for Distributors using Le-Lisp. Knowledge rep — production rules which can be grouped into packages and can use variables. Inference method — forward chaining. Interfaces to — software written in Le-Lisp.

Developer: : Act Informatique.

Distributor: Logotron.

14. Expert Ease

An induction expert system builder. Information on attributes and examples are entered into spreadsheet-like tables. The system then induces a decision tree of rules for each table.

Machines: PCs (UCSD O/S) Coded in Pascal.

Cost: £100.

Features: Knowledge rep — example sets and decision trees. Inference method — backward chaining of decision trees.

Distributor: Intelligent Terminals.

15. Expert Edge (previously known as Tess)

Version: 4.0.

Machines: IBM PC/XT/AT with 512K. Coded in C.

Cost: £3700 includes 5 days training and consultancy. £200 run time licence.

Features: Bayesian probabilities, windowing facilities for user- interface, library of numeric functions, context-sensitive help, can change answers or volunteer information, log session. Knowledge rep — production rules, objects. Inference method — backward chaining, limited forward chaining. Interfaces to — Lisp, Prolog, C, Pascal, dBase III, Lotus 1-2-3, Visicalc, Multiplan, can run .Exe and .Com files, interactive video.

Distributor: Helix.

Notes: Thorn EMI may sell their own modified version of Expert Edge called Expert 2000.

16. EXSYS

Version: 3.0.

Machines: IBM PC/XT/AT, SUN, HP9000, VAX (Unix & VMS). Coded in C.

Cost: $400 for PC run time licence $600 $5000 for VAX run time licence $10000.

Features: Knowledge rep — production rules, frames. Inference method — forward and backward chaining, frame inheritance. Interfaces to — dBase III, Lotus 1-2-3 and others.

Distributor: EXSYS Inc.

17. ExTran 7

Can induce rules from examples and converts these together with user defined rules into Fortran 77 routines. These are then run to produce the consultation.

Version: 7.2.

Machines: XT (DOS 2.1 or later), AT (DOS 3.0 or later), SUN, MicroVAX, VAX (Unix or VMS). Coded in Fortran 77.

Cost: £2000 for PC. £5000 for SUN, MicroVAX. £18000 for VAX.

Features: Knowledge rep — rules, example sets and decision trees. Inference method — forward and backward chaining. Interfaces to — external routines and databases.

Distributor: Intelligent Terminals.

18. FLOPS

Version: 1.3.

Machines: PC/XT/AT 512K RAM recommended, VAX.

Cost: $200, $500.

Features: Fuzzy systems theory — fuzzy logic, fuzzy numbers, fuzzy sets, and fuzzy predicates; built-in fuzzy truth maintenance. Blackboard system; calls to programs written in FLOPS or in other languages, relational format for blackboard data.

Distributor: Kemp-Carraway Heart Institute.

19. GEST (Generic Expert System Tool)

Expert system developed and technically supported by a university.

Version: 3.0.

Machines: Symbolics 3600 series, TI Explorer, VAX (VMS). Binary and source versions available.

Cost: Object licence $15000. Source licence $45000.

Features: Blackboard architecture supporting parallel knowledge source execution, forward and backward inferencing, frame matching, knowledge rep — frames, rules, facts and functions; multiple conflict resolution strategies; built in certainty factors; user-friendly interface, easily customised by the user; embeddable in user programs as a subroutine library; tutorial.

Distributor: Georgia Tech Research Corporation.

20. Goldworks

Hybrid expert system building tool, offering frames, rules and object oriented programming in a single integrated system.

Machines: AT or 386 with 512K base memory, 5MB (10MB recommended) extended memory and 10MB free hard-disk storage.

Cost: £5500.

Features: Frames, rules and object-oriented programming. Interfaces to Lotus 1-2-3, dBase, C and networks. Three level interface: For inexperienced user — menu driven interface with browser, control panel and screen. Can enter frames and rules and debug system. Provides on-line help and on-line tutorial. At middle-level is the toolkit layer, providing access to Goldwork's knowledge representation language. Supports frames organised in hierarchy with multiple inheritance. Forward and backward rule-based reasoning with access to lisp. Object programming supports message handlers and demons. Also a certainty factor mechanism, and dependency network for truth maintenance. Common Lisp development environment — providing interpreter, GMACS editor, and Lisp debugger.

Developer: : Gold Hill Computers.

Distributor: AI Ltd.

21. GURU

An expert system shell intended for integrating business software, such as SQL queries, data bases, text files, spreadsheets, graphics, forms, etc.

Version: 1.1.

Machines: PC, VAX (Ultrix & VMS), SUN, MicroVAX. Coded in C.

Cost: PC £4800+, SUN, MicroVAX $1700 , VAX $34000 - $60000.

Features: Knowledge rep — production rules, rules can access GURU's procedural language. Inference method — Forward and backward chaining, with switches to control inference process, certainty factors. User interface — there is a choice of four interfaces for the end-user: a menu interface, customised procedural templates, a command language, or a natural language interface. Interfaces to — dBase, Lotus 1-2-3, KnowledgeMan/2 (mdbs's own database product).

Distributor: Micro Data Base Systems.

Further refs: Review in AI Expert November 1986.

22. G2

Tool for building real-time expert systems. Designed for applications where hundreds or thousands of variables are monitored at the same time. For use in fields such as process control, computer integrated manufacture, financial trading, network monitoring and automatic testing.

Machines: TI Explorer, Symbolics, VAX (Lucid CL), Sun-3, Sun-4. Coded in Common Lisp.

Cost: $45000 ($3600?) for off-line development system with simulation $60000+ for on-line version.

Features: KB created and edited via graphical schematic of objects and their relationships. Heuristics, and attributes are defined using a structured 'natural' language. Includes temporal knowledge representation, supports state variable dynamic models, supports on-line data acquisition, and a truth maintenance system which considers time duration as well as changes in data. A graphical display for dynamic simulations allows knowledge testing under hypothetical scenarios.

Distributor: Gensym Corp.

Notes: Optional on-line modules allow G2 to distribute intelligence across a number of expert systems, data servers and graphics systems. Other modules exist for linking G2 systems together and interfacing them to data sources, data-bases and other external devices.

Further refs: New Products in AI Magazine, Fall 1987. News review in Expert Systems, November 1987.

23. Humble

A rule based and object oriented expert development system written in Smalltalk-80.

Machines: Xerox, Tektronix 4400 Series, Sun-2, Sun-3, Apollo, AT (1MB of extended memory), Mac. (Need Smalltalk-80). Coded in Smalltalk.

Cost: £600 + cost of Smalltalk-80 (£3000 on Suns & Apollo).

Features: Combines rule-based and object oriented programming; forward and backward chaining; a modular certainty system; user interface with graphical browser; and programmer interface.

Developer: : Xerox

Distributor: AI Ltd.

Further refs: Review in AI Expert, November 1987.

24. Insight 2+

A standard expert system development shell, with its own procedural language — a version of Pascal.

Version: 1.3.

Machines: IBM PC/XT/AT and 512K memory MS-Dos 2.0 or later, VAX (VMS) Coded in Turbo Pascal.

Cost: PC version $485. Run time licence $95 per copy.

Features: Knowledge rep — production rules, hierarchical goals specification, context control operators, procedures. Inference method — forward and backward chaining inference via procedural rules and operations. Interfaces to — dBase.

Distributor: Level Five Research.

Further refs: Review in AI Expert, December 1986.

25. Intelligence/Compiler

Hybrid expert system development tool.

Machines: PC. Coded in Pascal.

Cost: $1000.

Features: Knowledge rep — frames (with multiple inheritance), rules, logic, and procedures. Inference method — forward and backward chaining.

Distributor: IntelligenceWare.

26. KDS 3+

A frame-based expert system shell offering blackboard and maths features.

Machines: IBM PC/XT/AT (MS-DOS), 512K RAM and a numeric coprocessor, (hard disk recommended). Coded in 8088 assembler.

Cost: $1500. Run time licence available.

Features: Knowledge rep — frame based, object oriented. Inference method — forward & backward chaining, "blackboard" features for combining results of different aspects of problem-solving. Distributor and end-user communicate with system using structured English-like natural language. Permits interrupt calls and interface to exe. Comprehensive maths support.

Distributor: KDS Corporation.

27. KEATS (Knowledge Engineers Assistant)

A toolkit developed by the Open University and British Telecom under the Alvey programme.

Machines: Symbolics.

Features: Consists of four main tools: ET, and Editing Tool, for browsing & editing of on-line knowledge elicitation sessions. GT, a Graphics Tool which can convert sketches of an expert's knowledge structure and diagnostic structure into code. FT, a Frame-based Tool, providing inheritance, multiple contexts, procedural attachment, and type checking. RT, a Rule-interpreter Tool, which provides pattern directed invocation and access to FT structures.

Further refs: News/Review in Expert Systems, February 1987.

28. KEE

A hybrid toolkit for developing knowledge-based systems. Whereas ART has a bias towards a rule-based approach, KEE is inclined towards an object-oriented approach.

Machines: 386-based PCs, Symbolics, TI Explorer, Xerox 1100, Apollo, SUN, MicroExplorer, MicroVAX, HP9000.

Cost: $40000 on workstations, $15000 on 386-based PCs, Educational discounts.

Features: Knowledge rep — facts, objects (frames), rules, inheritance. Inference — forward chaining, backward chaining, truth maintenace, hypothetical reasoning using worlds. Elaborate window, icon, graphical based interfaces.

Developer: : IntelliCorp.

29. KES (Knowledge Engineering System)

Version: Version 2.4 Februaury 1988.

Machines: IBM PC, XT (MS-DOS), Apollo, Sun, Tektronix 4400, AT&T 3B2, Micro Vax (VMS & Ultrix), VAX (VMS & Unix), IBM mainframes (MVS & VM), HP9000, Unisys 5000, NCR Tower, Prime, Silicon Graphics, and Gould. Coded in C.

Cost: PC version £2500 , Workstations $7000 - $10000, Mini/Mainframe $10000 - $60000.

Features: Consists of 3 sub-systems: PS (Production System) — object oriented production rule system; backward chaining, Shortliffe type certainty factors. HT (Hypothesise & Test) — descriptive frames based system; minimum set cover theory using symbolic probabilities. Bayesian Inference — Bayesian statistics. Interfaces to — dBase III and Lotus 1-2-3; can be linked via OS calls or by embedding it in other software.

Distributor: Software A&E.

30. Knowledge Craft

A hybrid toolkit for developing knowledge-based systems. Composed of three sub-systems: CRL — a frame-based representation language; CRL-OPS — a foward chaining rule component; and CRL-Prolog — a backward chaining rule component.

Machines: SUN, TI Explorer, Symbolics, VAXstation, VAX.

Cost: $27500 - $46000. Educational discounts.

Features: Knowledge rep — facts, schemata (frames), rules, relationships, inheritance. Inference — forward chaining, backward chaining, hypothetical reasoning using contexts.

Distributor: Carnegie Group.

31. Keystone

Intended to be largely compatible with IntelliCorp's KEE 2.1.

Machines: AT (with optional 386 HummingBoard) with 512K base memory, 5MB of extended memory, and 10MB free disk space; also need Golden Common Lisp 286 Distributor.

Cost: $10000.

Features: Object oriented programming, multiple inheritance, rule objects and rule classes, backward and forward chaining, methods, demons, windows, graphics, images, mouse-driven interface.

Distributor: Technology Applications Inc (TAI).

32. Leonardo

Machines: IBM XT/AT with 512K memory, MS or PC Dos 2.00 or higher and VAX. Coded in Fortran and Assembler.

Cost: Level 1 — £150; Level 2 — £700; Level 3 — £2000; Run time licences £2000 for 10, £10000 for 100. VAX £4000 — £12000.

Features: Three levels of product Leonardo 1, 2 and 3 increasing in complexity. Knowledge rep — rules, frames, procedural language (resembles Pascal & C). Level 2 adds support for multiple structured knowledge bases, with a co-ordinating agenda. Level 3 includes support for inheritance amongst frames and supports uncertainty with — Bayesian statistics, fuzzy logic, certainty factors, and accumulation of evidence. Inference method — backward and forward chaining, access to procedural language, demons. Other facilities — while testing or running applications supports interrogation — How?, Why?,

Expand?, and What if? Interfaces to — Dos, ASCII files; network support for DOS 3.10 and above.

Distributor: Creative Logic.

Further refs: News/Review in Expert Systems, August 1987.

33. MUSE

Development tool designed particularly for real-time applications and embedded systems.

Machines: Sun (Unix) at least 4MBytes memory. Coded in PopTalk (an object oriented version of Pop, written in C).

Cost: £15000 single-user, £25000 network license.

Features: Fuse system sits on top of PopTalk, provides: collections, relations, databases, demons, knowledge sources, notice boards, agenda-based scheduling, and data capture channels. Two rule-based languages (FPS and BCS) are provided within Fuse, supporting forward and backward chaining production rules. Window-based structure editor for creating and editing object structures. Interface to Emacs editor, and to the Unix Source Code Control System (SCCS). Also a comprehensive debugging tool. Real-time support facilities include agenda-based priority scheduling, interrupt handling and fast data capture.

Distributor: Cambridge Consultants.

Further refs: News/Review in Expert Systems, August 1987.

34. Nexpert Object

A hybrid expert system building tool, supporting both rules and object-based programming.

Machines: Mac +, Mac SE, Mac II; IBM AT, PS/2, 386 (with Microsoft's Windows); VAX 2000, II, or III (VMS/UIS); Unix workstations eg. Sun, Apollo, HP, and IBM RT (with X-windows). Coded in C. Also runtime versions.

Cost: Mac, PC versions. $5000, Educational & quantity discounts. VAX versions $8000 - $15000, Educational and quantity discounts.

Features: Knowledge rep — rules (same rule format for both forward and backward chaining rules), objects (methods, classes, meta-slots, multiple & user-defined inheritance, dynamic creation of objects). Inference method — integrated forward and backward chaining, declarative access to control structure, event-driven architecture, calls to external code. Graphical browsing interface permits editing of objects, rules and control structures. Rules can directly communicate with databases. Supports user-defined uncertainty methodologies. Keeps track of logical dependencies.

Distributor: Neuron Data.

Further refs: Review in AI Expert November, 1987. News review in Expert Systems, November 1987.

35. Nexus

Consists of an expert shell component, rule editor, and procedural component, based on Modula-2.

Machines: XT/AT with 640K, PC/MS Dos 2.0 or higher, 2 disk drives, hard disk recommended. Mac with 512K, Mac Plus, minis (Unix) Coded in Modula-2.

Cost: £5000. £400 for run time licence.

Features: Knowledge rep — production rules and procedural actions. Inference method — forward and backward chaining, procedural actions affecting kb or rules. Interfaces to — databases, spreadsheets, and wordprocessors can be built using procedural language of Nexus.

Distributor: MindSoft.

36. Personal Consultant Easy

Introductory level expert system shell.

Machines: VAX (C), MicroVAX (C), PC/XT/AT with at least 512K memory.

Cost: $500.

Features: Backward chaining rules (no frames); certainty factors; trace and explanation facilities; "natural-language" interface. Systems of up to 500 rules; access to DOS and dBase files; facilities to incorporate graphical images as part of the user interface; tutorial-style manual and extensive examples.

Distributor: Texas Instruments.

Further refs: New Products AI Magazine, Spring 1987. Review of PC Easy in AI Expert, March 1987. Review in IEEE Expert Winter '87.

37. Personal Consultant Plus

Hybrid expert system building toolkit.

Version: 3.0.

Machines: VAX/MicroVAX (VMS, C), Explorer (Common Lisp), 8088/286/386 machines, with 640K memory and hard-disk (delivered in PCScheme or C).

Cost: $3000 Run time diskettes $100 each or twenty for $1000.

Features: Knowledge rep — frames (with inheritance and active values), rules, meta-rules to control inferencing, and procedures. Inference method — forward and backward chaining, confidence factors. Other facilities — access to PCScheme interpreter and compiler, will support up to 2MB of extended memory, 'natural language' interface : rules can be written in English-like Abbreviated Rule Language (ARL), rules can be viewed in English, ARL, or Scheme; rule tracing, end-user explanation facilities, graphics image capture and display, context sensitive help, mouse support. Interfaces to — C, dBase, Lotus 1-2-3, DOS files, .EXE or .COM programs, communication packages, and interactive video-disk. Enhance with PC Images ($500) which provides active images; interactive dials, gauges, forms and selection images. PC Online ($1000) allows direct interaction with process data.

Distributor: Texas Instruments.

Further refs: New Products in AI Magazine, Spring 1987. Review of PC Plus 2.0 in AI Expert March, 1987.

38. RuleMaster 2

A rule-induction based expert system. Uses ID3 algorithm on case examples or decision tables to produce optimised decision trees which can be compiled into C or Fortran code.

Machines: PC, SUN, Apollo, HP9000, VAX, IBM S/370, Cyber. Coded in C.

Cost: PC version $500, Workstation $7500, Mini/Mainframe $17500 - $28000.

Features: Knowledge entered as rules or examples; C and Fortran source code generators so that systems can be embedded in other software; backward and forward chaining as well as uncertainty are supported; KBs can be ported between DOS, Unix, and VMS operating systems; English-language explanations for end-user; two interfaces — development and user; user interface supports windows and menus, with a screen design tool kit to support quick and easy design of custom end-user screens; ASCII file import facility permits interfacing to database and spreadsheet packages.

Distributor: Radian Corporation.

39. Savoir

Machines: XT, Apricot, Prime, GEC, MicroVax, VAX, IBM mainframe (VM and MVS) Coded in Pascal.

Cost: £1000 on PC rising to £15000 on IBM mainframe.

Features: Knowledge rep — propositions, formulae, fuzzy logic, demons. Inference method — forward and backward chaining, and demons. Interfaces to — IVS-100 Videotex, Smart Datamanager, dBase III, Mic 2000 Videodisk, Fortran, Pascal, Auditor, Norbatch.

Distributor: Intelligent Systems International (ISI).

40. SD-Advisor

Machines: PC, VAX (VMS & Unix).

Cost: £1500 for PC.

Distributor: Systems Designers (SD-Scicon).

41. Super Expert

A revised, upgraded and repackaged version of 'Expert Ease'. An induction expert system builder. Information on attributes and examples are entered into spreadsheet-like tables. The system then induces a decision tree of rules for each table. These decision trees can be linked in forward and backward chaining manner.

Machines: PC/XT/AT (PC/MS Dos).

Cost: £700. Run time version £99.

Features: Knowledge rep — example sets and decision trees; can handle up to 1000 examples & 50 attributes; procedural attributes. Inference method — forward and backward chaining of decision trees. Interfaces to — Mirle Internationals 20/20 and via this to ASCII file-based packages like Lotus 1-2-3 and dBase.

Distributor: Intelligent Terminals Ltd.

Further refs: Review in Expert Systems User, Feb 1987.

42. Twaice

Machines: IBM/VM, IBM/VMS, VAX (VMS, Unix), MicroVAX, Tektronix 4404-6, Pyramid 90x, Nixdorf Targon 35, Sun, ISI, Apollo. Coded in MProlog.

Cost: $13000-50000.

Features: Includes MProlog system; English-like rules; incremental compilation of knowledge base, explanation facilities; two inference engines; access to MProlog and external procedures; frame-based taxonomy; on-line help; host editor interface.

Developer: : Nixdorf.

Distributor: Logicware.

43. VP-Expert

Rule-based expert system development tool with rule induction facility and interfaces to standard PC packages.

Machines: PC/AT/XT (DOS 2.** or 3.**) 256K. Coded in C.

Cost: $125. Run time licence available.

Features: Knowledge rep — rules developed by editing or induction from examples. Knowledge is represented by simple attribute value pairs. Inference method — backward chaining, and forward chaining. Interfaces to — external program calls to EXE, BAT & COM files; 1-2-3, dBase, other VP products. Other facilities — text and graphic rule tracing, confidence factors, floating-pt maths, built-in text editor, how/why and what-if commands supported.

Distributor: Paperback Software.

44. Xi Plus

Version: 1.50.

Machines: IBM PC/XT/AT with PC or MS Dos 2.1 and above, minimum of 512K memory (640Kb recommended), two floppy disk drives (hard disk recommended). Coded in MicroProlog and assembler. Available soon in C.

Cost: £1250; £2750 for 10 run time licences.

Features: Help, why, volunteer, "what if" (change previous answer). Knowledge rep — rules, facts, demons (continuously active rules) and queries. Inference method — forward (depth or breadth first) and backward chaining. Interfaces to — assembler and C languages; GEM Draw and Dr Hallo II graphics; DIF, SYLK, WKS and Comma Delimited file formats, and calls to other software.

Distributor: Expertech.

Further refs: Review in Expert Systems User, November 1986. Review in Expert Systems, February 1987.

45. 1st Class

Version: 3.5.

Machines: XT/AT. Coded in Pascal.

Cost: $500.

Features: Session report generator, spreadsheet like fill-in-blanks data entry form.

Distributor: Programs in Motion.

46. 1st Class Fusion

Enhanced version of 1st Class.

Version: 3.5.

Machines: PC.

Cost: $1300.

Features: Fill-in-the blank data entry forms; session report generator; graphics capture and display utilities; maths utilities. Interfaces to — dBase III, code generators for Pascal and C.

Distributor: Programs in Motion.

A.2   Distributors

Act Informatique,
12 Rue de la Montagne-ste-Geneviene, 75005 Paris, France,
Tel France 1 46 33 72 60.

Arity Corporation,
30 Domino Drive, Concord, MA 01742,
Tel USA 617 371-1243.

Artificial Intelligence Applications Institute (AIAI),
University of Edinburgh, 80 South Bridge, Edinburgh EH1 1HN,
Tel 031 225 4464.

Artificial Intelligence Ltd,
Greycaine Road, Watford, Hertfordshire WD2 4JP,
Tel 0923 247707.

Bonsai,
112-116 New Oxford Street, London WC1A 1HJ.

Cambridge Consultants Ltd,
Science Park, Milton Road, Cambridge CB4 4DW,
Tel 0223 358855.

Carnegie Group (UK) Ltd,
Coworth Park House, Coworth Park, Ascot, Berkshire SL5 7SF,
Tel 0990 872904.

Creative Logic Limited,
Brunel Science Park, Kingston Lane, Uxbridge, Middlesex UB8 3BR,
Tel 0895 74468.

Department of Artificial Intelligence,
University of Edinburgh, 80 South Bridge, Edinburgh EH1 1HN,
Tel 031 225 7774.

Expert Systems International Ltd,
9 West Way, Oxford OX2 0JB,
Tel 0865 242206.

Expertech,
Expertech House, 172 Bath road, Slough SL1 3XE,
Tel 0753 821321.

EXSYS Inc,
PO Box 75158, Contr. Stn. 14, Albuquerque, N.M. 87194,
Tel USA 415 961-4103.

Ferranti Computer Systems Limited,
Product Sales, Ty Coch Way, Cwmbran, Gwent NP44 7XX,
Tel 06333 71111.

GENSYM Corporation,
125 Cambridge Park Drive, Cambridge, Massachusetts 02140,
Tel USA 617 547-9606.

Gold Hill Computers,
163 Harvard Street, Cambridge, MA 02139,
Tel USA 617 492-2071.

Helix Expert Systems Ltd.,
190 Strand, London WC2R 1DT,
Tel 01 836 7788.

Inference Corporation,
5300 West Century Blvd, Los Angles, Ca 90045,
Tel USA 213 417-7997.

Intellicorp Knowledge Systems Division,
1975 El Camino Real West, Mountain View, CA 94040-2216,
Tel USA 415 965-5500.

Intelligent Environments Ltd,
Northumberland House, 15-19 Petersham Road, Richmond, Surrey TW10 6TP,
Tel 01 940 6333.

IntelligenceWare Inc,
9800 S. Sepulveda Blvd, Suite 730, Los Angles, California 90045.
Tel USA 213 417-8896.

Intelligent Systems International Ltd (ISI),
11 Oakdene Road, Redhill, Surrey RH1 6BT,
Tel 0737 71327.

Intelligent Terminals Ltd (Knowledgelink),
George House, 36 North Hanover Street, Glasgow G1 2AD,
Tel 041 552 1353.

Kemp-Carraway Heart Institute,
1600 North 26th Street, Birmingham, AL 35234,
Tel 205 226-6697.

KDS Corporation,
934 Hunter Road, Wilmette 12, Illinois 60091,
Tel USA 312 251-2621.

Level Five Research Inc,
503 Fifth Avenue, Indiatlantic, FL 32903,
Tel USA 305 729-9046.

Lithp Systems BV,
PO Box 65, 1120 AB Landsmeer, The Netherlands,
Tel 32-2908-4623.

Logic Programming Associates Ltd,
Studio 4, The Royal Victoria Patriotic Building, Trinity Road, London SW18 3SX,
Tel 01- 871-2016.

Logicware Inc,
5915 Airport Road, Suite 200, Mississauga, Ontario L4V 1T1,
Tel Canada 416 672-0300.

Logotron,
Ryman House, 59 Markham Street, London SW3 4ND.

or

Logotron Ltd,
Cambridge,
Tel 0223 811762.

MicroDataBaseSystems (Mdbs),
Imperial Buildings, 56 Kingsway, Holborn, London WC2 6DX.

Mind Path Technologies,
12700 Park Central Drive, Suite 1801, Dallas, Texas 75251,
Tel USA 214 233-9296.

MindSoft,
3 rue de l'Arivee, 75749 Paris, Cedex 15, France,
Tel France 1 45 38 70 12.

Neuron Data,
444 High St, Palo Alto, CA 94301,
Tel USA 415 321-4488.

Paperback Software Inc,
2830 Ninth Street, Berkeley, CA 94710,
Tel USA 415 644-2116.

Programs in Motion,
10 Sycamore Road, Wayland, MA 01778,
Tel USA 617 653-4422.

Radian Corporation,
PO Box 9948, Austin, Texas 78766,
Tel USA 512 454-4797.

Software A&E,
Sussex Suite, City Gates, 2-4 Southgate, Chichester, West Sussex PO19 2DJ,
Tel 0243 789310.

Systems Designers (SD-Scicon),
AI Business Centre, Pembroke House, Pembroke Broadway, Camberley,
Surrey GU15 3XD,
Tel 0276 686200.

Technology Applications Inc,
6621 Southpoint Drive North, Suite 310, Jacksonville, Fla. 32216,
Tel USA 904 737-1685.

Teknowledge Inc,
1850 Embarcadero Road, Palo Alto, CA 94303,
Tel USA 415 424-9955.

Texas Instruments Ltd,
Manton Lane, Bedford MK41 7PA,
Tel 0234 224260.

Xerox AI Systems,
475 Oakmead Parkway, Sunnyvale, CA 94086,
Tel USA 408 737 4815.

Bibliography

[1] *ILEA: NuPack, Cambridge Micro Software: Balance Your Diet.* 1983.

[2] Model based reasoning in KEE and SimKit systems. August 1986.

[3] *NUFFIELD:Home economics basic course*, Hutchinson, 1982.

[4] *Prolog standard - working draft 0.2, N21.* BSI wg17, UK.

[5] *STEM User Guide.* AI Ltd, UK, 1988.

[6] *Xerox Quintus Prolog users guide.* Xerox Corporation, 1985.

[7] J. C. Abegglen and G. Stalk. *Kaisha: The Japanese Corporation.* Business Books Inc., New York, 1985.

[8] J. Adams. A probability model of medical reasoning and the mycin model. *Mathematical Biosciences*, 32:177–186, 1976.

[9] V. Ambrosiadou and A. Boulton. Knowledge based systems for education in diabetes management. In *12th IMACS World Congress, Scientific Computation, Paris*, July 1988.

[10] V. Ambrosiadou, A. Boulton, and E. Masson. An expert system for education in diabetes management and complications. In *British Diabetic Association Workshop, Poster Session , Sterling, Scotland , September 1988*, 1988.

[11] P.K. Andow, A. Shafaghi, and F.P. Lees. Fault tree synthesis based on control loop structure. *Chemical Engineering Research and Design*, 62, March 1984.

[12] Ng A.Y.C. *A Validation suite for Prolog?* Dissertation in partial fulfilment of MSc, University of Salford, Department of Maths. and Computer Science, 1987.

[13] D. Bailey. *The University of Salford Prologix Reference Manual.* 1986.

[14] A. Barr and E. Feigenbaum. *The Artificial Intelligence Handbook vols 1 and 2.* William Kaufmann, 1981/82.

[15] V. Bassilli and A. Turner. Iterative enhancement: a practical technique for software engineering. *IEEE Transactions on Software engineering*, 9(6), November 1975.

[16] M. Bliss. *The discovery of insulin.* Paul Harris Publishing Co, Edinburgh, 1983.

[17] D. Bobrow and M. Stefik. *The LOOPS Manual.* Xerox Corporation, 1983.

[18] J. Bradshaw. *The P.R.O. Expert System Shell.* Master's thesis, Department of Computer Science, Rhodes University, Grahamstown, 6140, South Africa, 1986. Technical report 6/86, 1986.

[19] J. Branch. Towards integrated process design. *Processing*, 37–39, March 1985.

[20] I. Bratko and Lavrač.N. *Progress in Machine Learning.* Sigma Press, 1987.

[21] J. et. al. Breuker. *Model-Driven Knowledge Acquisition: Interpretation Models.* Deliverable Task A1, Esprit Project 1098, University of Amsterdam, 1987.

[22] J. Briggs. The Plan. 1985. Private publication.

[23] K Broda and S. Gregory. *Parlog for Discrete Event Simulation.* Technical Report DOC 84/5, Imperial College, Department of Computer Science, London, UK, March 1984.

[24] F.P. Brooks. *The mythical man-month.* Addison-Wesley, 1975.

[25] J.S Brown and R.R Burton. Diagnosing models for procedural bugs in basic mathematical skills. *Cognitive Science*, 2, 1978.

[26] L. Brownston, R. Farrell, E. Kant, and N. Martin. *Programming Expert Systems in OPS5.* Addison-Wesley, USA, 1985.

[27] B. Buchanan and E. Shortliffe. *Rule Based Expert Systems.* Addison-Wesley, 1984.

[28] B.G. Buchanan and E.A. Feigenbaum. DENDRAL and Meta-DENDRAL:their applications dimension. *Artificial Intelligence*, 11(1-2):5–24, 1978.

[29] Buchanan, B. et. al. Simulation assisted inductive learning. In *Proceedings of AAAI*, 1988.

[30] A. Bundy. How to improve the reliability of expert systems. In S. Moralee, editor, *Research and Development in Expert Systems IV*, pages 3–17, Cambridge University Press, 1987.

[31] J.R. Carbonell. AI in CAI: an artificial intelligence approach to computer assisted instruction. *IEEE transactions on Man-Machine Systems*, 11:190–202, 1970.

[32] K. Carden. *Explanation facilities in the P.R.O. System*. Master's thesis, Department of Computer Science, Rhodes University, Grahamstown 6140, South Africa, 1987.

[33] P. Chalk. Prolog-based computer-aided learning environments. *Programmed learning and educational technology*, 2:102–107, 1987.

[34] R. N. Charette. *Software engineering environments:Concepts and technology*. Intertext, New York, 1986.

[35] E. Charniak and D. McDermott. *Introduction to Artificial Intelligence*. Addison-Wesley, 1985.

[36] C Chatfield. *Statistics for Technology*. Chapman and Hall, London, UK, 1978.

[37] R.C. Christopher. *The Japanese Mind*. Pan Original, London, UK, 1984.

[38] W. J. Clancey and R. Letsinger. Neomycin: reconfiguring a rule-based expert system for application to teaching. In *Proceedings of the seventh IJCAI*, 1981.

[39] W. Clocksin and C. Mellish. *Programming in Prolog*. Springer-Verlag, 1987.

[40] C. Cole. Using a microcomputer to process data for classroom scientific research. *PEGBOARD*, 1:19–33, 1986.

[41] R. A. Corlett. Explaining induced decision trees. In J. Fox, editor, *Expert Systems 83*, pages 136–142, 1983.

[42] P. Cox and R. Broughton. *Micro Expert Users Manual (Version 2.1.1)*. Redhill, Surrey, UK, 1981/1982.

[43] O. J. Dahl and K. Nygaard. SIMULA – an Algol-based simulation language. *Comm. ACM*, 9:671–678, 1966.

[44] J. De Kleer and J.S. Brown. A qualitative physics based on confluences. *Artificial Intelligence*, 7–83, 1984.

[45] N. Dean. *FISHFARMER: An Aquaculture Expert System*. Honours Report 88/36, Department of Ichthyology and Fisheries Science, Rhodes University, Grahamstown, 6140, South Africa, 1987.

[46] N. Dean, J. Bradshaw, and M. Bruton. The aquaculture system. In *International conference on alternative life history styles of fishes and other organisms*, Grahamstown 6140, South Africa, June 1987.

[47] J. Doores, A. Reiblein, and S. Vadera. *Prolog Programming for Tomorrow.* Sigma Press, 1987.

[48] R. Duda, J. Gaschnig, and P. Hart. Model design in the prospector consultant system for mineral exploration. In D. Michie, editor, *Expert Systems in the Microelectronic Age*, pages 153–167, Edinburgh University Press, UK, 1979.

[49] R. O. Duda, J. Gasching, and P.E. Hart. Model design in the prospector consultant system for mineral exploration. In Michie D., editor, *In Expert Systems in the Microelectronic Age*, pages 153–167, Edinburgh University Press, 1980.

[50] R.O. Duda, P.E. Hart, and G.L. Sutherland. Semantic network representation in rule-based inference systems. In D.A. Waterman and F. Hayes-Roth, editors, *Pattern Directed Inference systems*, pages 203–221, Academic Press, New York, 1978.

[51] Slatter P. E. *Building Expert Systems: Cognitive Emulation.* Ellis Horwood, 1987.

[52] R. Ennals and A. Cotterell. *Fifth generation computers: Their implications for further education.* Technical Report, Further Education Unit, UK, 1985.

[53] Sowa J. F. *Conceptual Structures: Information Processing in Mind and Machine.* Addison-Wesley, 1983.

[54] C.L. Forgy. Rete: a fast algorithm for the many pattern/many object pattern match problem. *Artificial Intelligence*, 19:17–37, 1982.

[55] J.W. Forrester. *Industrial Dymanics.* MIT Press, 1961.

[56] W. R. Franta. *The process view of simulation.* North Holland, New York, 1977.

[57] R.H. Fusillo and G.J. Powers. Computer-aided planning of purge operations. *AIChE*, 34(4):558–566, April 1988.

[58] J.H. Gallier. *Logic for Computer Science: Foundations of Automatic Theorem Proving.* Harper & Row, 1986.

[59] Gordon and E.H. Shortliffe. *The Dempster-Shafer Theory of Evidence*, pages 272–292. Addison-Wesley, 1985.

[60] J. Gordon and E. Shortliffe. A method for managing evidential reasoning in a hierarchical hypothesis space. *Artificial Intelligence*, 26:323–357, 1985.

[61] A. Grimshaw and J. Liu. Mentat:an object oriented macro data flow system. *Comm. ACM*, 1987.

[62] M. D. Grover. A pragmatic knowledge acquisition methodology. In *Proceedings of IJCAI*, 1983.

[63] J.Y. Halpern and Rabin M.O. A logic to reason about likelyhood. *Artificial Intelligence*, 379–405, 1987.

[64] P. Hammon. *Micro-Prolog for Expert Systems*. Prentice-Hall, 1984.

[65] A Hart. *Knowledge acquisition for expert systems*. Kogan Page Ltd, 1986.

[66] F. Hayes-Roth, D. Waterman, and D. Lenat. *Building Expert Systems*. Addison-Wesley, Reading, Mass., 1983.

[67] N. J. Holden. The development of the concept of communication competence in cross-cultural interactions. *R & D Management*, 17(2), April 1987.

[68] N. J. Holden. *The Development of the Concept of Communication Competence in Relation to Firms' Interactions in Overseas Markets*. PhD thesis, Manchester Business School, 1986.

[69] N. J. Holden. The Japanese language: a partial view from the inside. *Multilingua*, 2(3), 1983.

[70] D. Huntington. *The Exsys User's Manual*. 1984.

[71] M. Iri, K. Aoki, E. O'Shima, and H. Matsuyama. An algorithm for diagnosis of system failures in the chemical process. *Computers & Chemical Engineering*, 1979.

[72] A. James. Selection criteria for an integrated CAE system. In *I.Chem.E Symp. Series No 92, Process Systems Engineering '85*, Pergamon Press, 1985.

[73] R.J. Jarret. *Diabetes mellitus*. PSG INC., LITTLETON, MASSACHUSETTS, 1986.

[74] Rogers J.B. *Turbo Prolog Primer*. Addison-Wesley, 1987.

[75] Yong J.T.H. *A Validation suite for Prolog?* Dissertation in partial fulfilment of MSc, University of Salford, Department of Maths. and Computer Science, 1987.

[76] E. T. Keravnou and L. Johnson. *Competent Expert Systems*. Kogan Page, London, UK, 1986.

[77] A. L. Kidd. *Knowledge Acquisition for Expert Systems: A Practical Handbook*. Plenum, London, UK, 1987.

[78] T.A. Kletz. Eliminating potential process hazards. *Chemical Engineering*, April 1985.

[79] T.A. Kletz. *Hazop and Hazan - Notes on the Identification and Assessment of Hazards.* Institution of Chemical Engineers Hazard Workshop Modules, I.Chem.E., Rugby, 1983.

[80] L . J. U. Kohout and W. Bandler. Fuzzy expert systems. In *Proceedings ACM symp. on Expert Systems*, Brunel University, 1982.

[81] P. Kotler, L. Fahey, and S. Jatusripitak. *The New Competition.* Prentice/Hall International, Englewood Cliffs, New Jersey, 1986.

[82] M. A. Kramer. Malfunction diagnosis using quantitative models and non-boolean reasoning in expert systems. *AI ChE*, 1986.

[83] B. Kuipers. Qualitative simulation. *Artificial Intelligence*, 29:289–338, 1986.

[84] S.A. Lapp and G.J. Powers. Computer-aided synthesis of fault-trees. *IEEE Transactions on Reliability*, R-26:2–11, April 1977.

[85] C. Lee. A comparison of two evidential reasoning strategies. *Artificial Intelligence*, 35(1):127 –134, 1988.

[86] F.P. Lees. *Loss Prevention in the Process Industries.* Butterworths, London, UK, 1980.

[87] A. Loukaidis. *Health education and logic programming.* Dissertation, South Bank Polytechnic, 1988.

[88] R. S. Mazze and P. Zimmet. Computers in diabetes care and patient education an overview. *Prac Diabetes*, 4(1):8–11, January/February 1987.

[89] J. McDermott. R1: a rule-based configurer of computer systems. *Artificial Intelligence*, 19:39–88, 1982.

[90] K. A. Meadows, B. Fromson, C. Gillespie, A. Brewer, G. Carter, T. Lockington, G. Clark, and P. H. Wise. Development validation and application of computer linked knowledge questionnaires in diabetes education. *Diabetic Medicine*, 5:61–67, January 1988.

[91] R.S. Michalski, J.G. Carbonell, and T.M. Mitchell, editors. *Machine Learning: An Artificial Intelligence Approach.* Tioga, Palo Alto, 1983.

[92] R. Miller, H. Pople, and J. Myers. Internist-1, an experimental computer-based diagnostic consultant for general internal medicine. *New England Journal of Medicine*, 307:468–476, 1982.

[93] M. Minsky. A framework for representing knowledge. In P.H. Winston, editor, *The Psychology of Computer Vision*, McGraw-Hill, New York, 1975.

[94] R. Muetzelfeldt, M. Uschold, A. Bundy, N. Harding, and D. Robertson. An intelligent front end for ecological modelling. In *Working Conference on Artificial Intelligence in Simulation*, Belgium, 1985.

[95] F. Neelamkavil. *Computer Simulation and modelling*. Wiley & Sons, 1987.

[96] M. Newman. *DAPES Phase II Fault Diagnosis Strand: Intermediate Representation Stage report*. Unpublished club report DAPES II-NCC0012, NCC, Manchester , UK, 1987.

[97] J. Nichol, J. Dean, and J. Briggs. Teachers encounter Prolog. *Journal of Computer Aided Learning*, 2:74–82, 1986.

[98] P. Norbury and G. Bownas, editors. *Business in Japan: A Guide to Japanese Business Practice and Procedure*. The Macmillan Press, London, UK, 1974.

[99] J. O'Keeffe, D. Danilewitz, and J. Bradshaw. *The River Conservation System - A User Manual*. CSIR, Pretoria, 1986.

[100] J. O'Keeffe, D. Danilewitz, and J. Bradshaw. The river conservation system - an automated 'knowledge assistant' to help in determining the conservation status of south african rivers. In *Proceedings of the Conference on Freshwater Wetlands and Wildlife, Charleston, South Carolina*, pages 24 – 27, March 1986.

[101] T. O'Shea and J. Self. Learning and teaching with computers. In *Artificial Intelligence in Education*, Harvester Press, 1987.

[102] Wimbourne P. Record of project work at Hydeburn School. *PEGBOARD*, 1:106–112, 1986.

[103] A. Papoulis. *Probability, Random Variables and Stochastic Process*. McGraw Hill, second edition, 1984.

[104] E. Post. Formal reduction of the general combinatorial problem. *American Journal of Mathematics*, 65:197–268, 1943.

[105] H. Prade. A synthetic view of approximate reasoning techniques. In *Proceedings of the 8th IJCAI*, pages 130–136, 1983.

[106] H. Purchase. *P.R.O. version 2*. Technical Report 87/26, Department of Computer Science, Rhodes University, Grahamstown 6140, South Africa, 1987.

[107] H. Purchase, De Moore, I., and M. Bruton. Pisces - an expert system for the control of the introduction of exotic fish species into south africa. In *International conference on alternative life history styles of fishes and other organisms*, Grahamstown 6140, South Africa, 1987.

[108] M.R. Quillian. Semantic memory. In M. Minsky, editor, *Semantic Processing*, MIT Press, Cambridge, Mass., 1968.

[109] J. R. Quinlan. Discovering rules by induction from large collections of examples. In D. Michie, editor, *Expert Systems in the Micro-Electronic Age*, pages 168–201, Edinburgh University Press, 1979.

[110] J. R. Quinlan. Inferno: a cautious approach to uncertain inference. *Computer Journal*, 26:255–269, 1983.

[111] J. R. Quinlan. Learning efficient classification procedures and their application to chess and games. In R. S. Michalski, J. G. Carbonnell, and T.M. Mitchell, editors, *Machine Learning: An AI Approach*, pages 463–480, Tioga Press, Palo Alto, C. A., 1984.

[112] J.R. Quinlan. Discovering rules by induction from large collections of examples. In D. Michie, editor, *Expert Systems in the Microelectronic Age*, pages 168–201, Edinburgh University Press, 1979.

[113] Davis R and Buchanan B.G. Meta-level knowledge: overview and applications. In *Proceedings of the 5th IJCAI*, pages 920–927, 1977.

[114] E. O. Reischauer. *The Japanese*. Charles E. Tuttle, Tokyo, 1984.

[115] Duda R.O., Hart P. E., and N. J. Nilsson. Subjective bayesian methods for rule-based inference systems. In *Proceedings of the 1976 National Computer Conference*, AFIPS Press, 1976.

[116] D. Robertson, A. Bundy, M. Uschold, and R. Muetzelfeldt. *The EcoLogic System*. Technical Report Technical Report TP-1, Department of Artificial Intelligence, University of Edinburgh, 1988.

[117] D. Robertson, A. Bundy, M. Uschold, and R. Muetzelfeldt. *Synthesis of Simulation Models from High Level Specifications*. Technical Report Research Paper RP-313, Department of Artificail Intelligence, University of Edinburgh, 1987.

[118] D. Robertson, S. Bundy, M. Uschold, and R. Muetzelfeldt. Helping inexperienced users to construct simulation programs: an overview of the eco project. In S. Moralee, editor, *Research and Development in Expert Systems IV*, 1987.

[119] D. Robertson, R. Muetzelfeldt, D. Plummer, M. Uschold, and A. Bundy. The eco browser. In M. Merry, editor, *Research and Development in Expert Systems II*, pages 416–423, Springer-Verlag, 1985.

[120] D. Robertson, M. Uschold, A. Bundy, and R. Muetzelfeldt. The eco program construction system: ways of increasing its representational power and their effects on the user interface. to appear in International Journal of Man Machine Studies , Also available as D.A.I. Research paper 380, 1988.

[121] W. Royce. Managing the development of large software systems: concepts. In *Proceedings of WESCON*, August 1970.

[122] G. Shafer. Belief functions and possibility measures. In J.C. Bizdeck, editor, *The Analysis of Fuzzy Information 2*, CRC Press, 1987.

[123] G. Shafer. *A Mathematical Theory of Evidence.* Princeton University Press, 1976.

[124] B. Sheil. Power tools for programmers. *Datamation magazine,* 29(2):131, 1983.

[125] J. Shiozaki, H. Matsuyama, E. O'Shima, and M. Iri. An improved algorithm for diagnosis of system failures in the chemical process. *Computers & Chemical Engineering,* 1985.

[126] E. H. Shortliffe. *Computer-Based Medical Consultations: MYCIN.* American Elsevier, New York, 1976.

[127] D. Sleeman and J. Brown. *Intelligent tutoring systems.* Academic Press, 1982.

[128] D. Sriram and M.L. Maher. The representation and use of constraints in structural design. In *Proceedings of the 1st International Conference on Applications of Artificial Intelligence in Engineering Problems,* Southampton University, U.K., April 1986.

[129] A. Starfield, S. Adams, and A. Bleloch. *A Small Expert System Shell and its Applications.* Technical Report, University of the Witwatersrand, 1984.

[130] A. Starfield and A. Bleloch. Expert systems: an approach to problems in ecological management that are difficult to quantify. *Journal of Environmental Management,* 16:261–268, 1983.

[131] Steel,Jr. G.L., S.E. Falham, R.P. Gabraiel, D.A. Moon, and Weinreb D.L. *Common Lisp Reference Manual.* Digital Press, Massachussets, 1984.

[132] K. Steer. Testing data flow diagrams with parlog. In Kowalski and Bowers, editors, *Proceedings of 5th International Conference and Symposium on Logic Programming I,* 1988.

[133] L. Sterling and E. Shapiro. *The Art of Prolog.* MIT Press, 1986.

[134] M. Stubbs and P. Piddock. Artificial intelligence in teaching and learning: an introduction. *Programmed learning and educational technology,* 2:150–157, 1985.

[135] J.R. Taylor. An algorithm for fault-tree construction. *IEEE Transactions on Reliability,* R-31(2), June 1982.

[136] G. Tecuci, Y. Kodratoff, and Z Bodnaru. DISCIPLE: an expert and learning system. In S. Moralee, editor, *Research and Development in Expert Systems IV,* 1987.

[137] R. Turner. *Logics for Artificial Intelligence.* Ellis Horwood, 1984.

[138] M. Uschold, N. Harding, R. Muetzelfeldt, and A. Bundy. An intelligent front end for ecological modelling. In T. O'Shea, editor, *Advances in Artificial Intelligence*, pages 12–22, North Holland, 1986. Also in Proceedings of ECAI-84, and available from Edinburgh University as Research Paper 223.

[139] S. Vadera. A theory of unification. *Software Engineering Journal*, 3(5), 1988.

[140] R. Walmsley and M. Bruton. Aquaculture: a development plan for South Africa. In R. Walmsley and J. As, editors, *Aquaculture 1986 , Occ. Ser. No. 15, Ecosystems Programmes*, FRD, CSIR, Pretoria, 1987.

[141] A.J. Waters and J. Ponton. Qualitative simulation and fault propagation in process plants. under review for Chemical Engineering Research and Design.

[142] P. J . Watkings. Long term complication of diabetes. *Clin Endocrinol Metab*, 15:715–1003, 1986.

[143] A. White. Inference deficiencies in rule based expert systems. In M. Bramer, editor, *Research and Development in Expert Systems II*, pages 39–51, Cambridge University Press, 1985.

[144] P. H. Winston and Horn B.K.P. *Lisp*. Addison Wesley, third edition, 1988.

[145] P. H. Wise. Computer applications in diabetes education. *Prac Diabetes*, 4(3):111–113, May/June 1987.

[146] P. H. Wise, D. C. Dowlatshahi, S. Farrant, S. Fromson, and K. A. Meadows. Effect of computer based learning on diabetes knowledge and control. *Diabetes Care*, 9(5), September/October 1986.

[147] W.W. Woods. What's in a link? foundations for semantic networks. In D.G. Bobrow and A. Collins, editors, *Representation and Understanding*, Academic Press, New York, 1975.

[148] L. A. Zadeh. Fuzzy logic and approximate reasoning. *Synthese*, 30:407–428, 1975.

[149] L. A. Zadeh. Fuzzy sets. *Inform. and Control*, 8:338–353, 1965.

[150] M. Zimmerman. *Dealing with the Japanese*. George Allen and Unwin, London, UK, 1985.

Index

272